T. S. Arthur

Out in the World

A Novel

T. S. Arthur

Out in the World
A Novel

ISBN/EAN: 9783744711210

Printed in Europe, USA, Canada, Australia, Japan

Cover: Foto ©Thomas Meinert / pixelio.de

More available books at **www.hansebooks.com**

OUT IN THE WORLD.

A Novel.

BY

T. S. ARTHUR,

AUTHOR OF "LIGHT ON SHADOWED PATHS," ETC. ETC.

NEW YORK:
CARLETON, PUBLISHER, 413 BROADWAY.
M DCCC LXIV.

OUT IN THE WORLD.

CHAPTER I.

UNDISCIPLINED, wayward, sometimes petulant — pure, warm-hearted, loving. Life was simple feeling. Such was Madeline Spencer when she took upon herself the vows of wifehood. Her husband, Carl Jansen, was older by five or six years; a young man of placid exterior and thoughtful habits, but sensitive and proud. He had, by long continued effort, learned to govern himself; or, in exacter phrase, to hide what he felt from observation — to maintain a calm outside, even under strong interior excitement. He was considerate of those around him, as well from naturally kind feelings as from a certain ground of principle; but, there was also in this consideration, a desire to stand well in the opinion of others. This love of approbation had been, in fact, a strong element in the work of self discipline which had for years been in progress.

Jansen was selfish, as are all men, no matter of what culture or training, who have simply developed on the natural plane of life under natural motives. He had controlled his passionate impulses, not because they were evil in themselves, but because their exhibition would shadow his good name, or hurt his worldly interests. He was polite, deferential, calm, orderly, kind; in a word, gentlemanly in his whole deportment; but not from Christian ethics. It was not because he desired the well being or happiness of others, that he was so considerate of their comfort, convenience, or pleasure. It is questionable whether he ever regarded this. How will it appear?— what will be thought? Herein lay the boundary of motive; but not the conscious boundary, — let this be said in Jansen's favor. He thought himself better than he was. We say it not in reproach — he did not know himself.

No matter to what extent this culture of man's natural mind may go, the good exterior will only be an assumed beauty. The root will draw nutrition from the soil of selfishness. Out in the world, the man may counterfeit the saintliest virtues. At home, he will be what he is; and the reactions of home, if against his weaknesses and desires, will give another form to his life — hard, harsh, angry; it may be cruel. He will not prefer another to himself, as on the social plane, where he bids for fair opinions; he will not yield, in seeming bland good nature, the point of argument; will not consider and excuse faults of character nor read human nature against himself.

Undisciplined, wayward, petulant, yet pure, warm-hearted and loving. Such, in brief, was Madeline Spencer when she became Mrs. Jansen. And the young husband was exteriorly placid and thoughtful, but sensitive and proud. Such unions do not afford large promise of happiness; but they quicken all the elements of life — give rapid growth of character — and make men and women stronger for good or evil. They eliminate the saint or develop the fiend.

An observer, writing in a kind of playful seriousness, on the phenomena of love, says that one man is enamored of a curl, another of a graceful ankle, a third of blue or brown eyes, a fourth of a swan-like neck, a fifth of a Grecian profile, and so on; the real character and quality of the enchantress rarely if ever coming into view, thus making marriage something akin to blind guess-work. Alas for many, when the curl loses its crisp circles; when the ankle's fine symmetry departs; when the blue eyes grow leaden, and the brown eyes swim in tears; when the neck shrinks into lines and angles, and the fine profile mocks an expressionless or peevish face!

It was the beauty of Madeline that first attracted Jansen; the beauty of her whole face when life flowed into it — the life of joy. Her complexion was of that pure, transparent pink and white, seen occasionally, and always so charming if accompanied by regular features; in her case made more striking by hazel eyes, close brown eyebrows, and long lashes of the same color. If the eyes had been blue, Jansen might not have been captivated. The brown eyes did the final work. Love takes for granted almost everything. The curl represents grace of mind; the blue eyes tenderness; the brown eyes depth of feeling; the nobly formed neck dignity of character; the clear cut profile internal symmetry. Love takes all for granted. Never questions — never doubts; and goes blindly to the altar.

Undisciplined, wayward, and sometime petulant, for all the pinky flesh and chestnut eyes! Jansen might have seen this; he did see it in fact — but, in his infatuation, doubted the evidence. There was an error in the observation, he thought, some false adjustment of the instrument. It was impossible for imperfections like these to dwell in a casket so fair to look upon.

After the wedding day — after the honeymoon, came the sober realities, the plain facts of married life; and none escape them. The worshiped divinity steps down from her pedestal and becomes a woman; still fair, beloved, and worshipped, but not at the old distance. If she be a true, disciplined woman, unselfish (in the ordinary acceptance of the term,) and generously inclined to minister in all things to her husband's happiness, comfort, and convenience, there will be, unless he is a tyrant or a brute, a home in which peace can fold her wings. But, if she be not so disciplined and unselfish, but petulant, wayward, thoughtless, the chances are all on the other side. If, back of this petulance, and thoughtless waywardness, lie purity, truth, and a generous loving nature, the husband will be equally to blame with the wife, if clouds instead of sunshine hang over their dwelling place — nay, more to blame; for by virtue of his mental constitution, he may lift himself into regions of calm thought more easily than his wife, and so, rise out of the blindness of mere impulse. She loves and feels most; he dwells most in thought — and should let reason give clear sight and a just self control.

Now, in the case of Jansen, there was, as we have seen, a habit of self-control. But, we have seen also, that this was not grounded in any spiritual motive; but was simply natural — that is, selfish. He loved the good opinion of others — liked to stand fair with the world; and so guarded himself, lest at any time he should betray unmanly weaknesses, passion, ill-nature, or hardness of character. The self-control, therefore, was not a restraint of wrong impulses, lest they should prove harmful to others; but a restraint lest they should, through some reaction, hurt himself. Just so far, and no farther, had Carl Jansen gone in the great work of soul-discipline, at the period of his marriage. As for his beautiful young wife, she had not yet taken her first lesson in self-command. Her impulses were her rulers. As she felt, so she acted. Her early training had not been wisely ordered. Her father had been indulgent, and her mother blind and weak. Naturally gifted, her mind imbibed rapidly, and she was better educated than most young women of her age. For music she had a passion. She performed with a taste and skill rarely acquired, and sang with a richness of vocalization, and absorbed feeling, that always drew a crowd around her when in any large company, she sat down to the piano.

In this passion for music, Carl Jansen had no share. A few notes, or a few bars, when they first struck on his ears, came in waves of sweetness; but, like honey to the taste, this sweetness soon palled on the sense. After a few minutes, he would fail to perceive any response in his soul; and thought would wander from the vibrant strings, no longer discriminating chords or passages, and merely dwelling, half conscious of their presence, in a maze of sound, that disturbed rather than tranquillized his feelings. He generally experienced a sense of relief — particularly in social companies — when, to use his own words, "the piano ceased its humdrumming." He had never said this to Madeline before marriage. Oh no. That would have been inconsistent with his world-side character. On the contrary, he affected a polite enthusiasm for music, and would stand, as if entranced, by the piano, asking her to play piece after piece, even while wearied with the sound of jarring chords, and impatient of her long-continued beating of the keys. This he called politeness, and consideration for those with whom we associate. It was on the plane of his assumed gentlemanly bearing towards the world; but its mainspring was selfishness. He was enamored of the maiden; he was the lover and the wooer; and every act was designed to conciliate her favor — as every act before the world was to win the world's regard.

Herein lay the danger to happiness. This outside, with Carl Jansen, did not present the real man. That shrunk away and hid itself under smoother and compliant exteriors — looked out stealthily from blinds — was always standing on guard. It was different with Madeline. She had no concealments — never tried to veil her petulance or waywardness, more than her loving impulses. Every heart-beat showed itself in her transparent countenance. You saw the state of her feelings in her eyes. It was not a mirror only, it was a crystal window. You could look down through it into her soul. In every changing state, the past state with her was forgotten — she lived so wholly in the present. She was pure — she was true; but ignorant of the world, impulsive, wayward, and, for lack of discipline, self-willed. As to hereditary quality she was a better woman than Jansen was a man — more sincere — less concealed. Yet, with all this, there lay undeveloped with her, strength of character — power of endurance; and a pride not easily quickened, but having latent elements that, once infilled with life, would make her inflexible as iron.

CHAPTER II.

AFTER the wedding day — after the honeymoon came the sober reality, the plain facts of married life; and none escape them. The worshiped divinity steps down from her pedestal, and becomes a woman; still fair, beloved, and worshiped, but not at the old distance. We repeat these unwelcome sentences — unwelcome to many, because the words will bear to them a meaning beyond their literal sense.

It was not long before the divinity of Carl Jansen's new home stepped down before his eyes, and revealed herself as human, in whom were human weaknesses and human faults. The all-compliant lover was not merged, gracefully, into the all-compliant husband. Why should there be wooing, after winning and possession? A new order of things must follow marriage; an entire change of relation between the woman and the man. Before, the will of Madeline was his law; now, his will must be her law. There is a vast difference between the two relations; and the substitution of the one for the other cannot take place without a jar. If Jansen had been less selfish, and thence clearer seeing — able to change in perception, his stand point for that occupied by his young wife — the shadow of a cloud, dark enough to hold a tempest in its bosom, need not have fallen so quickly upon their lives. But, he had a cold, inflexible nature, which, to the world, veiled itself under warm and soft exteriors — and had so veiled itself to the maiden, Madeline. To her, he had ever seemed warm and yielding. Nothing hard, icy, or exacting, had appeared in all the happy months of waiting for the blissful day that was to make them one. She felt that he was all tenderness, all love; and that she could rest on his manly strength, and hide herself, like a tired child, when life had weary or sad moments, in sweet abandonment on his breast.

Alas for her disappointment! She awoke with a start — a shock — a wound — arose shuddering, yet in anger, and with a new consciousness of strength. There had been disturbances in her sleep — a troubled sense of pain and wrong — strange dreams that hurt and frightened her — a kind of vague nightmare, changing all at once to a gibbering phantom on her breast, when she awoke with a cry, — awoke, never to sleep the old tranquil sleep again!

Let us come to particulars. The awaking was in this wise. Keep in mind the two characters with which we are dealing. The one undisciplined, impulsive, self-willed, independent; the other cold, orderly, inflexible, and sensitive to the world's opinion. How will it appear? governed his life in its social aspect. Is it right, and agreeable to myself? governed hers. She rarely, if ever, thought about what others might say or think of her — while he felt himself to be under constant observation.

It was five months after their marriage. During that time, the young husband had been gradually changing in the eyes of his wife, and putting on new forms of character. The honey-moon had scarcely passed, ere a jar was felt. Pain and surprise followed — vague questionings,— bewilderment, doubt,— Madeline pondered the fact, not comprehending it — pondered it sitting in the edge of a shadow that was advancing, black and cold upon her life. Another jar — more questioning — deeper bewilderment — strange doubts — the shadow still advancing. What was meant? What portended? She had entered a new region, and was losing her way. The path along which her feet had moved in dancing measure, grew all at once narrower, and she began looking to her steps; and then, as her eyes from a vague instinct of danger, ran forwards, the path lost itself to vision. She trembled and grew afraid — sat down and wept. And this happened ere two months had passed since the bridal kiss lay sweet upon her lips.

How imperfectly do we understand each other. We move side by side, dwell in the same household, commune together, enter into the most intimate and sacred relations and yet, continually misapprehend and falsely interpret one another. Each is a mystery — a human temple, into the penetralia of which none but God may enter. In just the degree that we selfishly live our own lives — that is, seek our own pleasures, and do our own will, are we in danger of misapprehending and misinterpreting others. Their acts, (all we really see of them,) if they fail to square with our rule of thinking — if they touch our sense of propriety, or interfere with our comfort or convenience, are read against them as signs of perverseness, moral defection, wrong intent, or evil desire; and we respond, in our action, to the assumed meaning of theirs.

In so responding, were the truth really known to us, we should find ourselves wrong twice in three times. But we too rarely get down to the truth in these things. Our reactions upon assumed perverseness or evil, are met by counter-reactions, and we grow blinder and falser in our judgments. Pride and anger rise up to cloud still more our better reason, and too often, alas! we lift the hand to punish where there has been no sin. If men and women made it a rule always to suppose good instead of evil touching the doubtful actions of those to whom they bear intimate relations, there would be peace and unity with tens and tens of thousand, who now perversely wound and hinder one another — turning the honey of their lives into vinegar and gall.

Both Jansen and his wife were strongly marked as to individuality of character, living so completely in their own ideas of life, as to render adequate sympathy with the peculiar ideas and sympathies of another nearly impossible. Herein lay the ground of danger. This was the barrier to unity and happiness. He was always guarding and hiding from the world his weaknesses and peculiarities — dropping down a veil when he appeared abroad — questioning as to how it would sound or seem, ere the impulse to speak or act found ultimation. She, on the contrary, was a standing revelation of herself. Never on her guard — never asking what this one or the other might say or think — ruled by her impulses — sunny, showery, petulant, tender, passionate. Her heart beat along the surface of her life, and you might count the pulsations. It was this perpetual revelation of herself that constituted the veil of mystery, beyond which the eyes of Jansen could not penetrate — caused his misinterpretations, and stimulated his impatience. He could not understand her character — far less, sympathize with her.

At the end of five months — after a troubled sleep, in which strange dreams had hurt and frightened the young wife — there came a full awakening. The stealthy, intruding, suffocating, weird nightmare, suddenly revealed, as we have said, its hideous form, and she sprung from sleep, with a cry of fear. It was in this wise: —

Beautiful, gifted, fascinating in manner, social, and gratified with the attentions that were lavished upon her, Mrs. Jansen was not in the least inclined to withdraw herself from the pleasant circles wherein she had shone as a star. Now, this did not please her husband. He wanted her more for himself, and felt disturbed when he saw her enjoying the company of other men. Hindrances had been thrown in her way which only annoyed instead of impeding her. He watched her narrowly when in society, and she was constantly detecting the half-suspicious glances of his cold, wary eyes, a circumstance that did not cause reflection or concession, but only awakened pride, and led her farther away from the paths in which he desired her to walk.

Carl Jansen was a merchant, living and doing business in the city of New York. As our story has nothing to do with his business life, we shall not weary the reader with dry descriptions of his store, his clerks, or his customers. In regard to personal appearance, a few words must suffice. In stature, he was five feet eight inches — not stout — straight and symmetrical. He was always well dressed;

had dark, fine hair, a little wavy; and clearly defined, smooth eyebrows, handsomely arched. Eyes nearly black. Side whiskers, just a little wavy, like his hair, and similar as to color. His profile was almost classic, and like chiselled marble in its pure outlines; but the face itself was nearly as pale and cold as marble. "A perfect face," was often said, when the eyes first rested thereon; but, the more you studied it, the less you were satisfied — the less perfect it seemed. There was defect in something that gave the sign of a true and noble manhood. You had an impression of narrowness instead of breadth — of littleness instead of grandeur. It was a face, the calm surface of which was rarely broken. There might be a tempest below, but few signs thereof would be revealed in his placid countenance. He knew, perfectly, the art of hiding what he felt; of restraining the flow of passionate blood ere it put a stain of betrayal on his cheek. Such men get credit for virtues not always possessed.

Carl Jansen left his store one evening in November, a little before six o'clock. It was almost dark. He took a stage in Broadway, just above Wall street. Two or three vacant places remained — one at the forward part of the stage, to which he passed. Before reaching John street, the stage had its complement of twelve passengers. The last man who entered, was a person well know to Jansen. A gentleman sitting next to him recognized this person as he came in and made room for him. He did not observe Jansen. There was some defect in the stage lamp, and it went out soon after passing the Astor House; in consequence, the faces of the passengers were all in deep shadow. The last comer had not observed our merchant, who sat crowded into the corner of the seat, and who, being a smaller man than his immediate neighbor, was quite concealed. The two men were, it soon appeared, intimate acquaintances. The one known to Jansen was named Guyton. He was a small Wall street broker, of no very fair record, but a specious, insinuating, shrewd, self-determined man, who was making his way in the world, and did not mean to fail through lack of wit and effort. He had a smooth tongue, a gracious manner, a rhinoceros skin, and a conscience without scruple.

"You will be at the club to-night?" Jansen heard his immediate neighbor say to Guyton, as they were passing Barclay street.

"No; I have something better than the club on hand."

"Ah! What?"

The two men drew close together, speaking almost into each other's ears. The rattle of the stage prevented their voices from being heard by the passengers sitting opposite; but, Guyton's face being turned towards Mr. Jansen, he by leaning and hearkening with an almost breathless attention, managed to get nearly every word that was spoken.

"A party at Mrs. Woodbine's. Were you not invited?"

"The Woodbines and I don't take to each other. They are very nice people, no doubt; but, a little stuck up, since Woodbine ventured into the California trade, and came out winner instead of loser."

"It's the way of the world, you know," said Guyton "But they give fine entertainments, and you meet some charming people there."

"Who?"

"There is one in particular. Do you know Carl Jansen?"

"Of Maiden Lane?"

"Yes; at least, I know of him."

"Have you met his wife?"

"Never."

"They've only been married a few months. But she is lovely! Wears the sunniest face you ever looked upon. A perfect enchantress! I am going to meet her."

"You are!" Jansen did not fail to note the surprised tone in which this response was made.

"Yes: she's the attraction. I wish you could hear her sing. She has the most perfect voice I ever heard in a woman. It is divine."

"Does the lady respond to your admiration?"

Just then, in making way for a down-coming stage, the one in which they were riding turned short towards the pavement, and the hind wheels grinding against the curbstone, drowned the voice that answered; and so the eager, tingling ears of the surprised husband did not catch the reply. What he did hear from Guyton's companion, was not calculated to soothe his feelings. The sentence was this:—

"A little vanity in so good looking a fellow as you are may be pardoned. If, however, an old stager's advice be worth anything, let me suggest prudence. Trouble is apt to come of these things. Honesty is found to be the best policy in the long run, whether a man's gold or his wife be considered. You'd better come to the club."

"No, thank you! Not small beer when I can get the flavor of wine."

"How is Erie to day?" Guyton's companion changed the subject.

"Flat," was answered.

"Hudson river?"

"Advanced a half. If you have a few thousands to spare, now is your time. It's on the upward move."

"Do you think so?"

"I know so."

Jansen shrunk back into his corner of the stage with a mingled feeling of pain, anger and mortification. Nothing more of what passed between the two men reached his ears. Did a suspicion touching his wife cross his mind? No — not the shade of a suspicion. He believed her to be true and pure, and it almost maddened him to think that the breath of such a man as Guyton should fall upon her cheek. The particular attentions of this man to Madeline on two or three recent occasions had not escaped his observation. He understood something of their meaning now.

But, how was he to deal with Madeline? How save her from contact with a person whose eyes he saw, in fancy, looking at her with the greed of a sensualist and a villain? The two men left the stage before him, and, unembarrassed by their presence, he pondered this new question, that seemed more difficult of solution with every repeated effort to reach an answer. Madeline herself had proved an enigma. He had, so far, failed to comprehend her character. She did not seem to reflect — had no worldly wisdom — no suspicions — no prudence. Her feelings were her leaders, and carried her whithersoever they would. Every effort so far made, whether gentle or firm, to hold her back from the social life in which she found so much enjoyment, had been fruitless. The feeble arguments he could educe on the side of "moping at home," as she said, were to her as weak as gossamer. She blew them away at a breath.

"Life was given us to enjoy, Carl," she sometimes answered him in playful seriousness, "and we cannot enjoy it alone. The heart is social. It must have friends. Home is sweet — but the sweetest and purest lake that ever smiled back into the blue sky, or reflected the light of stars, will grow vile and death-breeding, if its waters be not renewed and agitated by the influx of streams. Because we have created a home, shall we retire into it and selfishly shut the door — letting none pass over our threshold nor crossing it ourselves? This would indeed be folly! No, no, Carl! We must not imitate the folly that is making so many homes in our land little better than gloomy cloisters. Does the marriage vow involve a renunciation of the world? Is the wife a simple devotee? — a nun? — I must be pardoned for thinking differently."

Carl might as profitably have talked to the wind as to argue against his wife. All this was, with her, a matter of perception. She saw it; and reasons to the contrary were to her as words without meaning. In all his efforts to draw her to his way of thinking — where it ran counter to what she saw and felt to be right — he had, so far, entirely failed. There was either a playful setting of him aside, or a more sober, but resolute, advance along the ways in which she saw it right to go. These were not perverse, doubtful, or dangerous ways; but simply the old ways amid social pleasures wherein she had walked for a few bright years; where Carl had walked also; and where they had met as lovers. In his eyes she had graced these ways once — was their most beautiful ornament — but now, she seemed out of her sphere there. It had been well enough for the maiden, but was not for the wife. The conversation just heard in the stage, confirmed all his objections to her love of society. But he was not clear as to the propriety of reporting this conversation — at least not for the present. His experience with Madeline caused him to hesitate. He was never certain of the way in which she would respond to a communication in any manner bearing upon her conduct. In most cases, she had acted in clear opposition to his way of thinking.

Carl Jansen, on reaching home, found his wife in the midst of elaborate toilette preparations, though it was yet full two hours before Mrs. Woodbine's guests would begin to present themselves. His face did not light up with its accustomed smiles on meeting her. He was too sober — too annoyed — for smiles. His eyes clear and cold at all times, were particularly cold now; his face clouded; his lips compressed with unusual firmness. His presence, to the warm, light heart of Madeline, fell like a shade.

"What's the matter? Are you sick?" she asked, resting her eyes on his face, and trying to read every line of expression.

He said something about a slight headache; but his manner was reserved. As this was not the first time her husband had come home in a strange humor, on a like occasion, Madeline partly guessed the cause. A state of irritation followed. Jansen saw this change of feeling writing itself in her tell-tale eyes and face, and it sobered and discouraged him still more. Excess of feeling, while it blinded her, stimulated her self-will. He had gained experience of this already.

"There is no use in opposition," he said to himself. "She will go, spite of anything I can say."

He might have told her of what he had heard in the

stage. But, that would have been no reason for her remaining at home; only for a guarded demeanor towards Mr. Guyton. As the communication of this incident, at the time, would effect nothing, Jansen felt constrained still to keep it in his own possession. He would, of course, not lose sight of Madeline for a moment — would linger near her as much as possible; and watch Guyton with eagle eyes.

In this spirit he went with his wife to Mrs. Woodbine's.

CHAPTER III.

THEY were silent by the way — he, from a brooding, questioning, bound state of feeling; she, partly from the intrusion of his unhappy condition of mind, and partly, because she knew that to speak of her pleasant anticipations would meet with no cheerful response.

Mrs. Woodbine's elegant suite of drawing-rooms, from the last of which opened her choicely stocked conservatory, were almost filled with guests when Carl Jansen and his wife arrived. They had entered, Madeline leaning on her husband's arm; been received by Mr. and Mrs. Woodbine; and were moving down the room, amid richly attired women and their attendants, when Mr. Guyton presented himself with a face all smiles and courtesy, and said, with the assured familiarity of a favored friend —

"Ah, Mrs. Jansen! I've been looking for you! Good evening, Mr. Jansen! Let me take the care of your lady off of your hands."

And before Jansen had time to think, Madeline's hand had been withdrawn from his arm, and she was moving away, leaning on the arm of the very man whom of all men living, he at that time most detested. What was to be done? Anything, or nothing? For once in his life, there were red stains of passion in his cheeks. He knew it by their burning glow; and, in fear lest he should betray the almost maddening strife of feeling that seemed as if it would bear him beyond self-control, he moved out of the circle of observation as far as possible. But, he did not lose sight of his wife. How perfectly at home she was with Mr. Guyton! How familiarly did she lean towards him, looking up into his face, and answering him with sunny smiles and bright laughing eyes! He was an attractive man; taller in stature than Mr. Jansen, and altogether of a more imposing exterior. His manners were polished — his tastes cultivated; and he had fine conversational powers. Altogether he was a man to shine in society — one that fascinated women.

As Jansen's eyes followed them, a cold, dull sense of fear, that hurt as it stealthily intruded, crept through his heart. What did this mean? The unhappy man looked inward, searchingly, and found a new sensation, full of pain. Love had taken the alarm; and, suddenly, a mailed knight was by her side, with sword unsheathed. Under the half shut visor, you saw the gleam of a cruel eye. It was Jealousy.

Now, in most cases, jealousy sees through an obscuring medium, and gives false report of every act. The purest smile is an invitation to step aside from paths of virtue; the simplest motion a betrayal of design; a foregone admission of evil distorts and changes everything.

Like a dissolving view, almost suddenly, yet by a strange, gradual blending with, and substitution of one thing for another, the scene before Carl Jansen put on new features, and a new significance. There was a dangerous tempter beside his wife — she was in peril. There was safety only in her withdrawal from his alluring sphere. This idea took entire possession of Jansen's mind. But, how was this withdrawal to be effected? He was yet in the midst of his perplexed and troubled thoughts, when he observed Madeline and her companion pass from one of the drawing rooms into the conservatory. As he was moving to follow them, he found himself face to face with a lady acquaintance, who said, as they recognized each other —

"I've been looking at your wife, Mr. Jansen. She is lovely."

The lady was not a flatterer; but a frank outspoken friend, well enough acquainted to assume liberties of speech.

"I've never seen her look better than she does to-night," she continued. "Perfectly charming. Everybody is in love with her! I wonder you are not jealous. I should be, were I a man and had such a beautiful, fascinating creature for a wife."

"A poor compliment to both yourself and wife that would be, taking the supposed case as real," said Jansen, trying to answer indifferently. But, his voice had no music in it. The tones were dull and husky.

"I believe you are jealous!" said the lady, in playful banter, passing her fan lightly before his face. "For shame!"

Once more, a rare thing for Jansen, the color rose to his cheeks, and he felt that he was betraying himself. A third person joining them at the moment, there was opportunity for dropping a theme which to him had proved almost painfully embarrassing. Full twenty minutes elapsed before he could disengage himself from these two ladies. During this time his watchful eyes had been upon the door leading into the conservatory; but his wife had not yet reappeared.

Jealousy moves, always, with circumspection — has stealthy, but quick-seeing eyes. — Veils alertness under forms of indifference. — Pretends not to observe, when every sense is acute. Jansen entered the conservatory with the air of a half absent-minded person, and stood near the door, in pretended admiration of a flowering-cactus. He bent to the curious, irregular mass of vegetation — touched its fluted sides — felt of its prickly spines, and stooped to its crimson blossoms as if to find some odors there; yet, thought was scarcely noticing the plant, and his eyes, as he leaned over it, were looking between its branches, and along the green-house alleys. But their search was not satisfactory. A little farther away from the entrance depended a basket, in which an air plant was imitating a butterfly; and so perfect, at first sight, was the semblance, that Jansen was half deceived, and stepped closer to solve the illusion. The bright eyes and painted wings were but the coloring of a leaf.

"Isn't it exquisite, Carl?". Jansen started to find his wife near him. She was still in the company of Guyton. Her face was alive with beauty and feeling. She looked more lovely than she had ever appeared. "You will find some rare and beautiful things here," she added. "I have enjoyed them so much. Be sure to look at Mrs. Woodbine's pansies, at the lower end. Such richness and variety in the coloring, I have never seen."

In the next moment, she had vanished with her attendant, passing again to the drawing-rooms, and leaving her husband to the companionship of flowers. For a short time, he stood bewildered; then advanced a little way down the conservatory — stood, apparently, in admiration of a large orange tree; and then, turning, went back to the parlors. Through these, he searched in vain for his wife. She was no where to be seen. Presently music was heard. It came from one of the upper rooms. A few, who loved music, left the crowded apartments below, and went up stairs. Jansen stood in the hall, near the stair-way, in a state of indecision. A voice, clear and sweet, stole out on the air above, and came floating down. There was a pause in the movement about Jansen — a pause to listen.

"That's your wife," said one who happened to be near the young man.

At this moment, another voice, rich and deep, swelled out, in accord with the fine soprano.

"And that's Guyton," added the same person. "He's a glorious singer. Come!"

The speaker moved to the stairs, and Jansen accompanied him. They went up, and following the rich sounds, entered a large front chamber, which had been arranged as a music room for the occasion. The sight which there met the eyes of Jansen was in no respect calculated to soothe his disturbed feelings. The piano was so arranged that you could see the performers' faces.

Madeline was seated at the instrument, and Guyton standing beside her. They were singing a duet. Guyton turned the music, and in doing so, bent, with a closeness of contact, and a familiarity of manner, that struck the husband as an outrage; sometimes dropping, during a pause in his part, a word in the ear of Mrs. Jansen. At the conclusion of the piece, Madeline, who seemed to be conscious of no presence but that of her companion, lifted to his her bright eyes and glowing face, and received, with evident signs of pleasure, the compliments he lavished.

Jansen was on fire! With difficulty he restrained an impulse prompting him to cross the room to where the performers were engaged, and invite his wife to accompany him down stairs. The act would have been an outrage; and he was able to see this clearly enough to prevent the folly. For nearly half an hour, he was doomed to the sufferings of a purgatory. The singers were enchanted with the music, and as he read their feelings in their countenances, with each other also. Madeline had never looked to him more ravishingly beautiful. Light flashed from her face and eyes, and floated around her glossy curls and gemmed head-dress, like a halo.

Dancing had commenced in the parlors; and this was gradually diminishing the company gathered in the music room. Jansen was among those who lingered. A brilliant little Italian song had been sung by Madeline, and she was sitting quietly for a moment in the pause that followed, when Guyton bent down and said something. Smiles of consent and pleasure danced over her face, and she arose from the music stool and took his proffered arm. They were half across the room, when Jansen stood in their way, and looking coldly, almost sternly at his wife, said, in an undertone —

"I want you for a moment." Then bowing with an excess of formality to her companion, he said to him —

"Pray excuse her, Mr. Guyton."

Madeline looked seriously annoyed. Guyton was surprised, and stared at Mr. Jansen with falling brows, like one offended by a rudeness. He returned the bow quite as formally as it had been given, and left the young husband and his wife in the now almost deserted room.

"You are forgetting yourself, Madeline," said Jansen, as soon as they were sufficiently alone to escape particular notice. His eyes were riddles to his wife. What new, strange, dark meanings were looking out of them? They were full of accusation; were sharp with anger.

"I do not understand you," she replied; and she did not. The color had almost all gone out of her face, that was rosy as blushing May scarcely a moment back.

Jansen was excited and in mental obscurity.

"Perhaps I can make it clear," he said, speaking in a tone of irony.

"Do, if you please!" His hardness was communicating itself. Madeline looked at him with shut lips, and cold eyes. He had broken upon her happiness too suddenly and in a way that stirred her anger. She felt that there was something of outrage in his inexplicable conduct.

"There are some men with whom it is not prudent for a young wife to be seen in too close familiarity."

"Carl Jansen! Is it possible!" She was startled and indignant.

"I speak soberly," he returned.

"So much the worse," was answered quickly, and with a hot flushing of the face, which had grown so pale a little while before. "Your wife appreciates the compliment!"

"Don't make light of things that I regard as serious, Madeline; and, particularly, don't make light of this." He spoke in a warning way. "I am in no temper for trifling to-night. What I have seen and heard, justifies me in all I am saying and doing."

"And pray, sir, what have you seen and heard to-night?" demanded Mrs. Jansen, drawing a little away from her husband, and looking at him with flashing eyes.

"Enough," he said, "to warn me of danger to your good fame."

She turned from him with an offended air, and had receded a pace or two, when he moved forward to her side, and bending close to her ear, whispered —

"I am going home, and desire you to accompany me."

Madeline stood still instantly. She did not turn her face, nor look at him. Only a moment to reflection was given — no, not to reflection, but to the hindering of quickly springing impulse. Passion had sway; but passion hiding itself from common observation. She answered in a firm low voice —

"At one o'clock, I shall be ready to accompany you, not before."

"Madeline!" The tone was in warning.

"At one. Not a minute before." And she left him and went down stairs.

It was full twenty minutes before Jansen had sufficient possession of himself to venture into the drawing-rooms again. There was dancing, and his wife was on the floor — her partner, Mr. Guyton. He stood looking at them, as if under a spell. Every time the hand of his wife touched that of her handsome partner, a fiery thrill would run along his nerves, and strike on his brain with a shock. She moved before him, an image of surpassing loveliness — an embodiment of pleasure. There was nowhere to be read, on her joyous countenance, the faintest sign of troubled thought. It seemed as if the memory of what had passed a little while before was wholly obliterated from her consciousness.

"Is she heartless! Does she defy me! O jealousy! Blind, suspicious, cruel; how quickly dost thou lead the soul astray! Jansen moved back, and went into the hall, where he was out of sight of the dancers.

"I said that I was going home," he spoke with himself. "and what I say I mean. She made light of it. Very well! She shall know me better. My word is the law of my actions. I speak, and do. I said that I was going and I shall go."

It was one o'clock. Half the company had retired. The drawing-rooms were no longer crowded, as few except the dancers remained. For all the sunny face, and light, joyous manner of Mrs. Jansen, even as her husband looked at her in anger of this very joyousness, there was the weight, as of a leaden hand, lying on her bosom. And this had grown heavier and heavier, as the hours passed, until its pressure was almost suffocating. She had been dancing a set. The figures were completed, and the music ceased.

"I must find my husband," she said, partly aloud, and partly to herself, gliding away from her partner, and moving from room to room. Not seeing him, she passed to the hall, and then up stairs.

"Have you seen anything of my husband, Mrs. Woodbine?" she asked of the lady hostess, as she met her on the landing.

"No. Isn't he down stairs?"

"I think not."

"Perhaps you will find him in the music room. There are several gentlemen there."

But he was not in the music room. Mrs. Jansen went gliding down stairs, almost holding her breath. The hand that lay on her bosom grew heavier and heavier. Through the glass door of the conservatory, she saw figures moving among the plants. She went in, and along the fragrant aisles, but failed to meet the object of her search.

"Have you seen anything of my husband?" The question was asked of a friend whom she met on coming out of the conservatory.

"Not lately. Perhaps he is in the gentlemen's dressing-room."

"If you see him, please say that I have gone for my cloak and hood, and will be down in a few moments."

"Certainly." And the gentleman bowed.

It took Mrs. Jansen only a few minutes to get ready for departure. Cloaked and hooded she came down stairs, eagerly searching with her eyes among the gentlemen who waited in the hall for her husband. But he was not among them. Disappointed she drew back, up the stairs.

"Have you seen anything of my husband?" Again this question was repeated. She spoke to Mr. Woodbine.

"Indeed I have not, Mrs. Jansen."

"Wont you be kind enough to ascertain for me if he is in the gentlemen's dressing-room?"

"With pleasure."

"Say, if you please, that I am all ready."

A sofa stood in the upper hall. Mrs. Jansen was feeling very weak. Her limbs trembled. She went up from the landing, on which she had met Mr. Woodbine, and sat down on the sofa.

"Why, how pale you are, Mrs. Jansen!" exclaimed a lady who had come up at the moment. "Don't you feel well?"

"Not very," Madeline answered, faintly.

"You have danced too much. I feared you would overdo yourself." The lady friend drew a bottle of smelling salts from her pocket, and handed it to Mrs. Jansen. The pungent odor, stimulating her brain, partly revived her.

"You should have been more prudent. It was on my lip to suggest this two or three times. Where is your husband?"

"I am expecting him every moment. Mr. Woodbine has gone to the dressing-room to tell him I am ready."

Two or three ladies by this time stood before Madeline.

"What's the matter?" "Is she sick?" "How very white she is!" These short sentences passed from one to another.

"I can't find anything of your husband," said Mr. Woodbine, joining, soon after, the group. One of my servants says that he went out nearly three hours ago, and that he doesn't remember having seen him since. And now that I think of it — Bless me!" His tone and manner changed instantly. "Catch her! She's falling!"

Madeline's head had dropped suddenly on her bosom, and she was slipping to the floor. Eager arms caught her, and laid her back on the sofa. She was colorless as marble, and insensible!

CHAPTER IV.

FOR two months Madeline lay ill at Mrs. Woodbine's. A portion of the time there had been despair of her life. Then she was removed to her own home.

More than one sweet hope died in her heart during these never-to-be-forgotten days. She came out of them, changed for all the time to come. What guarded explanations of his conduct her husband unbent himself to make, in no degree satisfied her. She did not, indeed, comprehend them. She could not get to his stand-point, and from thence view herself. Her very innocence and artlessness obscured all perception of wrong.

On the part of Jansen, there was regret for the consequences which had followed his too hastily determined withdrawal from the party, and he blamed himself for what he had done. But pride kept back from his lips and manner a confession of regret, or an acknowledgment of blame. On the whole subject, he was coldly reticent;

trying, as it were to throw a veil over the affair, as something that could not bear the light. So far as Madeline was concerned, she was ready to answer for herself in everything — had no desire for concealment — would have justified herself to the last particular, because she knew herself to be loyal and pure. But, her husband never gave her this opportunity. If the truth, in regard to him, could have been exhibited in clear light, it would have shown such a state of keen sensitiveness touching the world's opinion of what had taken place, as to overshadow considerations that lay at the very foundations of peace and happiness. And this sensitiveness to the world's opinion did not regard his wife's reputation so much as his own. He wished to appear blameless in the eyes of all men; and must we say it, desired, in his secret heart, that Madeline should stand convicted of wrong rather than himself!

Always Carl Jansen was consciously in the world's presence. Keep this trait of character in mind. He was an actor on life's stage, and the men and women he knew and mingled with socially, or in business, were the audience. He acted badly, you will say, at Mrs. Woodbine's. So he did, and no one knew that better than Jansen himself. It was the smarting consciousness of this that made him cold and unforgiving towards Madeline. He blamed her for what he suffered; and failed adequately to pity her suffering, because he deemed it deserved and salutary.

Out of sharp mental agonies most persons arise with a clearer moral vision. It was not so with Mrs. Jansen. True, her thought had a wider range; she had developed in some directions in a remarkable degree. But, touching her true position as a wife, perception had not grown clearer. She felt that she had been wronged in her husband's heart, and wronged by him before the world. Nothing was clearer to her than this. She could see it only in one light. What had she done? Nothing evil. In not one line had she swerved from honorable thought or feeling. There had not been the least variableness nor shadow of turning in the needle of her love, which pointed to her husband as its polar star. As of old, she had entered with all the outflowing impulses of her nature into the night's festivities. She had sung with that sweet abandonment of soul common with those who have a passion for music. She had felt the all-pervading sphere of pleasure that filled the atmosphere in which she moved, as she had felt it a hundred times before. That Guyton sought to monopolize her company was something to which she had not given a thought, until summoned so harshly by her husband and virtually commanded to retire with him from the house. Then, as a kind of self-justification, and from wounded pride, she permitted his further attentions. Had there been the feeblest motion of desire towards him — of preference above her husband — she would have started back from him in conscious fear and shame. But being, as we have said, loyal and pure, she did not, in imagination, invest him with any attractions that could hold her regard for an instant of time. He was a pleasant companion; that was all.

Alas for Madeline! Alas for her husband! that she had not come up out of the valley of pain and deep humiliation, with a clearer vision. Alas for them, that both were blinded by natural feeling, and that, alike, they saw obscurely — were alike disposed to self-excuses and mutual blame. There was no outward arraignment of each other

— no allusion, even remotely, to that one unhappy circumstance, the memory of which was as an ever present cloud in the horizon of their souls, dimming the sunlight; but, thought accused.

Each began to perceive in the other a sphere of coldness. The reserve that followed Madeline's restoration to health, increased rather than diminished. On the side of Madeline, this was attributed to a state of hardness towards her by her husband; on the side of Jansen, it was attributed to wilfulness and defect of love. To one thing the husband had made up his mind — reasoning from his own stand-point. It was his duty to guard his wife; to hold her as far as possible away from the allurements of society, and the dangerous association of attractive, but unprincipled men, and he meant to do this. If he had really known the artless, pure-minded woman who had promised to be true to him as a wife, he would not have seen his duty in this direction. But he did not know her, and what was worse, lacked the perceptive power by which to know her. He had no plummet line that would sound the depths of her real consciousness. And so, standing side by side with her, in the closest of all human relations, she was yet a stranger. For all this, he judged her as inexorably as if the book of her inner life were laid open to him, and he knew every page by heart.

On the return of health, the friends of Mrs. Jansen, who made up a large circle, drew her speedily back again into society. Deliberately, acting from what he conceived to be an imperative duty, her husband began throwing impediments in her way. She stepped over them without pause, acting in part from a spirit of womanly independence, in part from awakened pride, and with something of self-will; yet, chiefly, from an impelling necessity of her life. She was social, and felt drawn towards society with an almost irresistible impulse. There needed to be a warmer atmosphere — more demonstrative love — tenderer consideration — to give home the magnet's power over her. Even these could not have made her content with a semi-cloistered existence. She could love her husband (if worthy of her love); be true to him in all things; be faithful to every home-duty, and yet enjoy society with the keenest relish. But, such was the limited range of Jansen's ideas, that he was not able to understand how his wife could love society, without a decrease in her love of her husband and the love of her home.

"We cannot serve two masters," so he reasoned on the subject, as he turned it over and over in the circumscribed chamber of his thoughts. "If she prefers social life to home life, then she loves society better than her home. If she prefers the company of other men to the company of her husband, does she not put them above her husband?"

So he blinded, irritated, and hardened himself causelessly; and this, simply because he could not comprehend Madeline. On the other side, Madeline did not comprehend her husband. If she could have looked into his mind, and thus been able to understand something of his peculiar way of regarding things, the result of mental conformation and habits of life, she would have seen it best to deny herself in many things, in order that he might not read her actions as against honorable principles.

Selfish and arbitrary! Alas for domestic felicity, when

a wife so interprets her husband! Madeline was not able to give any higher interpretation to her husband's conduct on too many occasions, when, instinctively, self-will, stimulated by pride, nerved her to opposition.

Carl Jansen was not what we call an emotional man. He neither enjoyed nor suffered intensely — nor in paroxysms — never forgot himself in the overflow of pleasure or pain; but he was a brooding man, and would spread his wings over a false idea, warming it into vitality, and bringing into life a host of suggestions falser than the original; and what was worse, he too often acted on these suggestions as if they were truths. Self-poised, quiet, firm, resolute, he was one of those persons who, after adopting a line of conduct, generally pursue it to the end, bearing down — sometimes trampling down — whatever sets itself in opposition.

Madeline, on the other hand, was, as we have seen, emotional in a high degree. She could enjoy intensely, and she could suffer intensely; and what was peculiar in her case, the dominant wave usually effaced all marks of that which preceded. To her husband she was, on this account, inexplicable. Things that would have set him to brooding — that would have clouded him for days — passed with her as the morning cloud and the early dew. Now it was a rain of tears, and now a flood of sunshine. At dawn in the valley, and at noon upon the mountain top.

It was impossible for a man of Carl Jansen's range of ideas to comprehend such a woman. Narrow men are always exacting of prerogative. He was the husband and the head. Assuming this as the position of superiority, he saw very clearly that it was his duty as the head, to rule, and the duty of his wife to obey. The fact that she had defied his authority at Mrs. Woodbine's could never be forgotten — it was never forgiven. Often since then he had laid his hand upon her to hold her back, as she was moving in ways he did not approve; but as often, she had disregarded the intimations. Remembering the unhappy consequences which had followed the decided course taken at Mrs. Woodbine's, Jansen had hesitated on the question of assuming, and at the same time maintaining authority. Many times he had resolved to assert the right, held as he deemed, by virtue of the relation assumed in marriage, but not prepared for consequences that might follow, he yet hesitated. Madeline was a riddle to him. The laws of mental action, as educed from his own motives and consciousness, did not appear to govern in her case. He never knew how to determine the result of forces acting in her mind. It was a mystery to him that she had no sensitiveness to the world's opinion. This was his weak point — " How will it appear ? " " What will he think ? " or, " what will she say ? " Forever, with him, action was coming to this standard, while she lived, and moved, and had her being, in an almost entire unconsciousness of observation.

It must needs be that minds so diversely constituted come, sooner or later, into stern and unyielding antagonism. Nothing but genuine Christian virtues, the growth of self-denial, can save from this unhappy result, and in the case of Jansen and his wife, only natural feelings and considerations had influence.

CHAPTER V.

HE two months passed at Mrs. Woodbine's had not been useful to Madeline. Mrs. Woodbine was a person who generally managed to obtain considerable influence over young and ardent individuals of her own sex. She had a great deal of mental magnetism about her, attracting or repelling strongly. Tolerably well educated in the beginning, she had, by reading and intercourse with intelligent minds, enlarged her sphere of thought until it embraced philosophical and social themes. Not being a woman of well-grounded principles, it followed naturally that she lost herself in a region, the exploration of which had been attempted without chart or compass. It was a region however in which she saw much that appeared true, and in agreement with the laws of human life. But as she had accepted theories of social order not based on those immutable laws established for the soul by God, it was scarce-

ly possible for her to attempt the correction of social disorder without shattering, by her meddlesome hand, a hundred delicate fibres, where she brought a single one back into harmony.

Women of Mrs. Woodbine's peculiar character of mind, culture and temperament, have generally a large amount of sympathy with those of their own sex who are wedded to "brutes," and "domestic tyrants," and elect themselves advisors to all unhappy women who are indelicate or indiscreet enough to open their hearts to them. If they do any good, it is so largely counterbalanced by harm, that we shall scarcely err in unqualified condemnation of the class.

Of course, an incident so strongly marked as that which befel Mrs. Jansen, could not pass without comment. The fact that her husband went away and left her to return home alone at midnight, was too clear an indication of a serious quarrel, not to be accepted as evidence. Then, the brief conflict in the music room had been observed. Also, the nearly exclusive attentions of Mr. Guyton during the whole evening. A dozen little theories were started, first taking the shape of surmise, then assuming the form of positive declarations. The ears of Mrs. Woodbine were open to all those, taking them in greedily. It soon became a settled conclusion in her mind that Madeline had a self-willed, exacting young man for a husband, who, unless she early stood to her rights, might reduce her to the condition of a slave. Her beauty, her sweetness of manner, her spirit, her high social qualities, interested Mrs. Woodbine, and she determined to use whatever art she possessed, in order to save her from sinking into the condition of a host of wives, whom she pitied for their helplessness or scorned for their mean submission to a power which in her view they should have cast off and despised. As soon, therefore, as Mrs. Jansen began to recover from the worst effects of her sudden illness, Mrs. Woodbine commenced the work of poisoning her mind towards her husband. We use a strong but true word when we say poisoning. She did not in the beginning allude even remotely to Mr. Jansen, or the disturbed relation which she knew existed, but proceeded more cautiously, and by a surer way to success. In the first place, she spoke of the social inequality of men and women. She was well posted on this subject, and few men could listen for half an hour to Mrs. Woodbine, without a shame spot on the cheek. Men-made laws and customs, wherever they affected woman, would be shown by her to be the meanest of tyrannies, because they oppressed the helpless She had peculiar eloquence when on this theme, and was scarcely to be resisted.

Human nature is weak, and in nothing is this weakness — or, if you will, depravity — shown more widely than in a love of ruling or domineering over others. And it too often happens that your emancipated slave of a real or imagined tyranny, gives the first use of his freed hands to binding some weaker fellow. So it was at least with Mrs. Woodbine. She celebrated perpetually, her emancipation from marital subordination, by ruling her husband with a rod of iron. It so happened that he was a peace-loving man, and of inferior mind; one always ready to give way rather than contend. He had married Mrs. Woodbine, because he admired her brilliant mental qualities even more than her personal charms, and he had continued to admire her even though she too often made him appear mean and ridiculous in the eyes of the world. It was well for Mrs. Woodbine that such was his character. If he had been of a different spirit, they would have lived in fierce antagonism, or been driven apart.

"I am your friend, dear," she said one day to Madeline, who, a month after that unhappy evening, sat up in bed, with the soft glow of returning health just tinging her pale cheeks. Mrs. Woodbine kissed her as she spoke, and looked fondly into her eyes. "Nay, not a friend only," she added, kissing Madeline again — "that word is too cold to express my feelings. In the past few weeks, you have grown into my heart. I love you, my sweet child! You seem like one of my own flesh and blood. Confide in me, as if I were your mother."

Madeline was touched by this exhibition of tenderness, and accepted it as genuine. She had been lying with shut eyes, thinking sadly over the late unhappy affair, and with less of self-justification than before. Some rays of new light were stealing into her mind, and she was beginning to see the relation in which she stood to her husband as less favorable to herself than it had at first appeared. As a young married woman, she might not have acted with due reserve in company. Perhaps she had too completely ignored her husband during the late party. These thoughts were troubling her at the moment when Mrs. Woodbine touched her pensive lips with a kiss, and asked for her love and confidence. Tears filled Madeline's eyes as she looked up, smiling a sad, but thankful smile, into Mrs. Woodbine's face.

"What troubles you, darling? There is something on your mind." The lady drew her arm around Madeline's neck, and her head down against her bosom. Great sobs heaved the breast of Madeline; the pent-up trouble of her soul gave way. After a period of sobbing and weeping, she grew calm. In this calm, Mrs. Woodbine said —

"You are young, my child — have just stepped across the threshold of womanhood. Everything is new and strange. Already, I doubt not, your feet have found rough places — have been pierced, perhaps, by thorns. It is the lot of all. Your mother is not living,"

"O no. She died years ago."

"And your father?"

"He is dead also."

"Have you no near female relative?"

"None, except an aunt on my father's side; but, there is no sympathy between us. She never understood me."

There followed a pause. Then, speaking very tenderly, Mrs. Woodbine said —

"Let me be to you mother and friend. You have always interested me; and since, by a strange, perhaps not altogether unfortunate circumstance, you have been thrown into the very bosom of my family, my heart has gone out towards you with an irresistible yearning. There is something on your mind. You need a friend. You may confide in me if you will."

Madeline looked with grateful eyes at Mrs. Woodbine. No doubt shadowed her. She accepted the proffer of love and counsel, as if made by one who was the very soul of truth and honor. Ruled by the dominant impulse — such was her character — she lifted the veil that no wife should lift to a stranger; nay, unless in the rarest of cases, not even to a sister or a mother; and let this meddlesome woman of the world see what was in the most sacred chamber of her life.

"I thought so." This was the woman's ejaculation, after Madeline had uncovered her heart, and made a troubled confession of the doubts which had been intruding themselves. She was bewildered in mind, and spoke that she might receive counsel.

"I thought so." It is not surprising, that Madeline looked up at the woman's face, with a countenance full of questionings.

"What?" she asked, a shade dropping over her eyes.

"I thought the trouble was here."

"Where?" The shade was deeper in Madeline's eyes. Mystery always lays a weight upon the feelings.

"Dear child!" said Mrs. Woodbine, with a new ardor of affectionate interest in her manner, "you are accusing and tormenting yourself without cause. I cannot see that, as a wife, you have failed in anything. You are true to your husband in every thought and feeling. What more is possible? If more is demanded who has more to give? Not you, my child — not you!"

The large brown eyes of Madeline dilated. A look of surprise, mingled with vague questioning, came into them. She did not answer, but kept gazing at Mrs. Woodbine. Dimly the meaning of what was suggesting began to appear. Had she not been true in every thought and feeling to her husband? What more was possible?

"Men rarely understand women." The tone in which Mrs. Woodbine said this was gentle and regretful, her voice falling to a sigh on the last word. "This, however," she added, "is scarcely a matter of surprise; their training, education, and associations are so different. A false idea, strong from generations of predominance in the public mind touching the position of woman, warps the judgment of every man. He thinks himself superior. Assumes to be the head, in marriage, with the right to rule. Most women — a souless herd, if I must say it — accept this doctrine, and passively submit. A few, of nobler essence, stand firm. Generally, the waves rush against them. Some are swept away — many abide to the end in their noble defiance of wrong; calm, enduring, grand in their assertion of equality. I have known many such, and I love and honor them."

The countenance of Mrs. Woodbine glowed with fervor.

Her fine eyes were full of enthusiasm. Mrs. Jansen looked at her in a kind of maze; half surprised — half startled — half in admiration.

"You, my dear, are one of the noble sisterhood."

Madeline did not start in surprise when Mrs. Woodbine ventured upon this remark. She was in the sphere of the woman's strong magnetism. Nay, instead of being thrown instantly on her guard, she felt something like a glow of pleasure in being so classed.

"Do not understand me, my dear," added Mrs. Woodbine, in a low, penetrating voice, "as assuming that your case is an extreme one, as meaning to prophecy a life of antagonism towards your husband. I do not think him made of the hard stuff out of which some masculines are built into the image of manhood. But, he is a man, and all men have in them the germ of tyrants. If you permit him to be the master in everything, he will not fail to accept the office of ruler. If you let him see that you are co-equal — possess a soul as distinctly individual, and of right as self-asserting as his own — he will admit your claims, and you will be co-ordinate and harmonious. There will, in the nature of things, be an occasional jar. There has been already. But, if you continue true to yourself; firm in the maintenance of what is your right by nature ; never yielding to command — yet always faithful in clearly defined duties, you need have no fear about the result."

"So far," answered Madeline, carried away by her dangerous friend, and seeing in the light of her eyes — "I have not yielded to arbitrary demand. It is not my nature. If I perceive a thing to be wrong, I will not do it. If I see it to be right, and only an arbitrary opposition is set up against me, I cannot be held back. It is my nature."

"So I have read you, my child; and therefore it is that I say you are one of the noble sisterhood."

Poor Madeline! This woman, at the very first effort, had succeeded in drawing her completely within the circle of her dangerous influence. The proffered friendship was accepted — the solicited confidence given. From that day during the three or four weeks that elapsed before Madeline could be safely removed to her own home, this enchantress threw deeper and deeper spells around her. For hours she talked with her on the absorbing themes to which she had given so much thought. — On the social disabilities of her sex — on man's dreadful wrongs to woman — on the false ideas that prevailed touching just equality in the marriage bond — on the wife's duty to herself — and topics of a kindred nature.

Unhappily for Mrs. Jansen, Mrs. Woodbine first taught her to think and reason. So far in life, she had been mainly the child of feeling and impulse. A reflective being, in any high sense, up to this time, she was not. She felt, she perceived, and she acted. That was the simple process. But, during these few weeks, Mrs. Woodbine had lifted her into another region — had opened the door into another chamber of her mind. A theory, sustained by facts and reasonings that seemed clear as noonday, had been presented and accepted; and she only wondered that her own thoughts had not long ago leaped to like convictions. A few intimate friends who sympathized with Mrs. Woodbine in her peculiar ideas, were admitted to the chamber of Madeline, and she heard many conversations on the subject to which we have referred, and listened to them eagerly. Thus her mind was led to dwell upon them, and thought to gather arguments in favor of that womanly independence her nature prompted her to assert. When, at last, returning strength warranted her removal, she went back to the home of her husband, changed and matured to a degree that caused her often to look down into her own consciousness and wonder.

We shall not linger to trace all the progressive steps of alienation that too steadily separated the lives of Mr. and Mrs. Jansen. The causes have been made apparent. Two such minds, acting without concession, and without self-denial, must, in the nature of things, steadily recede from each other. And so, unhappily, did they recede.

CHAPTER VI.

THEY had been married for nearly two years. In all that time, the process of separation went on. This was not apparent to common observers — a few only saw the growing incompatibility. The fascination thrown around Mrs. Jansen by Mrs. Woodbine continued. This woman held her almost completely under her influence. Jansen understood Mrs. Woodbine's character, and did all in his power to draw his wife away from her sphere; but in this he failed altogether, only increasing Madeline's misapprehension of motives by the pertinacity of his opposition.

One day some scandalous reports reached his ears, in which the name of a lady was used whom he knew to be an intimate friend of Mrs. Woodbine, and a constant visitor at her house. Mr. Guyton's name was also mentioned. There was, or at least Jansen imagined as much, something in the relator's thought behind his speech, not felt proper to communicate, and his quick inference was that his wife's name had been in some way connected with the scandal.

"There must be an end of all this!" So he said resolutely, speaking with himself. I have opposed, remonstrated, argued, but to no effect. Madeline has set my wishes and my will at naught. But, this woman must be given up! I can no longer permit an association that is hurting my wife's reputation, if not corrupting her heart. If she be without suspicion and without prudence — if she will not look at danger though it stand in her path, my duty as a husband compels me to interfere. If love and persuasion avail not, authority and force must come as a last resort."

Jansen felt himself to be the superior and the stronger; and scarcely doubted, that, under a stern assertion of prerogative, would come submission. Within an hour after hearing the scandalous report, he met his wife on the street.

"Where are you going?" he asked, in a tone that was so full of the right to ask, that Madeline's spirit rebelled.

"Shopping," she coldly answered.

Jansen turned and walked in the direction she was going.

"I wish to say a word or two." His manner put his wife on her guard.

"You are not going to Mrs. Woodbine's," he said.

"Yes, I shall, in all probability, go there while I am out.

"No, Madeline, not there any more. Scandals, touching persons who visit at Mrs. Woodbine's are abroad, and I cannot have your name connected with them. But, we will talk all this over when I come home. In the meantime do what I say."

Madeline was silent.

"You understand what I mean," said her husband. There was, in his voice, an assumption of authority that roused the pride of his wife.

"Good morning!" she said, abruptly, turning from him and crossing the street.

Jansen was confounded; then indignant; then angry. He read this action on the part of his wife, as a defiance of his assumed prerogative. If there had remained with him any tenderness of feeling towards Madeline, it retired beyond all range of perception, or died out.

In the evening, after tea, he asked, in cold, but repressed voice —

"Were you at Mrs. Woodbine's to-day?"

They had met in mutual reserve, and remained, until this time, almost silent.

"Yes." A simple, quiet, almost indifferent "Yes."

"After what I said?" There was little change in Carl Jansen's tone of voice.

"Yes," in the same indifferent voice.

"I said there were reports abroad touching the good fame of a lady who visited there."

"Well? What of that?" She looked him strongly in the face. Her voice was firmer.

"I have your good fame in keeping — "

Madeline's eyes flashed instantly.

"So, it is my good fame that is compromised! Well, sir!" — Her suddenly rising excitement carried her away, and she became almost tragic in her manner. — "And did you assert your manly right to defend your wife's honor, and punish the false defamer?"

"If my wife," replied Jansen, not undeceiving Madeline, "in the face of warning and remonstrance, persists in associating with persons of questionable reputation, I shall not be Quixotic enough to quarrel with every one who may happen to class her with the company she keeps."

"You make a false assertion, sir!" Madeline was growing more excited.

"Take care, madam!" Jansen spoke in warning.

"I say, that your assertion, that I keep company with persons of questionable reputation, is false!" She spoke in a calmer voice, but with deeper anger, and more defiance.

"You must not use such language to me," answered the husband. His usually colorless face was now almost white. But he showed no agitation of manner.

"Guard your own tongue, then," answered Madeline, sharply.

"Surely, if I see a wolf on your path, I may speak without offence! What folly is this to which you are giving yourself over? I am amazed!"

"It is easy enough to cry wolf," retorted Madeline. "But, I do not choose to have my friends so designated. So, I pray you give better heed to your speech. It does not suit my temper. And further, Carl, let me say to you once and forever, that any assumption of authority on your part will not be favorably regarded on mine. You cannot influence me in the slightest thing by word of command, unless it be to act squarely in opposition. So take heed! I will walk in the world by your side, as your wife and your equal; but not a step behind, in submissive acknowledgment of inferiority. I am no slave, sir!"

Madeline drew herself up proudly.

Now, to Carl Jansen, taking his views of the marriage relation, which placed man at the head, as the wiser and stronger, and woman below him, as the weaker vessel, there was outspoken rebellion in this. They had been sitting face to face, the one looking steadily in strong self-assertion at the other. Half confounded, Jansen arose and crossing the room, stood with his back to his wife, thinking rapidly, yet with thought obscured, and so groping in partial blindness.

Naturally calm and proud — with no great depth of feeling — of a persistent nature, and sternly resolute in walking the ways he thought in the line of right and duty, Jansen was standing now on the Rubicon of his own and his wife's destiny. Was it possible for him to yield in this open contest? Should he move back or pass over? Behind him, he saw humiliation — the abandonment of right and prerogative — submission to an inferior power, involving disgrace and loss of self-respect, — beyond this Rubicon was a dark void, into the bosom of which sight could not penetrate; yet he knew it to be full of evil things — an abyss of suffering to himself, and of sorrow and shame for his wife.

For a moment, as he stood thus pondering, a good angel uncovered the past, and flooded his soul with the tenderness of early love. He saw Madeline as she had once looked in his eyes, the embodiment of all sweet conceptions — pure, loving, joyful as a summer day. His heart swelled with old emotions. He was beginning to move back from the Rubicon. But a darker spirit was near and shut the page from view. He was cold, stern, resolute again.

"I cannot sink my manhood! If she drags down ruin

upon her head, the blame and the consequences are her own." So he spoke firmly with himself. Turning, at length, he came back, and sat down in front of his wife. She had not moved. He looked at her, and she returned his gaze, with wide open eyes. There was no change in her manner; no sign of weakness. This pricked his feelings like the keen entrance of a dagger point. He felt irritated.

"We cannot live in open conflict, Madeline," he said.

She did not reply.

"For one I could not endure such a life. It would be a hell on earth."

Still she made no answer.

"Madeline!" The tone was too imperative; too full of the man's self-assertion. There had just come stealing into Madeline's heart a softer feeling — her true woman's nature was stirring. But the lifting wave swept back under this wind of authority.

"Madeline! unless we are both true to our marriage compact — unless the just, heaven-ordained relation of man and wife be faithfully regarded — there is no hope of peace, far less of happiness for you or for me. Consider! Pause, I implore you! Do not advance a step farther in the way you are going. Do not utterly defy me. I cannot bear such a defiance; nor be answerable for the consequences."

The head of Mrs. Jansen assumed a prouder attitude.

"Defiance? I do not understand you?" she returned, in a clear, steady voice. "Does the stream defy the obstructing stone that casts itself blindly into the free current! — or the stone defy the stream?"

She paused for him to answer. But her question only

annoyed him. He saw its application, but held the allusion to be irrelevant. There was, on his part, only a gesture of impatience. He grew blinder and harder.

"Equal, Carl, equal!" said Madeline, seeing that he did not answer. "There can be no other peaceful relation between us. From the beginning, you have treated me as though I were an inferior; and my whole nature has been in revolt. For a time, I bore with an assumption of authority over me not warranted by our relation to each other — an authority that was irritating and offensive. But, I shall bear it no longer. You must step down from your attitude of command, and if you wish to influence me, come with reason and suggestion. No other way will suit me. As to the word defiance, as applied to my conduct, I pray you, never again let it pass your lips. You may influence me by gentleness, by kind consideration, by love, Carl, such as you promised me; but never by command. I do not comprehend the word obedience, as touching my free thought and act, except as referring to God!"

"I think," answered Jansen, in a cold, cutting voice, "that the words of the marriage ceremonial, to which you deliberately responded, were, 'Wilt thou obey him, and serve him; love, honor, &c.' The form was not mine. The church made it, and all good men and women subscribe to it as expressing the true relation of man and wife. There was no compulsion. You went of your own free will, to the altar, and so registered your marriage vows. If you choose to cast them to the winds, the evil and the responsibility must rest on your own head. But I pray you in heaven's name, to pause! You have lived with me, now, for two years, and in that time gained some knowledge of my character. I am not impulsive, nor given to quick changes; but I am, by nature, inflexible. I endeavor always to walk as close to the right as possible; and when I am assured as to the right, I move onward, never stopping to question about consequences."

"I have only one thing to answer," said Madeline, her voice dropping to as cold a tone as that which her husband had used. "Take my advice, and stop where you are to question of consequences; or, when too late to question, you may regret your inflexibility. Remember, that 'love has readier will than fear.' Remember, also, that there are natures so organized that they cannot yield to force. Mine is of that order."

She ceased, and waited for him to reply. But he remained silent. For all his consciousness of right, and for all his natural inflexibility, there was something in the tone and speech of his wife, that gave him a warning to pause. He clearly understood her to be in earnest; and saw the abyss that lay before them grow darker and more appalling. So, in doubt as to what he should say, Jansen remained silent. During this silence, Madeline retired from the room, and the subject was closed for that time.

Sleep did not give a clearer mind to either Carl Jansen or his wife. As to Madeline, her intercourse with Mrs. Woodbine and other persons of her school, whom she met in the frequent visits made to that lady's house, had seriously warped her views touching her relation to her husband. The idea of submission in anything, was scouted among these wise women as a degradation of the sex. Of the essential difference between what was masculine and feminine, and therefore of the true relation of husband to wife, they were in complete ignorance. Their ideas of equality gave to woman a range of mental powers exactly similar to a man's, and also a position, if she would but assert her right, side by side with man in every worldly use or station. The mental difference, so apparent to even a child, as exhibited in the ends and actions of the two sexes, was not referred by these philosophers to any essential difference of spiritual organization, that limited the uses of each within certain spheres of life, but to false customs and habits, and to arbitrary social laws. And they had resolved among themselves to assume a larger liberty than woman usually enjoyed, and especially to maintain an individual independence so far as each was concerned.

Grafting these views upon her natural love of freedom, Madeline's will sent out strange branches, that soon blossomed and bore fruits of bitterness; and now she was lifting her hand to pluck and eat them. If her husband had been a wise man — one of a broader and warmer nature — he might easily have withdrawn Madeline from the influence of these bad associations; but he was narrow, cold, brooding and *sensitive* about his rights and prerogatives, and, what was more fatal to happiness in the *sensitive* relation held towards his wife, he had morbid views of duty, and a false conscience. He could be hard, inflexible, cruel, even, and yet stand self-justified. Of his own acts, he always judged approvingly — always took care, as he said in his thought, complacently, to be right. There was with him also the pride of consistency, and the conceit of a superior manliness, in not being subject to change.

"I am not one to be driven about like a weathercock, by every changing blast of opinion," he would often say of himself proudly.

Such they were, and now in antagonism, resolutely face to face, in the crisis of their destiny. The chances for yielding on either side were small; yet, one or the other must give way, or the most disastrous consequences would follow.

On the next morning, after a silent breakfast, Jansen said as he arose from the table —

"I must say one word, Madeline, before I go out."

There was an effort to speak softly — even in a tone of appeal; but far more apparent in voice and manner was the assertion of a right to expect his wife's compliance with what he was about saying. Madeline lifted her head quietly and gravely. Jansen saw, when he looked into her clear brown eyes, an unshaken spirit. For a moment he was in doubt — for a moment he hesitated; then he passed with a blind desperation over the Rubicon on which he had been standing.

"Don't be seen at Mrs. Woodbine's again!" The softness had died out of his voice — the tone of appeal was gone. He spoke as one in authority.

The color went from Madeline's face instantly; her eyes grew hard and fearful; slight twitching convulsions played strangely for a moment about her mouth; then, still as stone she sat, not now looking at her husband, but in a fixed stare past him, as if contemplating the dark future of her life.

Jansen was not moved to any change by this appearance, it rather made resolution sterner; he had stretched forth his hand to the plow, and would not look back.

"Remember that I am in earnest!" he said, in a warning voice, and went out, leaving the stony statue of his wife sitting at the breakfast table.

CHAPTER VII.

AT his desk, that morning, as Carl Jansen sat over the letters of correspondents, the writing would fade under his eyes, and in its place there would look up towards him the stony image of his wife, as he parted from her at the breakfast table. He could not read the newspaper for that interposing image. It overlaid the prices current; the report of the stock exchange; the sales of real estate; the foreign news. If he opened a ledger to examine an account, he soon found himself gazing at his wife's statue on the page, that concealed all the figures, and hindered the results for which he was searching. He found it in his check book, his bill book, his day book; among invoices, and accounts current; on bits of paper taken up casually. Everywhere he encountered it. The eyes did not look into his; but, with a strange, fearful expression, past him, at something beyond.

Jansen went out upon the street; partly for business purposes — partly to escape the haunting image. But it pursued him everywhere. Looking at him, or rather past him into the dark beyond, from the faces of men and women — from pictures in shop windows — from all objects, animate and inanimate towards which his eyes were bent. There was no change of expression in the countenance — none in the hard, fearful eyes — none in the marble attitude. He went back to his store, to find the spectre there, among books, papers, accounts — among articles of merchandise — in customers' faces — standing out bodily, in the atmosphere.

But, he had crossed the Rubicon of his own and his wife's destiny. There might come regret, fear, even a shuddering sense of approaching evil, but no return. Carl Jansen could not go to his wife and say, "I was wrong!" — could not take back the words last spoken. They must stand, though hearts broke, and the home-temple fell into a shapeless ruin.

At dinner-time, as Carl laid his hand upon his own door, there came a brief cessation of heart-beats — a brief stoppage of the breath. Then he passed in. He did not find his wife. She had gone out, the servant said, several hours before, and had not yet returned. Jansen felt uneasy. Then a weight dropped down upon him, so heavy as to produce a feeling of suffocation. Doubts began to obscure his mind. What if he had driven this sensitive, high-spirited woman to desperation? What if she had gone away, never again to return, except through his confession of wrong, and consequent humiliation of himself to a woman? This last thought, coming in with doubt and fear, stung his pride, steadied his shaking nerves, and restored him to inflexibility.

"If she is strong enough," he said, bitterly, to himself, "surely I am! If a woman accepts this ordeal, shall a man shrink from it? No — no! By all that manhood claims of strength and superiority — no!"

Thus, he further entrenched himself in the position he had taken. Pride sustained him through natural weakness. Pride helped him when pity, tenderness, mercy, and the old love assaulted his strong places, and gave him the victory.

On the bureau, in their chamber, he found a letter. As he reached forth to take this letter, his hand shook — shook in spite of all his natural impassiveness and habitual self-control; shook so that he laid it down and moved back some paces. But, he could not endure suspense in this great crisis. The letter was in his hand again, and as he unfolded the sheet, the irrepressible tremor of his nerves made it rattle in the air. The writing was Madeline's; clear and accurate at the beginning, but irregular, blotted, and bearing evidence of deep feeling in the progress and conclusion.

"MY HUSBAND — I fear that we have come to a place in life where our paths must diverge: not however through my desire or my election. As I look out into the world, and dimly realize what I must be, and do, and suffer, living apart from my husband, I faint in spirit — I shudder at the prospect. My heart turns back, fain to linger in the sheltered home where it took up two years ago its rest in peace and joy. But, you have dictated the only terms on which I can remain in this home. I must be inferior and obedient. You must be lord, and I serf. The free will that God gave me, I must lay at your feet. Alas for me! I cannot thus submit. As your equal, I can walk by your side, true as steel to honor, virtue, purity, and love; as your inferior there can be no dwelling together for us in the same house.

"To-day, you have laid on me a command, and, deliberately, in face of all consequences, I resolve to act as freely as though it had not been spoken. At the same time, I shall give you credit for being in earnest, and refrain from coming back, after I leave your house, until you send me word that you desire my return. I go, because I will not live with you in strife; and the terms you dictate render concord impossible. I pray you not to misunderstand me! Too much for both of us is involved. I do not go away from you, because I desire to repudiate our marriage contract, nor because there lives on this earth a man whom my heart prefers before you. I go, because you will not let me live with you in the freedom to which every soul is entitled, and in the equality that I claim as right. Here is the simple issue, as Heaven is my witness! In whatever you elect to do, keep this in mind, Carl! Your wife asks for love, and will give love in return; but if you command obedience, love dies. She cannot dwell with you as a slave, and will not dwell with you in open contention.

"My heart is full, Carl, and my eyes so dim with tears, that I can scarcely see the page on which I am writing. If I were to let my feelings have sway, there would go to you such a wild, such an impassioned appeal, as no man living, whose heart was not of stone, could resist. The words are pressing nay, almost imploring, for utterance. But, I press them back, and keep silence, for I will not be a beggar for the love you promised, nor a craven to submit. Equal, Carl! We must stand side by side as equals, or remain forever apart.

"It is vain to write more. If you cannot comprehend the stern necessity that is on me, after what I have said, further sentences will be idle. I go, because you have declared terms that make it impossible for me to remain. I will return, if you write a single line of invitation. If you say " come back," I will take it as a hopeful assurance for the future. If you keep silence, this separation is eternal! If you wish to see me, or write to me, call or send to number 560 ——— street.

"MADELINE."

After reading this letter, in an excited and prejudiced state of mind, Jansen threw it from him, under a first impulse of indignant rejection, and sat for some time in stern isolation of spirit — hard, angry, accusing, implacable. In the reading, pride had recognized only an assault upon himself and his rights as a husband; and he chafed in spirit. A calmer state succeeded. He read the letter again; but still failed to comprehend its true meaning. In his view, it was rebellious and defiant; proudly stating terms to which he must submit, or his 'wife would permanently abandon him. If he had read this letter a third time, he might better have comprehended Madeline, and the true, pure, loving woman he had driven from his heart and home. But, he folded it with a stern spirit — crushing the paper unconsciously — and threw it into a drawer away from sight.

"If she thinks I will stoop to solicit her return — that I will humble myself at her feet — she is grievously mistaken!" he said. "I am not made of that kind of stuff. If she had known me, she would never have tried this mad experiment. It will fail — miserably fail! Go to her! Solicit her to come back! Promise to be submissive to her will! Give up manhood — self-respect — prerogative — duty — rights! — No, never! I shall stand just where I stand. I am her husband, and this is her home. If she, of her own choice, abandon both, what then? She persists or repents — I am passive. So all rests in her hands. I did not thrust her from my door, and it shall never be closed against her, so long as her life is without stain. But, I cannot solicit her to come back — I will not solicit her!"

Jansen was not a man of half purposes; nor of the disposition that reviews determined lines of action, hesitating, doubting, repenting. There was something of the gypsum quality in his mind; determinations "set" quickly, and were not resolved again into free thought. Madeline was not wholly ignorant of this, when she took bold issue with her husband. She knew him to be narrow, selfish, proud, and stubbornly persistent in any line of conduct he might adopt. Yet, she braved all consequences, in her blindness; abandoning duty, love, ease, comfort, and that independence of the world, the absence of which is so wounding to all women of sensitive feelings and high spirit.

As men and women are — born with selfish inclinations, and inherited peculiarities — mutual concession is an essential rule of action in marriage. If this rule is not observed, strife must come. Were we in original purity of soul — or, through observance of divine laws restored to that purity — then no conflicts could arise. Love would be the governing law. In the degree that any individual is so restored, or regenerated through a life according to the Divine Word, so far will that individual, even in the case of a woman unhappily married, submit to things unjust and hard to bear, rather than abandon all, trusting by patience, gentleness, and a loving observance of every duty, to lift her husband into a juster perception of the relation they bear to each other. She will give up many innocent things, because his warped or narrow views will not let him regard them as allowable. Nay, even submit to arbitrary rule and dictation, rather than grapple with him in a conflict that can only end in submission for one, perpetual strife, or separation. And what is true of the woman, whose soul is rising out of the dominion of natural evils, is in like manner true of the man. He will bear and forbear — will yield and even submit in much — rather than break the most sacred of all bonds. And all this may be done without any real abandonment of that free will, whose highest office is to reject evil and choose good.

But, where there is no law of spiritual life, in the soul, leading to concession for another's good, then let the law of truth in the understanding, which every one may accept, act as a controlling force, and hold all things in fealty to higher duties, though the way in which the feet must walk be difficult, often going down into the vale of humiliation.

Madeline was wrong. Both were wrong. False views, stimulated by passion and self-will, had made a breach between them. Neither had the spirit of concession, but, instead, the spirit of accusation; and there was no angel in their hearts to bridge the widening chasm with love.

Jansen had acted with inconsiderate haste, pressing an interdict upon his wife while she was yet too blind to see all that she might have seen of duty and prudence, had he dealt with her more tenderly and wisely; and Madeline, with equal haste and lack of regard for her husband's excited state of mind, had set him at defiance. So, in mutual blame, they had been driven asunder.

CHAPTER VIII.

IF Carl Jansen could have annihilated that statue-like image of his wife, as he last parted from her at the breakfast table, he would have felt better; but, let thought turn towards Madeline when it would, thus he saw her. By an effort of will, other images might be projected before his eyes; but they faded out quickly, leaving the stony statue in their place. It was so all through the first agitated, but resolved evening following Madeline's departure; so through all the succeeding days and weeks. Even years had no power wholly to cover and hide that strange, fearful spectre, which, for a few moments, held his vision like an enchanter's spell.

No word, no sign from either. Both lived, for weeks, in blank suspense; yet wrapped about in pride, and without thought of concession.

Poor Madeline! She had gone out into the world alone. Who were her faithful friends? Upon whom, now, was she to lean? Over the threshold of what home might her feet pass confidently, and with the firm tread of one who had a right to enter? Alas for the bewildered, erring young creature! She had not counted all the cost of this wrong act. When she left her husband's house, she went directly to Mrs. Woodbine's. But, with what a different feeling from any experienced before did she enter the residence of her specious friend. The old feeling of independence and equality had strangely departed from her. Now she was a homeless wanderer, coming to ask for temporary shelter. So keenly did she feel this as she stood at Mrs. Woodbine's door, that, but for having rung the bell, she would have turned away, and gone home to reconsider the step she was taking. But, she heard the servant's feet along the hall, and it was too late to retreat.

"Ah, my dear Mrs. Jansen!" With this heartily uttered welcome, Mrs. Woodbine entered the drawing-room where Madeline sat awaiting her, and, catching her hand, pressed it warmly. "But, bless me, child!" she added, in a changed voice, "what's the matter? You're as pale as a sheet?"

Madeline tried to answer; but there was only a dumb motion of the lips.

"Are you sick?"

Madeline shook her head.

"Nothing wrong with your husband, I hope?"

"Yes." The tone was faint, and, even on this monosyllable, betrayed a tremor.

"What is it child?" asked Mrs. Woodbine.

"I have left him."

"No!"

"It is true, Mrs. Woodbine!" The heart of Madeline

was not strong enough. She sobbed out aloud, and hid her face.

"This is a serious matter, my dear," said Mrs. Woodbine, as soon as her visitor grew calm. "Left your husband! For what?" She looked sober.

"He positively forbade my coming to see *you*. That was going too far. I will not be commanded as a slave! I am here, acting in open disobedience; and do not mean to return until he signifies his wish to have me do so, promising, at the same time, to treat me as his equal in all things."

"Forbade your coming to see *me!* On what ground, pray?" There was a stain of anger on the face of Mrs. Woodbine.

"Somebody has been making slanderous reports."

"About whom?" demanded Mrs. Woodbine, growing excited. Something looked out of her eyes at Madeline, which caused the latter's heart to shrink. She had never seen that expression in them before.

"I cannot tell," replied Madeline in a confused way. "No name was mentioned."

"What was said?" The manner of Mrs. Woodbine grew hard and almost imperious.

"Nothing that in any way touched your reputation," answered Madeline, trying to soothe the anger which had been aroused.

"Who's then?" Still she was imperative; and still she looked down upon Madeline with that strange, evil gaze, which made her heart shrink and shudder.

"I cannot answer, because I do not know," replied Madeline, showing distress, and speaking in tones of deprecation. "I think it was more than half pretext on the part of my husband. He never liked our intimacy; and, finding that I was not going to give up my friends to gratify his whims and prejudices, has taken this course in order to effect his object. There is evil speaking everywhere. The best are not free from misrepresentation. Especially are women who take the independent stand you and others have taken, liable to false judgment. Somebody has spoken lightly of somebody who visits at your house — the light words repeated, have reached my husband's ears; this has given him a chance, as he supposes, to break up our intimacy. But he has not found me as clay in his fingers. It was a base pretence, I am satisfied — nothing more.

The evil look faded out of Mrs. Woodbine's eyes. Her face grew softer. She accepted the explanation. But, to Madeline, she did not assume the old cordial, winning air.

"I understand it all now," she gravely answered. "It was, as you affirm, a base thing in your husband. But my child, you have taken a serious step. What do you propose? Have you friends who will receive you?" Mrs. Woodbine gazed searchingly into Mrs. Jansen's face.

"I trust that I am strong enough to be my own friend," bravely, and with just a pulse of indignation in her voice, replied Mrs. Jansen even though her heart was growing like lead in her bosom. The change in this lady's manner struck her with a painful surprise.

"Of course you are — every true woman is strong enough for that." Mrs. Woodbine spoke with a certain air of approval, yet still with a reserve that chilled the feelings of her visitor. "And you are equal, I trust," she added, "to the contest on which you have entered. If your husband is the unemotional, strong-willed and wrong-willed man I think him, that contest must be a severe one, and may end in a permanent separation. Does he yet know of the step you purpose taking?"

"He will know of it when he returns home at dinner-time."

"Not till then?"

"No. He will find a letter, advising him of my purpose to live separate, unless he consent to treat me as an equal. If he ask me to return, I will go back and make a new trial. If he remains silent, the separation must be permanent. As I said to him, I will not live in strife, nor will I humble myself to the station of an inferior. Equal and peaceable, or not at all! He will be in no doubt of the issue when he reads my letter."

"I am afraid," answered Mrs. Woodbine, "that you have acted hastily. What if he make no reply?"

"I have counted that cost."

"Ah, indeed! Well you will be rich in resources if you prove able to meet it."

"How so?" Madeline might well ask in surprise. What could be the meaning of this changed spirit in her friend — the friend who had first counselled resistance to her husband's encroachments, and so often urged her to maintain her womanly freedom? She was puzzled, hurt and distressed by a circumstance that seemed inexplicable. "How so?" she repeated.

"In the first place, you give up an elegant home, and money to any fair extent that you may see fit to demand. Have you rich relatives, who will, in turn, supply these? Your good name is to-day, unsullied before the world. Abandon your husband, on almost any pretext, and though your life be pure as an angel's, the soil of slander will be

4

cast over your garments. You have now ease, comfort, and complete independence in worldly matters; how will it be if you cast them all behind? My dear young friend, you stand this hour in the most momentous crisis of your life. I would not have advised this step. As society is now constituted, the woman who breaks the marriage bond is misunderstood and misinterpreted. Public opinion ranges itself against her, and a hundred impediments are thrown in the way of her honorable independence. A man cast loose upon the world if he have strength and will, finds all things conspiring to his success; but a woman so cast loose, finds all things conspiring against her. I speak soberly, my dear young friend, and earnestly, for I have a larger experience of the world than you. No — no! this is not the way. Hold to your legal position as Mr. Jansen's wife, but maintain your independence. If he seek to put on the tyrant, set him at naught, but hold to the material rights acquired in wedlock. If you abandon him, you abandon everything; but if he abandons you, the law will give alimony, and so leave you independent. You see, child, that I take a sober, common-sense view of things. I look to the main chance. Understand me; I counsel no submission. You are his equal, and if skilled in the use of your native strength, fairly matched with him in any contest he may precipitate. The home you purpose abandoning is as much yours as his. Don't lose the advantage its possession gives you. Put on triple armor for defence, if that be needed; call to your aid all a fertile woman's resources, as I have done, and victory will surely perch on your banners. But don't — don't take this hazardous step. Your husband is narrow in his views — cold and stubborn. I do not believe he will send or come for you. He thinks woman weak, and will trust to your repentance. To return to him after the final breach, would be a shame and a humiliation."

"I would die first," said Madeline, with aroused indignation.

Here the interview was interrupted by a visitor — a small, pale-faced, high-browed, dark-eyed woman, whose faded countenance yet self-reliant air, showed a person who had seen some service in the warfare of life.

"My dear Mrs. Windall," exclaimed Mrs. Woodbine, rising and advancing to meet her as she entered the drawing-room, "I'm so glad to see you this morning! Just in time to help me advise our young friend, Mrs. Jansen."

"Ah, Mrs Jansen!" said the new comer, turning from Mrs. Woodbine — "I did not anticipate this pleasure. In trouble, child! What's happened?"

Before Madeline could speak, Mrs. Woodbine answered for her —

"Yes, she's in trouble, and we must see her through it, if possible."

"What kind of trouble?" asked Mrs. Windall.

"With her husband, of course. Oh, dear! these miserable husbands! they're the curse of our lives!"

A shadow dropped over the pale face of Mrs. Windall: her brows fell; her dark eyes grew intense; she looked angry — almost cruel —

"The curse of our lives! You may well say that." She spoke in a kind of panting undertone, like one in strong excitement.

"Well, dear?" turning to Madeline, "what has happened? A quarrel with your tyrant, of course! I can guess that much."

"We shall never quarrel again," replied Madeline, with a calmness of voice not expected by Mrs. Woodbine.

"Ha! what does that mean?" The eyes of Mrs. Windall flashed. There was apparent in her manner a thrill of excitement.

"It means that we have parted company," said Madeline.

"Of your own choice?"

"Yes; I will not be a slave, nor will I dwell with any man in perpetual strife."

"Spoken like a brave, true woman!" said Mrs. Windall, grasping Madeline's hand — "and I welcome you to the sisterhood of those noble ones who can suffer, but not endure bonds. It would be better for our sex if there were many, many more of your spirit. My ear catches the ring of the true metal, and the music is sweet. I kiss you, dear, brave young woman, and receive you into our circle." And Mrs. Windall pressed her lips to Madeline's forehead. They were almost like the touch of marble lips — so cold — giving a chill instead of warmth.

"There is the cost to be counted," said Mrs. Woodbine, now interposing. "Always it is best to count the cost. Mrs. Jansen has left her husband. What next? Where is she going? What will she do? Who are her friends?"

"All true women are her friends," responded Mrs. Windall, becoming heroic in manner.

"She will need something beyond mere friendship."

"True friendship is full of service," answered Mrs. Windall.

"In my opinion," said Mrs. Woodbine, speaking in a firm asserting tone of voice, "the highest office of friendship towards Mrs. Jansen is to advise her to go back to her home and maintain her rights there. I have said this to her already, and my hope was that you would say the same. There she will possess all external advantages — every luxury and comfort she desires — a liberal supply of money — ease and independence, if she will assert and maintain it. There are plenty of ways in which a bright, resolute woman may rule, instead of being ruled by her husband, and thus hold in freedom all the advantages of her position. Go back, Mrs. Jansen; that is my advice."

"I am not so mercenary as you seem to imagine," replied Madeline, flashing her beautiful eyes into the face of Mrs. Woodbine. There was an air of defiance in this, quite offensive to the latter, whose love of having things her own way never calmly brooked a spirit of opposition. Madeline had been, up to this time, a docile learner in her new school of woman's rights; but now that she was asserting a right to think and act for herself, Mrs. Woodbine felt that her superior judgment was being set at naught, and this was more than she could calmly bear.

"But a great deal sillier than I imagined," came in sharp retort from her lips. "You must live! How, pray? That's the question. Have you the answer ready?"

"The world is wide," said Madeline, her tones less impassioned. "And I shall find my place in it. I am strong enough, I trust, both to do and to dare in whatever work or strife befall me. But, I will not dwell in contention with my husband. I hold the marriage bond as too holy a thing for this. I loved my husband — I still regard him above all other men"— her voice gave way, but she recovered it quickly, and went on — " and I will not meet him in open war, wounding and receiving wounds. There may be women who glory in battle; but I am not one of these. My spirit will not brook tyranny; so I flee from the tyrant's presence and seek to dwell in peace."

"You are not a woman of my stamp," retorted Mrs. Woodbine, with a half contemptuous motion of the head. "No tyrant shall drive me from the place assigned me by natural right, and by law. If the question come as to who will leave this house by voluntary act — my husband or me — be sure that I will remain at any cost. He can go if it so please him; but not I. I thought you had more pluck, child. Pshaw! Cast these romantic notions to the wind. Love! Dont talk of that. When a husband puts on the tyrant, love vanishes."

Madeline had entered the house of Mrs. Woodbine, intending to remain there temporarily. She had expected a far different reception. Had looked for sympathy, succor, and encouragement. Alas! How suddenly this admired and almost worshipped friend had become transformed. Now, she arose, as if to depart.

"Don't go," said Mrs. Woodbine. But there was no feeling in her voice — no actual invitation to remain.

Mrs. Windall arose at the same time. Her eyes were on the face of Madeline. She was reading it with keen, but sinister glances.

Mrs. Jansen did not reply to the remark of Mrs. Woodbine, but drew her shawl to her shoulders, and stepped back towards the door. Mrs. Windall did the same.

"My dear young friend! I trust you will reflect deeply on what you are about doing," said Mrs. Woodbine, in a tone of warning.

"Be advised by me. Go home. Sleep for another night on this question, remembering that it is to affect for good or ill your whole life. I am your friend. Don't forget this. Your true friend, who seeks to save you from calamity. Mrs. Windall! Join me in admonishing her to beware of a step, which, once taken, cannot be retraced, and may lead to untold evils."

"Come home with me, dear," said Mrs. Windall, turning to Madeline. "As Mrs. Woodbine intimates, the most vital things are concerned, and every step should be well considered. We will go over the whole matter together, and see what is best to be done. Trust me, Mrs. Woodbine" — looking towards that lady — "I will counsel her as faithfully as if she were my own child. Good morning! Come, dear!"

And without giving time for interposition, even if that had been in Mrs. Woodbine's thought, she hurried Madeline away.

"Faithfully!" Mrs. Woodbine spoke with herself, standing alone in her drawing-room.

"Aye, as the hawk deals with the dove! Foolish young creature! I wish she were safely back in her home again. What strength has she for the battle that is before her? — what endurance for the storms that will beat upon her fair young head? Well! well! Some natures are incomprehensible! Some spirits move blindly upon ruin. You cannot counsel them — you cannot hold them back. As for Mrs. Jansen, I wash my hands clear of all responsibility. Be her future what it may, no blame shall rest at my door."

CHAPTER IX.

RS. WINDALL was, as we have said, a small, pale-faced woman, with dark keen eyes and high forehead. She was rather showily dressed, in cheap, faded finery, the soils and creases therein marking her as an untidy person. She was one of those who, affecting a scorn for things feminine, have yet a weak love for gaudy attire, but neither taste nor neatness. So in her wardrobe she made herself noticeable, but did not elicit admiration. Years before she had quarreled with her husband, and they had ever since lived separately. As to the blame, it was about equally divided. Both had hung out false colors, she pretending to be an heiress, and he a thriving man of business. The mutual cheat was never forgiven on either side, and after a brief but stormy attempt to live before the world as man and wife, they had broken their fetters and swept asunder.

Previous to her marriage, Mrs. Windall had lived with a distant relative; but, on separating from her husband, the door of her old home did not open for her again. The fact was, she had been a burden to this relative, who felt no inclination to take it up again. Mrs. Windall, therefore, in leaving her husband, went out into the world alone. Just how she had managed to live for the past five or six years, no one knew. Frequent changes of boarding places, left with some the inference that she was either difficult to please, or for some cause was not considered a desirable guest. The truth was, she had a slender purse, and did not pay as she went. The question of ways and means had become one of vital interest to Mrs. Windall. She would not, however, descend into any of the vulgarly useful employments, preferring to get money through appeals to sympathetic strangers, in whom she managed to excite pity for her wrongs and destitution. She had "boarded round" and "begged round" in Philadelphia for nearly two years, until she became so well known that both doors and sympathy were shut against her. Then she found means to procure from three clergymen and two editors, letters of introduction to as many individuals in Boston of the same professions, whither she went, and on the strength of these introductions, managed to get into respectable society. But she was both a moth and a drone, consuming yet not producing. For a time, she interested people of some cultivation, for her mind was active, and she was a fluent talker. In Boston, she met with a number of men and women who were absorbed in social theories, joined their circle, and for awhile became a leader among them. Gradually, however, something in her was felt as repulsive. The circle did not harmonize with Mrs. Windall so near the centre, and by tacit consent, she was gradually pressed to the circumference. She could talk glibly of "broad humanities;" of "noble aims and ends;" of their "high mission in the world;" of the "new gospel" they were sent to preach; but those who had the means of knowing her best, saw that she was idle and selfish — a taker on all sides, but not a giver.

For over two years Mrs. Windall managed to keep afloat in Boston; then she found it necessary to emigrate. Gradually the circle of her friends had diminished, and as it lessened, the character of her associates were of a lower grade. Light scandals touched her fame — whether justly or not we cannot affirm. In the end, a few weak but well-meaning individuals, who pitied her destitution, obtained for her letters introductory, and a sum of money, with which she passed to New York. Here she had flourished for a while, but was now getting to be so well understood, that she found it difficult to hold her own.

Such in brief was the woman into whose hands Mrs. Jansen had fallen. Coldly had the friend on whom Madeline counted turned from her — the very friend who had first taught her the new doctrines of equality and independence, on which she was now acting. The friend on whom she had counted for everything in this the great crisis of her life, turned from and left her with a woman whose sphere had always been repellant, and holden by whose hand she was now stepping out into an unknown and untried world. The air of this new region struck upon her with a chill, and she felt an inward shudder as she walked away from Mrs. Woodbine's door, accompanied by Mrs. Windall. Had she been alone, most likely her feet would have turned back towards her own house. But she was committed to a degree that left retreat out of the question. She was too young and too strong in her self-will for a cool counting of the cost — for that sober reflection and hesitation which years of life-experiences, with their sufferings, are sure to bring. Pride was a dominant passion — this also held her to the course upon which she had so madly entered.

Mrs. Windall was boarding at No. — Washington street, in a house and neighborhood quite below the range of respectability in which Mrs. Jansen had been living with her husband. The latter held back, and gave her companion a look of surprised inquiry, as they stopped before a dingy dwelling.

"This is my home for the present, dear," said Mrs. Windall, with an encouraging smile. "Not as elegant as I could desire, but the people are so very kind that I can't take heart to leave them. Come!"

Mrs. Windall's hand was already on the bell. Madeline felt an impulse to turn away, and run as if for life; but she had not strength enough to break the spell that was upon her, and so stood passive, with her eyes cast down and half-closed, instinctively shutting away the unpleasing objects that were before them.

"Come dear!" The door had been opened by a sharp looking Irish girl, who glanced keenly at Mrs. Jansen as she entered on this invitation of her friend.

"Is my room in order, Kitty?" asked Mrs. Windall, when they stood in the narrow hall, the atmosphere of which was heavy with dining-room and kitchen odors.

"No ma'am," answered Kitty, with a curtness of tone that did not escape Mrs. Jansen.

"Will you put it in order right away, Kitty?"

Kitty did not give a verbal negative, but her manner said emphatically — "No!"

"Walk into the parlor, Mrs. Jansen," said Mrs. Windall, turning from the servant, whose sharp, curious eyes had already closely scanned the visitor's face.

The parlor was a small front room, of cheerless aspect. The air was close and impure, the furniture dingy, the painted walls dirty with head and hand marks. An old sofa, with a broken spring shining through the rent haircloth, stood on one side. In the centre was a small round mahogany table, on which was a carcel lamp, surmounted by a globe, cracked on one side, and with a crescent-shaped piece scalloped out of the top. The odor of sperm oil struck the nostrils as the eyes rested on this lamp. It was not imagination. Five ancient looking stuffed chairs were ranged about the apartment. The carpet, of English Brussels, had once been handsome; but that was a long time ago. It would have been difficult now to make out the figure clearly, the pile was so completely worn off in large spots, thus exposing the coarse grain of the canvas. Paintted shades, which could hardly have seen less than ten years' service, darkened the windows. On the mantelpiece stood a small French clock, the pendulum motionless. This article of ornament was flanked by two small, curiously spotted shells, the only clean and fresh looking things in the room. A few pictures, so called by courtesy, hung on the walls, the most noticeable being a savage looking Judith and Holofernes.

"We'll sit here for a short time, until the servant gets my room ready," said Mrs. Windall, taking off her bonnet, and tossing it in a careless way on to the table, where stood the carcel lamp, untrimmed since the last night's burning.

If it came off free of an oil spot, so much might be counted as gain. "She didn't expect me home so soon, or it would have been all right. When I go out in the morning I hardly ever get home until dinner-time. And now, my child, while waiting for Kitty, we can talk."

Mrs. Jansen glanced towards the folding doors, that stood closed between the front and back rooms.

"There's no one there," said Mrs. Windall, understanding the significance of the glance.

A movement in the adjoining room contradicted her assertion, and she dropped her voice, as she remarked —

"Only a servant, I presume. But, we can talk low. And now let me repeat the assurances already made, that I am your friend, and feel deeply interested in your case. Do you know, dear, I've always felt drawn towards you. There's something about you so frank and outspoken — so womanly and so independent — so true to yourself. The step you are taking is a most painful one; but it is in pain that higher principles are born. We must go through the fire to purification. We must get strength for noble work by braving the tempest. Dear, dear child! don't give way to a weakness that is unworthy of the duty to which you are called!"

Poor Madeline! Her heart had failed her. Looking into the face of things as they were beginning to present themselves, she shuddered in affright. Her answer to Mrs. Windall was a trio of sobs, and a gush of tears.

"I know it is a hard thing for you, my dear," said Mrs. Windall, in a tenderly sympathizing voice, drawing an arm as she spoke, around Mrs. Jansen. "So young — so hopeful — so loving, yet so terribly disappointed! These wrongs to our sex set my blood on fire. I grow fierce with indignation when I see them. Poor child! This is but a momentary weakness. I understand how it is, for have I not also been in the furnace? You will be stronger in a little while."

"It is cruel — so cruel!" murmured Mrs. Jansen.

"All men are cruel. It is their nature," said Mrs. Windall. Flatter them — yield to them in everything — call black white to humor their whims, and they can be as gentle as lambs; but set yourself in opposition; dare to call your soul your own, and instantly the fangs are seen. But you haven't told me all about this unhappy affair. I could only get vague hints from our conversation at Mrs. Woodbine's. And, by the way, Mrs. Woodbine acted very strangely. I thought more highly of her. To recommend you to go back, just for the sake of money and position!

But you answered her nobly! Your language thrilled me with pleasure. I said, what a grand young soul! There was in your words the inspiration of a high purpose. I felt that the priestess for our new temple had come. And so I drew you away from the unworthy contact of such a woman as Mrs Woodbine."

This speech was not without influence on Mrs Jansen. She was pleased rather than disgusted, and so made blind instead of clear-seeing in regard to her friend. Her emotion had already subsided; calmness and strength were born of momentary weakness.

"How was it? Tell me all," said Mrs. Windall, resuming. Trust me, as one who loves you — as one who will make your cause her own — as a daughter would trust her mother."

Mrs. Windall could attract strongly. If one come fully within her sphere, that one was captive, at least for a time.

Already Madeline was beginning to feel the influence of this subtle sphere. As she looked into the woman's face, its expression changed. What had been hard and repellant, was softened by more graceful lines. There was tenderness in the cold dark eyes, from whose strange intenseness she had so often turned away with an inward shiver. Madeline was in her power.

"Tell me all," repeated Mrs. Windall. Her tones had in them now more of command than solicitation — not offensive command, but that expectation of consent, which, from its subtlety, is so much more certain to prevail. And Madeline opened all her heart. She kept back nothing.

"Now I can advise you understandingly," said Mrs. Windall, when in full possession of the case. "Of course you cannot go back, unless your husband consents to the equality you have demanded. That would be to sink below the former level you held in his house. It would be acknowledging yourself an inferior — a serf, a slave. He would be tenfold more the tyrant. No — no; you have entered a path in which there is no turning back without loss of everything a woman holds dear. And now, let me ask a plain question or two as to your connections and prospects outside of your husband. The better I understand things, you see, the better I can advise you. What of your relatives?"

"Apart from my husband," replied Mrs. Jansen, "I am nearly alone in the world."

"Ah!" There was a certain spring in Mrs. Windall's voice that indicated satisfaction.

"I lived with an aunt, my only near relative, at the time of my marriage. She has since died," added Mrs. Jansen.

"Have you an income? — Anything in your own right?"

"Nothing."

"So you stand alone in the world, trusting in your own strength?"

"Alone!" How the word echoed through all the chambers of Madeline's soul.

"And yet not alone," said Mrs. Windall. "As I have already affirmed, all true women are your friends; and you will find many noble spirits drawing to your side. They will encompass you as a defensive wall."

The parlor door was opened at this moment by Kitty, who had altered her first intention about Mrs. Windall's chamber.

"Your room is ready, ma'am," she said, with less curtness of speech than she had used when the ladies first came in.

"Oh! Thank you, Kitty," returned Mrs. Windall, with considerable blandness of manner.

After obtaining a good look at the visitor the observant Kitty retired.

The apartment to which Mrs. Jansen now ascended, was in the third story, back. Its furniture was in the ordinary style of second and third class boarding houses — meagre, dingy, cheerless. A cherry four poster, of scant dimensions and obsolete style, occupied a portion of the chamber. The bed was thin and covered by a faded calico spread, patched here and there with pieces of different patterns. There was no bureau. Two large trunks were, instead, the repositories of Mrs. Windall's clothing. A cheap mahogany framed glass hung against the wall, under which was placed a high and narrow pine dressing table. Two chairs, a small writing or work-table, a strip of carpet before the bed, a common maple washstand, and green paper blinds at the windows, made up the complement of furniture.

"It isn't very elegant," said Mrs. Windall, as she ushered her almost shrinking companion into this comfortless apartment. "But," she added, with affected indifference towards external things, "not in our surroundings does the heart find rest and satisfaction. Sweet peace, contentment, delight, come by an inner way. The poet who said, 'My mind my kingdom is,' understood life's true philosophy. How often do I repeat the words! How often have I repeated them in this poor little room, and felt their sublime meaning."

As she spoke, Mrs Windall untied Madeline's bonnet strings and removed her bonnet. The unhappy young creature was stunned and passive. She felt herself in a weird atmosphere, every breath of which fed a strange, scarcely real life. There was a spell on her, which it seemed impossible to break. She distinctly recognized a power in this woman against which she had not, in the present, strength to act. She felt herself like a broken branch on a stream, borne away she knew not whither.

"Don't look so miserable, dear," said Mrs. Windall, seeing in Mrs. Jansen's face a picture of wretchedness and vague alarm. "The first sharp pain will soon be over. Then you will feel calm, strong, and full of self-confidence! I have gone by this way, and know every foot of the ground. It leads to freedom — to self-repose — to honorable independence. Only the first steps are painful and difficult."

Mrs. Jansen did not reply. After her bonnet and shawl had been laid off, she sat down by one of the windows and looked out. The prospect was neither soothing nor clevating. Dirty brick walls, chimneys, roofs — a dull sky over head — below, not a green thing. It was a glimpse of New York out of a back third story window on the east side of Washington street. A dreary gaze — shut eyes for a little while — then Mrs. Jansen turned from the prospect without to the one within. The room seemed more desolate and repulsive than at the first glance. It was a comfortless cell compared with the luxurious chamber she had, until within a few hours, called her own. What a heavy weight rested on her bosom! She almost panted for breath. It seemed as if something were crushing her life out. Then came a strong impulse to break away — to run from this woman as from an enemy, and from this close room as from a prison. She even rose with a sudden resoluteness of manner, and crossed towards the bed on which her shawl and bonnet were lying. Mrs. Windall, who was on the alert, read what was passing in her mind, and moving quickly to her side, drew an arm around her and said —

"And now, my dear, going back to the subject of our conversation when Kitty interrupted us, take heart in the assurance that you do not stand alone. That all true women are your friends, and that purer and nobler spirits than you have yet known, will come to your side and claim you as a sister. Sit down again. I have a world of things to say."

And Mrs. Jansen, weak and bewildered, sat down; or, to speak more truly, permitted herself to be borne down upon the chair from which she had just arisen.

"And first, dear Mrs. Jansen! let me offer, with a free and loving heart, to share my poor room with you for a little while, until better arrangements can be made. A season of quiet is essential in your present state of mind. You need not join the family. I will arrange to have your meals sent up. Just as long as you may wish, shall you remain in perfect seclusion. In the mean time, we can survey the whole ground and determine your best course."

Mrs. Jansen, whose eyes had fallen to the floor, did not look up nor respond. She was thinking of the letter she had left for her husband, and whether he would send an answer. How was she to get the answer, if it were sent? She had given the number of Mrs. Woodbine's house, as that to which any communication for her should be directed. Could she go there again, after what had passed between her and Mrs. Woodbine? She felt, with keenness, the altered tone of this friend, upon whom she had counted for almost everything. She was hurt, alienated offended. When she passed through her door, on retiring, she had resolved never to re-enter it again. Of course, Mrs. Windall would call for her on the next day, and inquire for a letter! but, there came a hesitation in her thought — a certain want of confidence was felt. Though captive, in a degree, to the stronger will of Mrs. Windall, the instincts of her purer nature warned her against implicit trust. No, she did not wish any communication from her husband to get into the hands of this woman; nor, in case a letter was received, did she wish to read it in her presence. In such a case, she felt that she would not be free to act as her own heart and judgment might dictate.

"You do not answer me," said Mrs. Windall, breaking in upon Madeline's perplexed thoughts. There was just a shade of offended pride in her voice.

"Forgive me, my kind friend," answered Mrs. Jansen, rousing herself. She shivered as if a cold wind had blown upon her. "Be patient with me. I do not see clearly."

"No mother could be more patient, or more loving than I will be, dear Mrs. Jansen! It is because my heart is so full of your case, that I seem to be intrusive. I know how it is with you. I see just where you stand, and see, also, the way opening easily before you. Ah, dear, if your eyes could perceive what is so plain to mine! But that, in your present state, is impossible."

Mrs. Windall drew an arm around Madeline and kissed her. How cold the lips were! They sent a chill down her nerves.

Weak — passive — silent. The strength, born of indignant purpose; the half heroic enthusiasm which had led Mrs. Jansen out from the home of her husband; the dominant will, ready to accept anything but submission — were all failing now, as she stood face to face with these first repulsive facts of her new life. Anything so poor, so mean, so circumscribed as this chamber of her friend, had not come within the range of her anticipation. Sacrifice; endurance; self-dependence; stern conflict in the life-battle that was before her, going out thus alone into the world, she had nerved herself to accept. But in so far as imagination had realized anything as actual, there was in its pictures of the future a certain grandness and heroism, with its poetical compensations, that would give strength to a nature like hers. And here, at the initial step, as if to drive her back, she was met by a coarse and offensive reality, the first contact with which filled her with disgust. The admonition would have been effectual, had she not been under the influence of a will more subtle and powerful than her own. Weak — passive — silent she became, after a single effort to break away; and when, perceiving this state, Mrs. Windall urged her to lie down, she made no resistance.

After her head was upon the pillow, Mrs. Windall sat close beside her. Madeline shut her eyes and turned partly away. Her face was pale; her eyelids wet; her mouth full of sadness. Now a change flashed over Mrs. Windall's faded countenance — there was a gleam in her eyes — and the signs of an eager purpose about her thin, cold lips. With a repressed movement, she extended one of her hands, and laid it gently on Madeline's forehead. For nearly a minute she did not move this hand; then the fingers stirred, just as if the motion were involuntary. After that, she stroked the damp hair softly, gradually extending the touch down to the temples on each side. This was continued for some time, Mrs. Jansen remaining quiet. If the half unconscious woman, lying there with closed lids, could have seen the countenance of Mrs. Windall as it was now, she would have started up and fled in terror from the room. But she was fast losing herself. The motion of Mrs. Windall's hand went on, gradually increasing in quickness, while her eyes fixed themselves with a snake-like intensity upon Madeline. Five, ten, fifteen, twenty minutes elapsed, and still the hand of Mrs. Windall stroked the forehead and temple of the motionless woman lying before her — the expression of her face increasing all the while in its intense eagerness. At last she paused, still with her weird eyes on Madeline, and her hand held a few inches above the head she had been caressing. All remained silent as death. Even the breathing of Mrs. Windall was suppressed.

Now she stood up and bent over, so as to get a full view of Madeline's face. The result was satisfactory. A light flashed into her countenance, a strange, unnatural, evil light. Again she laid her hand on her head, and as she did so, called her name in a low voice; but no response came. Then an arm was gently lifted — it remained, as raised, after being released, not falling back upon the bed by its own weight. Mrs. Windall pressed upon the arm, and it went down slowly. Again that gleam of light flashed over the woman's face which was full of conscious power. An eager thrill of triumph seemed to pervade her soul. Her slight form swelled into fuller proportions.

"Mine!" she ejaculated, in a whisper. "Mine!" And still she stood looking greedily at the unconscious Madeline — a dove just flown from her cage, and so soon in the hawk's talons!

CHAPTER X.

THE whole aspect of Mrs. Windall was changed. At a first glance, even one quite familiar with her appearance might have failed in a clear recognition. Usually, there was about her an air of repose. Life did not flush the external of her being, but held itself, like a hidden spring, in fullness at the centre. Now it was leaping along her veins in unwonted currents, while every nerve was in a thrill. As she stood erect above the unconscious Mrs. Jansen, every part of her body was in motion, with that billowy grace seen in wild animals of the feline species; while her face glowed with an evil radiance. She stood over Madeline for a little while, and then crossing to the window, looked out for a moment; then turned and went back to the bed again — still with that rippling, springy grace of motion to which we have referred. Her eyes glanced towards her victim as she turned, with that glittering eagerness seen in the cat's eyes, half cruel, when she sports with her prey.

As if to reassure herself that Mrs. Jansen was completely spell-bound, she called her in a low voice; but the ears were dead to external sounds. Then she laid her hand on her temples — then lifted her passive arms, that retained, like pieces of wax, any position she gave them. A fuller satisfaction flushed her pale face — a keener delight burned in her calm, dark eyes — through every limb and muscle ran a stronger billowy motion. She was graceful in attitude as a wild beast on the alert for prey.

This flushing of all the externals of Mrs. Windall's life, consequent on gaining power over a weaker soul, whom she meant to render obedient to sinister purposes, continued for nearly an hour. During this long period, she was in almost constant motion, exhibiting the restlessness of a caged animal. Every now and then, she would stand over Madeline, and look upon her with an expression of intense satisfaction. There was no pity, no sympathy, no compassion in her cold face. She did not think of what suffering might lay in the path she was marking out in thought for this young creature's feet; but only of gain to herself.

After an hour, her exhilarant state passed, and Mrs. Windall became reflective. She sat down a little way from the bed, assuming in a short time the attitude of one who had pondered deeply. Sometimes her head moved in assent to a hidden thought, or slowly signed a negative, as some result was reached that did not find approval. And still the death-like sleeper lay with soul and sense imprisoned.

Almost another hour elapsed without change. At the end of that period Mrs. Windall stood over Madeline, not in the fearful aspect she had borne since the beginning of this infernal rite, but with her usual countenance, softened by looks of kindness. There were a few quiet passes and touches, and calls made in tones of tender interest; when the long still lashes quivered, the lips moved, the whole body showed a thrill of returning life.

"Dear Mrs. Jansen!" a mother's voice could hardly have so abounded in love as the voice of Mrs. Windall. "How sweetly you have slept."

Mrs. Jansen started up and looked around her in a scared way.

"Have you been dreaming, dear?" asked Mrs. Windall.

"Dreaming! dreaming!" murmured Mrs. Jansen, as one still but half awake. She looked strangely about the room, then timidly at Mrs. Windall.

"What a sweet sleep you have had! I've been watching you for more than an hour. I never saw anything so peaceful. It was like an infant's slumber." Mrs. Windall's arm was already around Madeline, who first shrank away, and then permitted herself to be drawn close to her side.

There came a rap at the door, which a moment afterwards was pushed open, and Kitty's sharp face peered in.

"Did you call, ma'am?" asked the servant, and as she spoke she advanced her body into the room, and fixed her intelligent eyes on Mrs. Jansen.

"No, Kitty," answered Mrs. Windall, in a slightly annoyed manner.—"I didn't call, and don't want anything."

"Will the lady stay to dinner, and shall I have a place for her?" Kitty held her ground, in spite of Mrs. Windall's intimation that she could retire.

"Oh, no — no," answered Mrs. Jansen, "I shall not stay to dinner. Is it so late?"

"It's going near on till two o'clock, ma'am," said Kitty.

"Impossible!" And Mrs. Jansen drew out her watch. "How strange!" she ejaculated — "Nearly two, as I live, and I thought it was scarcely twelve."

Kitty's eyes, full of curious interest, were reading every line and expression of Mrs. Jansen's beautiful young face.

"Yes ma'am," said the girl, "it's nearly two, and we have dinner at the hour. Shall I bring you up something?"

"No, thank you. Have I slept long?" And Madeline turned to Mrs. Windall.

"You can go down, Kitty," said the last-named person. "I did not call you. If my friend takes dinner with me, I will see to it. There — there —!" she added, in an imperative manner, as the girl still lingered. Kitty, with a look on her face that did not escape Mrs. Jansen, went out slowly.

"The most provoking girl I ever saw!" exclaimed Mrs. Windall, angrily, as Kitty shut the door. "She's always prowling about, and thrusting herself upon you in and out of season. But if you really want anything, she is very sure to have other engagements. Were you asleep long? Yes, dear. You slept for nearly two hours, and lay so quietly and peacefully that I could not find it in my heart to break the spell of slumber. You wont go down to dinner?"

"Oh, no — no, Mrs. Windall; I couldn't eat a mouthful."

"I'll have your dinner sent up."

"No, no; I would choke if I attempted to eat."

"But you can't go without food, dear. I'll find something delicate at the table, and bring it to you myself."

Mrs. Jansen only turned her head partly away, with that air of aversion which we sometimes see in the sick when pressed to take food. She had been sitting, since aroused from her unnatural sleep, on the bed. Now, rising, she walked in an unsteady way across the room, and stood at the window, from which she had already obtained so dreary a prospect of roofs and chimneys.

"I think," she said, turning suddenly around, "that I will ——" As suddenly as she had begun did Mrs. Jansen check herself.

"Will what?" asked Mrs. Windall.

"Oh, nothing; it was a mere thought," replied Madeline.

Mrs. Windall's forehead contracted. She looked sharply at Mrs. Jansen.

"Don't be afraid to speak out to me," she said. "I am your friend in everything. If you have doubts, questions, or rising purposes, don't hesitate about letting me see them. My heart is in your case, and, I will counsel or lead you as carefully as if you were my own child."

But Mrs. Jansen did not reveal her thought. Nay, hid it in her mind with care, lest it should be discovered. In vain did Mrs. Windall persist in trying to get at the meaning of that quick decision of her young friend's mind — for she saw that a decision had been reached — Madeline baffled her in every effort.

The loud clamor of a bell, jarring through the hall and stairways, announced dinner.

"You will not go down"? said Mrs. Windall.

"No."

"I will bring you up something."

Mrs. Jansen shook her head.

"But you must take food. A cup of tea and a piece of toast, if nothing else. Shall I bring these?"

"I'll take some tea," said Mrs. Jansen, with the manner of one who wished to get rid of importunity.

The instant Mrs. Windall left the chamber, Madeline's face lighted with a purpose. She listened intently to the sound of her retreating footsteps, to the opening and shutting of chamber doors, and the confused noise of feet down the stairs and along the passages. In a few moments all was still again. Now she got up quickly, and after a hurried arrangement of her hair, put on her shawl and bonnet. Her hand was on the door, which she pulled softly ajar. As she did so, her quick ear caught the sound of light ascending feet. Starting back, she threw off the bonnet and shawl, tossing them to the farther side of the bed from which she had taken them, and was sitting with an apparently absorbed air near the window, when Mrs. Windall opened the door and came in.

"They have some nice roasted fowl on the table," she said. "Now do let me send you a piece."

Mrs. Jansen shook her head, replying —

"No, Mrs. Windall; I cannot eat a mouthful. But, if it is not too much trouble, you may have a cup of tea made, and bring it up when you are through with dinner."

"And a piece of toast."

"Yes, yes; if I can eat it, I will."

Mrs. Windall lingered for some moments, like one haunted with suspicions, and only half satisfied. With quick but cautious glances, she surveyed the room, to see if there had been any change since she went down stairs. None met her eyes.

"I will bring the tea and toast in a little while," she said, as she moved back.

"Oh thank you. Perhaps I will feel better afterwards."

Mrs. Windall went out, shutting the door. The instant Mrs. Jansen was alone, a quiver ran through her frame, and her stooping body lifted itself to a firm erectness. She turned an ear, listening intently. Not the slightest sound was heard. Was Mrs Windall just outside of the door, or had she gone down with noiseless steps? A minute, that seemed like five minutes, passed before Mrs. Jansen stirred from where she sat. Then she went to the door, and opening it softly, peered out. There was no one in the passage. She stepped from the room, and moved to the head of the stairway. All was deserted and still. Assured of this, she went back quickly, and catching up her bonnet and shawl, drew them on, with scarcely a moment's pause for right adjustment. The finest ear would scarcely have detected her footfalls as she glided down the stairs. Unobserved, she had nearly reached the lower passage, when she heard some one coming up quickly from the basement, where the dining-room was located. Pausing, she held her breath, in a strange kind of fear. She felt like a criminal in the act of escape, and about suffering detection. All her mind was in confusion. A moment of suspense, and Kitty, the Irish girl appeared. Mrs. Jansen put her finger to her lip. The servant understood her, and nodded a quick assurance.

"Don't tell Mrs. Windall that I am going," whispered Mrs. Jansen.

"'Deed ma'am, I won't!" Kitty answered back in a whisper. "She's a horrid thing, any how," looking the disgust she felt, "and we all wish her a thousand miles from here. But get away with you, and don't be lingering. It's just my guess that she put you to sleep to-day. I've heard that she can do such things. Ough! I'd as soon let a snake touch me!"

"Kitty!" It was the voice of Mrs. Windall, calling up from the basement. At the same time, she was heard ascending.

"Go!" said the girl to Mrs. Jansen — "go right away; I'll keep her down there until you get out of the front door."

"Who were you talking to?" Madeline heard Mrs. Windall ask, as Kitty met her half way down the basement stairway. She needed no further incitement, but was in the street before Kitty, who had blocked up the stairs in front of Mrs. Windall, had given her evasive answer.

CHAPTER XI.

"I SAW your old friend Madeline on the street, to-day." The speaker raised his eyes from a book. He was a serious looking man, with hard lips, and gloomy, discontented eyes. The tone in which this remark was uttered, expressed no kind feelings. It was plain, that the "old friend" did not stand high in his regard.

"Ah?" responded his wife, who sat sewing. The husband had been reading to himself, and the wife, while sewing, thinking to herself. There was no light on his face as he spoke, and no light on hers, as she uttered her simple "Ah."

"Yes," said the husband, "and she looked like a crazy woman." There was a covert pleasure in his voice.

"Crazy, Mr. Lawrence!" The large dark eyes, gentle and tender, yet slightly veiled by pensive shadows, lifted themselves quickly.

"Crazy, or something else. She was driving along like a frightened bird."

"Alone?" said Mrs. Lawrence.

"Yes. All alone. I looked straight into her face, but she didn't notice me. In fact, I don't think she saw anything. There's trouble in her wigwam, I imagine. Why not? Jealousy on the one hand and free love on the other are by no means favorable to domestic peace."

"Indeed, Mr. Lawrence, you are unjust to Madeline!" said the wife, in earnest deprecation. "She may be gay and thoughtless — fond of admiration and society — but I will stake my life on her purity."

Mr. Lawrence shrugged his shoulders, and looked his doubts.

"How did she appear?" asked Mrs. Lawrence, returning to the fact mentioned by her husband. "Flurried, for one thing. Pale as a ghost for another. Half frightened into the bargain. There's something wrong, I can tell you, Jessie."

"What time was it?"

"A little before dark. I was near the South Ferry, and she had, to all appearance, just come over from Brooklyn. The thought struck me that she might have called here."

"O no. She wasn't here," said Mrs. Lawrence. "And you say she was pale and agitated?"

"Frightened is the true word," answered Mr. Lawrence.

"What can it mean?" Mrs. Lawrence spoke in a troubled voice.

"Simply, that she's reached the end of her tether, and been brought up with a shock. Such things are sure to occur sooner or later. To say the least, Madeline has been forward and imprudent. The public don't soon forget a circumstance like the one that happened with her a year or two ago — how she flirted with a man-about-town, whose character was patent to every body, to the disgust and indignation of her husband, who resented the outrage in a way that she did not soon forget."

"I never believed half of that story," said Mrs. Lawrence.

"You are less credulous than I am, Jessie. The fact is, to my thinking, the half was never told. There must be something very wrong between a man and his young wife, when he leaves her, in anger, at a large party, to make her way home after midnight as best she can."

"The hasty act of a jealous husband should never be held as conclusive against his wife," answered Mrs. Lawrence. "Jealousy has been blind and cruel from the beginning. I know Madeline better than all of you who are so ready to take up an evil report against her. She is a creature of impulse — strong-willed, and wrong-headed at times; but pure and true. It is not right to judge of all dispositions and temperaments by one rule. Minds are as different as faces. The very thing which in one would be an indecorum, in another might be as innocent as the deed of an artless child."

"I was never a believer in Madeline's artlessness," said Mr. Lawrence. "To me, she is a bundle of arts and coquetries. Nothing solid or truthful about her. And I'm not surprised at her being in trouble. How could it be otherwise?"

Mrs. Lawrence understood her husband well enough to know, that, from a spirit of opposition, if for no other reason, he would depreciate Mrs. Jansen as long as she continued the defence; so she kept back what it was still in her heart to say, and taking up the sewing from her lap, went on with her evening's work. Mr. Lawrence did not at the same time resume his book. The pleasure he had found in its pages was not strong enough to draw him quickly back from the pleasure of paining his wife by denouncing her friend — a recreation indulged in by a great many husbands — so, after a brief silence he went on, speaking with a virtuous indignation of manner, that did not deceive his wife. He had a pique against Madeline, and disliked her in consequence — the more, because Mrs. Lawrence would not turn against her.

"The fact is," said he, warming to his pleasant work, "Madeline has taken to bad company."

His wife dropped her needle hand with a start. A painful expression swept over her face.

"What is your authority for saying this?" she demanded, a low thrill of indignation in her tones.

"Common report," answered Mr. Lawrence, coolly.

"What do you mean by common report? I have heard nothing like this against her."

"Men who are about every day hear more than women who stay at home," said Mr. Lawrence. "There is a great deal of hard talk against Mrs. Jansen, and the people with whom she keeps company. They have a free love association at Mrs. Woodbine's; so the story goes."

"I don't like Mrs. Woodbine," said Mrs. Lawrence, "and I've told Madeline, often, that she was neither a sincere friend, nor a safe adviser. But this talk about free love is all a lie."

Mr. Lawrence really enjoyed his wife's excitement. So he answered —

"Very far from being a lie, let me tell you Jessie. I believe every word of the story. It's making a stir in the city. In last Sunday's Mercury, there was an article on the subject so pointed that several individuals were recognized, and their names bandied from lip to lip. 'A bright, dashing young beauty, whose husband would do well to look after her a little more closely'— so the article reads — evidently refers to your friend Madeline."

"Don't, don't say that!" replied Mrs. Lawrence, in painful astonishment. "A woman's reputation is too sacred a thing to be trifled with."

"And, therefore," said he, "a pure woman will not associate with the impure, lest an evil thing be said of her. We judge of people by the company they keep. Birds of a feather flock together. Similar things attract; dissimilar things repel. If Madeline were really the pure being you imagine her to be, she would keep company only with the pure; the fact that she does not, is evidence against her, and I accept it as conclusive. But, wrong ways always end in trouble to those who walk therein, and she is finding this out. She's had a flare up with her husband, probably. Some kind friend has informed him, no doubt, that his wife is the dashing young beauty referred to in the Mercury. People, you know, always have kind friends ready to tell them the latest bad news."

A servant opened the door, and said —

"There's a lady down stairs, ma'am."

"Who is it?" inquired Mrs. Lawrence.

"I think she said Mrs. Jankin, or Mrs. Janton. I asked her over again, but she spoke so low that I can't be certain."

Mr. and Mrs. Lawrence turned, with a slight start, and looked at each other.

"Don't see her," said the husband, in an undertone.

"Mrs. Jansen, perhaps?" Mrs. Lawrence spoke to the servant.

"Yes, ma'am, I guess that was it," replied the girl.

"Say that I will be down in a moment"—

"Jessie!" Mr. Lawrence uttered his wife's name in authoritative remonstrance; but she did not recall her words. The servant went out. As she closed the door, Mr. Lawrence said speaking resolutely —

"You must not see this woman!"

"Why not?" calmly asked his wife, who had already laid aside her work.

"I think reasons enough have been stated here to-night," replied Mr. Lawrence.

"Not satisfactory to my mind," was firmly answered. "You know that I am no summer friend — that when I have faith it is not easily shaken. My poor friend must be in sore trouble, or she would not come all the way from her home in New York to visit me at this late hour. Of course I shall see her. She can do me no harm, and I may do her much good."

And rising, she moved past her husband with a quiet firmness of manner that he made no effort to oppose, understanding, as he did, the strength of her will when she acted from love or duty.

"Why, Madeline! What has happened?" Mrs. Lawrence entered the parlor hurriedly, and stood face to face with her unhappy friend. A faint smile tried, for an instant to form itself on Madeline's lips, but lost itself amid lines of suffering. An effort to speak followed, but only mute signs were visible. Her face was pale and pinched, like the face of one who had been sick.

"What has happened, dear?" Mrs. Lawrence repeated her question in a tenderer voice, as she held tightly her friend's hand. "Have you been sick?" A new thought came, in explanation of this untimely visit and the strange appearance of Madeline. She had been ill, and wandering in mind, had risen and gone away from home without being observed. The thought thrilled her with a feeling of alarm.

"Have you been sick?" She asked the question again. "I am sick — sick! O yes, I am sick, Jessie!" sobbed out Mrs. Jansen, her eyes flooding with tears; and she bent down her face and hid it on the bosom of her friend, who drew an arm tightly around her. She was trembling like a frightened child. As she stood, shrinking down against her, Mrs. Lawrence perceived the tremor of her body growing less, and at the same time noticed the weight increasing, so that she had to brace herself to its support.

"Madeline!" she said, anxiously. But there was no reply. "Madeline!" she repeated. Even while the name parted her lips, she was grasping her poor friend tightly to keep her from falling to the floor. Drawing her to a sofa, she laid her down, and as her head fell back upon one of the cushions, Mrs. Lawrence saw that she had fainted.

CHAPTER XII.

"HE has thought better of this," said Carl Jansen to himself, as he walked homeward at evening. But, he did not feel the confidence his words expressed. A dead weight was lying on his heart. Might not all this be a terrible dream? Oh, that he could awake! A desolate silence appeared to reign through the house as he entered. The air had a real or imaginary chilliness, that sent a shudder along his nerves.

"No, she had not thought better of this! Carl did not yet clearly understand his wife's character. "I shall find her at home," he said to himself, many times, during that troubled afternoon. But, he did not find her at home. All was as he had left it at dinner time. Not a chair had been moved in the sitting-room, not a book taken from its place in the library, not a curtain drawn in their chamber. Not the slightest change in the strict order of things since he went away. How dreary it was! He asked no questions of the servants, and they, reading pain and mystery in his face, did not venture to question. But, they understood that something was wrong between him and his wife.

At the tea table, fronting him, Jansen saw, in the space vacant to material vision, that fixed, stony image which had been present to him all day, and in all places — his wife as he had left her in the morning. Eating was only a pretence. After taking a cup of tea, he went up stairs. What next? Should he go out, or remain at home? As to answering his wife's letter, or in any way communicating with her, that was not in all his thoughts. Pride, and a spirit of dogged adherence to any accepted line of conduct, prevented this. He did not even remember the place at which she had said a letter would reach her. Suffer what he might in this contest, from one purpose Jansen did not waver for an instant. He would not pursue his fugitive wife — would offer no persuasions to return — would remain silent and passive. He had done nothing to provoke the step she had taken — so he talked with himself — and, therefore, he had no apologies or concessions to offer. In her communication, she had dictated terms — that was his reading of her letter — and he would listen to no dictation from a woman, even if she were his wife. To yield in anything, was to yield all. This was her desperate venture for the supremacy; but she would find herself mistaken in his character — her venture would fail.

"If I say 'come back,'" Carl remembered this touching sentence in his wife's letter; but he did not feel its true meaning. "No," he spoke out sternly, "I will not say come back! I might as well yield everything; become an appendage to my wife, instead of her head and husband. No — no! I do not thus understand my duty. On the nature of things, on legality, on religion, I set my feet, and there I will stand. If Madeline ignores all these, and makes a desperate effort to drive me into ignoring them, she will find, to her cost, that I am not a willow wand that she can bend as she pleases, but a sturdy oak, defiant of her little strength."

So he fortified himself in his position. He did not believe that Madeline could, or would hold out for any great length of time. He thought it more than probable, that, ere bedtime, she would return home, humbled and repentant. She was subject to sudden and strong revulsions of feeling — was impulsive, and acted often under the first inspiration of an impulse. She had so acted on going away; and a change of feeling would bring her home again.

The hours passed, but Madeline did not return. Jansen found himself deceived. He did not grow softer, but harder, as the time wore on, and it became more and more clearly evident, that Madeline would not be at home that night.

Ten o'clock had been rung out by the time piece on the mantel, and Jansen was sitting, crouched in a large easy-chair — the image of calm repose without, but all agitation within — when he heard the street door bell. He did not stir, but listened intently. A servant passed along the hall. As she opened the door, he held his breath. A voice. Not a woman's voice! He felt a chill of disappointment. A man had entered, and the servant had shown him into the parlor.

"A gentleman wishes to see you, sir. Mr. Lawrence."

"Very well. I will be down."

The servant retired.

"Mr. Lawrence! What can he want, at this hour?" said Jansen. "It's rather strange!" His thought went naturally, to his wife, and connected her with the visit. Mrs. Lawrence was an old friend of Madeline's. After perplexing himself for a little while as to the import of this visit, Jansen went to the parlor carefully schooling his exterior, he met Mr. Lawrence with a quiet courtesy, that completely hid his real state of mind. For a few moments, the two men looked inquiringly at each other. In surprise at Jansen's manner, Mr. Lawrence at first thought the absence of his wife unknown to him.

"Mrs. Jansen, is at my house," he said, coming at once to the purport of his visit.

There followed no start — no look of surprise — no marked change of any kind.

"Is she?" The coldness of voice — the indifference of manner — chilled Mr. Lawrence. He moved back a step or two. Jansen did not ask him to resume the seat from which he had arisen.

"Do you wish to communicate with her?" asked Mr. Lawrence, uttering the first thought that came into his mind.

"No, sir!" Jansen shook his head, and shut his mouth closely. His voice and mien were icy.

"Good evening!" said Mr. Lawrence, bowing stiffly, and retiring towards the door.

"Good evening," returned Jansen, not relaxing a feature, or softening his tones.

"The next time I go on a fool's errand," so Mr. Lawrence spoke with himself as he shut the door behind him,

"I'll be a greater fool than I am now. I might have known how it was! He's turned her out of doors for vicious conduct; and I'm served right for meddling in the matter. All Jessie's geese are swans. She'll keep to her faith in this woman after her vileness is known to all the world. But, she shall not harbor in my house; I'm resolved on that. The air that my wife breathes shall not be polluted by one like her. Faugh! I'm mad with myself! What will Jansen think? He'll put my wife on a par with this woman. Their names will be spoken together!"

This thought chafed him sharply. He knew how pure and true his wife was, and he could not bear that her good name should be sullied by a slanderous breath.

"I'll settle this matter!" So he continued talking with himself as he hurried homeward, gathering hardness by the way. "Sick or well, in the morning she goes from my house. Jessie must stand aside. I will not be argued with, persuaded, nor set at naught. So vile a woman shall not poison the atmosphere of my home."

"I knew just how it was!" said Mr. Lawrence, angrily, on getting home and meeting his wife.

"Did you see Mr. Jansen?" asked Mrs. Lawrence, her voice choking a little.

"Yes."

"What did he say?"

"I told him that his wife was at my house; to which he answered, 'Is she?' as coldly as if I had mentioned the most trivial circumstance. He did not seem even annoyed. 'Do you wish to communicate with her?' I asked, and he said, curtly, 'No, sir?' My next words were, 'Good evening,' to which he replied, 'Good evening,' when I came away. Now, isn't that beautiful! What must a wife be — what must a wife have done — when her husband thus acts towards her? She has left him of her own will, or been turned out of doors, and he doesn't care a farthing what becomes of her. There's one thing certain, Jessie, she cannot remain here. I wont have your name mixed up with hers. On that I am resolved. To-morrow morning she must go away."

Mrs. Lawrence did not reply. She had dropped her eyes away from those of her husband, and was looking down at the floor. Her face, which had flushed eagerly as he came in, had already grown pale. She looked hurt — stunned — grieved.

"I knew she was a vile, wicked woman!" Mr. Lawrence spoke with indignation.

Mrs. Lawrence only shook her head.

"The devil would be a saint in your esteem, if —"

Mr. Lawrence stopped. The eyes of his wife had lifted themselves from the floor, and were resting steadily in his face.

"And this is all that passed between you and Mr. Jansen?" she said.

"All. And wasn't that enough? What more would you have had him say? A husband may not choose to denounce his wife."

"It is always safest to infer good," said Mrs. Lawrence.

"And so take a thief into your house, under the pleasant delusion that he is honest. No, Jessie, it is always safest to infer evil."

"And so hurt the innocent. I am no believer in this philosophy. Good or evil, Madeline cannot hurt me. But, evil I will not credit against her in the absence of proof."

"In the absence of proof! You amaze me, Jessie! Common report has long been against her, and now her husband has turned her from his house. What more do you want?"

"Report is no proof, Mr. Lawrence. As to her having been turned out of doors by her husband, we have only your inference. She may have left him of her own free will. More probably, in a state of partial derangement, which he did not perceive, and, therefore, remains blind and angry. I knew Madeline intimately, and cannot be mistaken in her. Be her faults and errors what they may, I do not believe her impure. Impulsive, strong-willed, thoughtless, imprudent, if you will; all these, but not evil. I must have very conclusive proof to credit this."

"Well, it's no use to talk, Jessie," answered Mr. Lawrence, in a most positive manner. "She is not going to remain in this house, after to-night. Bag and baggage, she must be off to-morrow morning. I don't want any of your 'ifs,' or 'buts.' I want you to see that what I say comes to pass."

To this, Mrs. Lawrence made no reply. Her face was clouded and troubled. She turned a little aside from her husband; not looking acquiescence. He saw this, and commenced walking the floor, fuming, and threatening magnificently, as weak men, who find themselves amid baffling circumstances, do sometimes. This was only "beating the air," as he felt, and his state of turbulence in a little while subsided.

Mr. Jansen sat down, after his visitor's hasty withdrawal, not feeling altogether satisfied with what he had done. To say the least, he had been neither courteous nor gentlemanly. He remembered, that Mr. Lawrence lived in

Brooklyn, a distance of over two miles from his residence in New York, and that the evening was far gone. Something was due to him. He had taken no small trouble in giving information about his wife. Jansen's love of approbation was hurt. He desired to stand well in the eyes of other people; to be always right before the world. But, he was not right in this — he stood self-convicted of an unpardonable rudeness.

This was not the only source of dissatisfaction. He was far from being indifferent in regard to his wife, or what concerned her. Instead, he was deeply interested, his inward sense hearkening after her departing footsteps with painful eagerness. Any sound, and sign, any shadow of intelligence would have been gladly received; only pride would not let him show the least desire, or take a single step in the direction his heart was going. He need not have taken a step in this case — need scarcely have asked a question. To his thirsty lips a cup had been raised, and in blind self-will he had dashed it aside.

"Over in Brooklyn, at the house of Mr. Lawrence! What can she be doing there?" So at last the burden of thought found relief in words.

He remembered Mrs. Lawrence as one of Madeline's early acquaintances. He had liked her, for her intelligence and womanly bearing; and had more than once regretted that in his wife's absorption among more showy and specious friends, she had virtually dropped this one. Mr. Lawrence, whom he met occasionally in business, he did not like.

What was she doing there? He might have known. The information he now so desired to possess, had been just within his reach — tendered, not asked — and he had put it roughly aside. The fact that she had gone to the house of Mr. Lawrence, was favorable to her in his eyes. As he thought of it, a sense of relief came. Mrs. Lawrence was a sensible woman — free from all modern fancies and transcendentalisms. One from whom good advice and good influence might be expected. She would counsel Madeline for her good — advise her to return to her husband and her duty. Jansen grew more confident of this, as thought dwelt on the fact that his wife was with this old and true friend. The case looked hopeful — Madeline would find no encouragement for her perversity with Mrs. Lawrence. Under her better influence, she would be led to see how wrong she was acting. She would come back, humbled and penitent; he would be vindicated. Pride, self-will, love of rule and predominance, conceit of superiority — all these would remain untouched. Master in his own house, with not a prerogative yielded, he would continue to be.

The satisfaction born of thought like this, was soon marred by questions as to how his unmannerly repulse of Mr. Lawrence would affect the case. Would it not give strong color to any representations his wife might make in regard to him, and tend to draw Mrs. Lawrence over to her side? There were probabilities in this view of the case that troubled him. But, there was no helping it now. He was not the man to concede anything; to humiliate himself by coming down from any assumed position. He could not write to Mr. Lawrence, nor go to him. Could not make the faintest sign without losing something that his narrow soul held dear. So he must stand still and wait. If Madeline came back, well; if she "persisted in her folly and crime," the consequences to him must be accepted and borne. He thought coolly to his conclusions, not wavering for an instant. With him, there was no quick fusing of thought into determinations, that hardened rapidly, then fused quickly again flowing into new forms. Nothing of the kind. He had no versatility of character, so to speak. All his ratiocinations moved in a narrow circle, with constant precipitations upon old ideas, which grew and grew into daily increasing importance in his eyes.

Another thought disturbed the tranquil state which had begun to settle over his feelings. Might not the utter indifference he had manifested in regard to his wife, have the effect to create unjust suspicions against her in the eyes of Mr. and Mrs. Lawrence? Might it not lead them to turn away from her, and so leave her adrift, to float with some evil tide on a disastrous shore? Well might this thought trouble him

CHAPTER XIII.

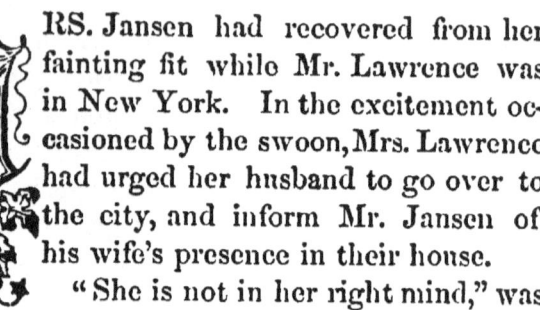

MRS. Jansen had recovered from her fainting fit while Mr. Lawrence was in New York. In the excitement occasioned by the swoon, Mrs. Lawrence had urged her husband to go over to the city, and inform Mr. Jansen of his wife's presence in their house.

"She is not in her right mind," was the appeal and argument. "I am sure that she has escaped from a sick room. Mr. Jansen must be in terrible suspense and alarm."

This did not seem altogether improbable, and so Mr. Lawrence went over to the city. His reception we have seen. During his absence Mrs. Jansen had recovered. The truth then came out, told with a mingling of sobs and tears — flashes of womanly anger and resolute words. Mrs. Lawrence listened in painful silence and with brimming eyes, not venturing in her friend's state of excitement, to offer counsel.

"I am a leaf, drifting away on a strange current, Jessie," said Madeline, in the calmness that succeeded, when she had told her story. "A tender thought of you, as one always loved, has borne me into the peaceful eddy of your home. Let me stay for just a little while — a very little while. I will then float off again into the current, to be carried, Heaven only knows whither!"

"We will talk of this to-morrow, dear friend," was answered. "The Providence which led you hither, will guide you in the future. To-night let thought rest, and all your hastily formed purposes recede, and be as if they had not been. Sleep gives a healthier tone to mind as well as body. You will be calmer and have clearer sight in the morning. I will leave you now." And Mrs. Lawrence kissed Madeline tenderly. Sleep came quickly. There was an opiate in the kiss which love had laid on lips and eyelids.

Madeline did not join the family at breakfast-time next morning. Mrs. Lawrence had gone into her room early, and found her waking and weeping.

"Do not rise yet," she had said. "We breakfast early, so that Mr. Lawrence may get off to business. I will come to you after he has gone."

"He is not pleased at my being here." Something in the voice of Mrs. Lawrence, as she mentioned her husband's name, betrayed to the quick ears of Madeline the truth. "I might have known this," she added, with a shade of bitterness — "all men are against us. But I will not trouble him long."

"Don't talk so, Maddy, dear; it does no good, and hurts your state of mind," returned Mrs. Lawrence, with increased affectionateness of manner. "Men do not always see as we see. How should they? They misunderstand us, and we, it is quite possible, as often misunderstand them. Let us be charitable — forbearing — not ready to think evil. We get down to the heart of a thing by a quicker way than it is given men to go, and should be patient with their slowness. If they are wrong-headed sometimes, we may often be perverse in feeling, and I have an impression that there is more hope of the wrong head than of the wrong heart. There! there!" And Mrs. Lawrence laid her finger on her friend's lips — "I did not mean to provoke a discussion: I was speaking only in apology for the other sex. Lie still for a little while longer. I will come to you in half an hour; then you shall rise and have breakfast; the day will be ours."

As Mr. Lawrence stood in the hall, with hat and gloves on ready to leave, he said to his wife —

"Now, understand me, Jessie, that woman is not to harbor here. I do not wish to find her in the house when I come home."

"Don't give yourself unnecessary trouble," was answered by Mrs. Lawrence, her quietness of tone contrasting with her husband's ruffled manner — "Madeline will not intrude herself. I think you will not find her here when you come home; but, if she leaves to-day, it will be against my wishes. *I* would rather have her remain for a week. Don't frown, and look so angry and impatient! It is for us to do good when God gives the opportunity. This opportunity He has now given. A woman, still pure and true to all high ends, as far as she can see them in the blindness of hurt feelings and under bad counsel, is cutting herself away from safe moorings. If she drift off into the world without chart or compass, there is danger of wreck and loss of everything. Ours may be the high privilege of saving her."

"Thank you! Don't say *ours!*" gruffly, yet weakly responded Mr. Lawrence. "If I have any 'mission' in the world, which I doubt, it doesn't lie in that direction: and I tell you once for all, Jessie, that I don't mean to have you mixed up with any of these things. Let her drift off, if she wants to; what is it your business or mine? If you stop to draw back into harbor every vagrant-souled woman that breaks from her moorings, you'll have enough work on hand for a legion of angels."

"If I can do, in a single instance, the work in which angels delight, will you step in between me and that work?" Mrs. Lawrence's calm eyes rested upon her husband. Her voice, clear and firm, yet impressive, subdued the captious spirit that dwelt within him. She stood brave and strong before him, not in personal defiance, but in the strength of a right will, that illustrated her husband's thought in spite of his prejudice and passion.

"You'll have it your own way, I suppose," he answered, fretfully. Women always do, husbands are nothing now-a-days. Good for working and providing — that's about all. But it doesn't signify. I set my face as steel against you all. Harbor the woman, if you will, but understand that in doing so you set your husband at defiance. You needn't expect me to play the smiling host. Keep her out of my way, if you don't want her insulted."

So, warming, as confused thought came into speech again, Mr. Lawrence talked after his irrational way when excited by opposing influences.

"My husband is too much of a gentleman," quietly answered Mrs. Lawrence, "to offer in his own house an insult to a suffering and helpless woman."

"Mr. Lawrence, an impatient sentence on his lips that his wife could not make out, turned off abruptly, passing through the street door, which he shut with a jar that was felt over the house.

After Madeline had risen and taken some breakfast, the two friends retired to Mrs. Lawrence's chamber.

"You blame me, Jessie, I know," said Mrs. Jansen; "but you do not comprehend my case. As a wife and equal, I would cling to my husband through good and evil report — in sickness, poverty and disgrace — under any and all circumstances of outside wrong and oppression. His love would bind me by cords impossible to be broken. As a slave, in confessed inferiority, I cannot remain in his house. Better for us to live apart than in strife. This issue I have made in going away. I left for him, written in plain, earnest tender words, a letter, clearly stating the case as it stands between us. If he answers that letter, and says return, I will go back, hoping and rejoicing. If he keeps silence, I shall never cross his threshold again."

"Purposes that involve so much ought never to be made under strong excitement," said Mrs. Lawrence. "A wife should bear and forbear a great deal, before taking the step that you have taken."

"I have borne until longer forbearance would be a crime against my sex," replied Mrs. Jansen, her eyes kindling.

"Touching the crime against your sex, Madeline, I hardly think that an issue in this case with your husband. The trouble is between you and him, and should not be complicated with remote considerations. You cannot determine your course wisely, on general principles or results.

Everything must be narrowed down to the relation existing between you and your husband."

"I am not so sure of that," said Mrs. Jansen. "No individual stands alone in the world; no act is without its good or bad influence on society. The rights and happiness of our sex should be dear to every woman. Too long have we disregarded them, leaving the weak without counsel or advocate. Now, the time has come when every true woman, if she does her duty, will see to it, that so far as her acts speak to the world, they speak against man's tyrannies. Mine shall, even though I be burned at the stake!"

"Madeline," answered Mrs. Lawrence, "nothing tells for good on society like right individual action. Not heroic action before the world, but self-denying and loving deeds in the sphere of private life. This separation from your husband, if it should, unfortunately, continue, will do an amount of harm to our sex, impossible to estimate."

"Harm! I do not understand you."

"The deepest wrong a woman can receive must always come from her own hand. Others cannot harm us vitally, if we are true to ourselves. They may assault and annoy us — may wrong us externally — keep back the rights and privileges to which we are entitled by nature — but cannot touch the inner life, if that be the dwelling-place of virtue, truth and purity. Your example in this act of separation, may lead others of our sex, not well based in principle, to follow in the same path, and so abandon their duty and harm their souls. The case must always be a hard one that justifies the step you are taking. Harder, a great deal harder, Madeline, than I am satisfied yours has been. Carl may have narrow views of his marital rights, and he may be self-willed and persistent in his assertion of these rights; all of which must chafe a woman of your temperament. But, he is a virtuous and an honorable man; and that is a great deal. I know pure, sweet, loving women whose husbands are brutalized sensualists, or men without honor. Their lot is a terrible one compared with yours; but, they do not abandon their places nor relinquish their duties, because the men they married of free choice, have proved unworthy. The compact is until death do part them. Their feet walk in difficult places — they have sore tribulations — but they are growing, daily, unto the beauty of angels; fitter for heaven. Every time I meet them, I perceive an odor of new blossoming flowers, the promise of immortal fruitage. They have not been hurt, interiorly, by their unhappy marriages, because they would not hurt themselves. Beware, then, my dear friend! If harm come, the blow will be from your own hand."

"I am not able to see in the light of your views," answered Mrs. Jansen. "They involve the old notions men are so fond of preaching about. They may be, and do, what they please; but women must be saints and angels! Now, I am human, and do not pretend to be anything else. I have human wants, human rights, human passions; and recognize the human right of self-protection. If I am assailed, I will defend myself — if wronged, I will seek to right the wrong. The assailer and the wrong-doer shall not have immunity and encouragement through my tame submission. No, no, Jessie! I am not one of your meek women-angels."

Mrs. Lawrence sighed, dropped her eyes to the floor, and remained silent. To argue with Madeline, in her present temper, would, she saw, only lead her into stronger states of self-justification. A few moments passed, when Mrs. Jansen continued —

"There have been martyrs to the right in all ages; and martyrdoms must continue so long as there is evil, and consequent wrong, in the world. Men set tyrants at defiance, battle for freedom, and achieve independence. They would be slaves, and unworthy of freedom, if this were not so. And shall woman be the only coward in the world! The only slave! No. By all that is just, by all that is heroic, by all that is right, no!"

Still Mrs. Lawrence kept silent.

"You do not see as I do," said Madeline, her voice dropping down from its enthusiasm.

"No; you see from one stand-point, and I from another," was replied. "As to whether your view or mine is best, depends on the relation of the stand-point to the object. We should never forget, that unless we change our position several times, we cannot look upon all sides of a question. Where momentous results hang upon our right decision of such a question, we should determine with great caution, and only after many changes of our stand-point. I pray you, dear friend, to have deliberation. Take counsel of doubt, rather than of partially enlightened reason."

"What would you have me do, Jessie? Go back and ask my husband's pardon?"

"No. A word on this unhappy incident in your lives need not pass between you. You can return and be silent. The dangerous impediment, that now stands like a mountain crag between you, is pride. He will not concede anything — nor will you. Without doubt, he has repented sorely of his part in the strife; but pride, resting on his narrow views of marriage, will not let him acknowledge his error. If you quietly return, your presence in the old places will, I am sure, make his heart leap with joy. He may hide this pleasure; doubtless will. But, in the future, he will be very careful how he pushes you to another extremity. All may yet be saved, dear Madeline! Oh, let me be your counsellor in this thing. Good will come of it, I know. A step or two farther in the way you are advancing, and all may be lost! A few steps retraced, and a whole life of peace may be secured. Go back — go back dear Madeline! Anything less than this will be fatal to your happiness."

"It has ceased to be a question of happiness," replied Madeline, her voice falling into a mournful undertone. "That is past. The question now is, Freedom or Slavery? I must decide for myself which will be most endurable. And I have made the decision. If my husband writes to me, and says, simply, 'Come back,' I will accept, it gladly, as an evidence, that I am to live with him as an equal. If he does not so ask my return — will not concede anything — then the die is cast. We stand forever apart."

"I had hoped, dear friend," said Mrs. Lawrence, with a sadness of tone she made no effort to conceal, "that better thoughts would have ruled in your mind. That you would have seen the duty of yielding something. Of going back a few steps in the wrong way so hastily taken."

"Not hastily, Jessie," answered Madeline. "Not in anger. For months I have looked to the issue that has come. I saw it approaching, and weighed and measured the consequences involved, until I understood their magnitude. They are coming upon me, and I accept them as lesser evils. I bow my head and stoop my shoulders to the new burdens I am destined to bear. They will be lighter for my spirit than have been those I cast aside. As our day may demand, so shall our strength be. I have faith in my power of endurance. I shall be equal to the destiny that awaits me. In suffering, the heart grows strong. Heroism is born of trial and pain."

"It is not heroism that you want," said Mrs. Lawrence, in reply — "I speak plainly as your true friend — but self-denial. Pride has risen in your heart, and made you blind to duty. You are thinking more of freedom, as you call it, than of a useful life. Of what is due to yourself, more than of what is due to others. You say that you love your husband; now, love forgets itself in desire to bless its object. It does not tend to separation, but conjunction. It will forgive much; it will endure much; it will suffer much. None are perfect here. The heir-loom in every life is error and evil. It is mine, it is yours, it is your husband's. We must look for inharmonious action in the contact of two lives — especially when the contact is so close as that between married partners. It is the offspring of our inherited defects. The worst remedy for this is antagonism, no matter from which side it may come. It is, in fact, no remedy at all; but a means of increasing the evil. If your husband has false views of marriage, love will enlighten him sooner than anger. If he vainly imagines that he is superior, let him discover how far above all self-assertion and pride of position, are self-control, and the patient endurance of a temporary invasion of rights for the sake of an ultimate and higher good."

But Madeline shook her head in strong rejection of all

this. It was in complete opposition to her state of feeling; and with her, feeling for the most part held reason in control.

"Men," she answered, "are in the love of ruling over the weak. They domineer and exact whenever in liberty to do so. To yield to them is to strengthen them. Submit to one set of manacles, and they immediately go to work to forge new ones, until the poor slave is bound in every limb and entirely helpless. If there be not resolute opposition, everything is lost."

It was all in vain. Mrs. Lawrence could not influence her mistaken friend; who, in every argument strengthened herself in the position she had assumed. At last, with a troubled feeling, she gave up all attempts to influence her. Naturally came next the question as to Mrs. Jansen's future life.

"If your husband does not say 'Come back,' what then, Madeline?" was asked.

Mrs. Lawrence saw, by the falling of light out of Madeline's countenance, that this question touched her closely. A sigh, half checked, betrayed the concern it awakened. She did not answer.

"If your husband does not, of his own free will, make a settlement on you, I scarcely think the courts will compel him to do so. Sufficient legal cause for a separation could hardly be shown."

There was a flashing of Madeline's beautiful brown eyes.

"And you think so meanly of me!" she said, half angrily, "Jessie! If I cannot be his wife and equal, I will not touch his money. No — no. I am not of the sordid quality you seem to imagine. I trust, that a high principle governs me in all that I am doing."

"You must live."

"He that feedeth the young lions will not see me lack," was bravely answered. "The world is wide. I shall find my place."

"What are your immediate purposes? It is my deep concern for you that prompts this question. Where are you going?"

Again the light faded out of Mrs. Jansen's countenance.

"The heroic is all well enough, Madeline; but nature has vulgar needs that will not brook delay. You must eat and drink — you must have clothing, and a home. If you cast yourself loose from the strong arm that makes provision and gives protection, you must look to yourself."

"I know all that. I have counted the cost, Jessie."

"Not all the cost, I fear. In the very first step you found pains and penalties not dreamed of."

"Why do you say that?" asked Madeline, in a tone of surprise. She had not spoken of her experience with Mrs. Windall.

"My husband saw you in the street yesterday. It was late. Your appearance was so singular, that it attracted attention."

"My appearance! What was singular about it?" asked Madeline, with a crimsoning face.

"Just how you looked, he did not say. But the impression made on him was strong. You were driving along, he said, like a crazy person. I was filled with painful anxiety on your account. If the first steps in this new way you have chosen, are so environed with difficulties, you may well tremble at what lies farther in advance. Where are you going? I ask that question again, for that is first to be considered. You left your husband's house yesterday morning, and at nine o'clock in the evening came here seeking shelter for the night. Don't be offended. I am coming down to the naked truth — calling things by their true names. It is best sometimes, and leaves no room for error. You know what befel during the unhappy intervening hours. I fear that you had much pain, much disappointment, much humiliation crowded into them. If it had not been so, you would scarcely have crossed the river, alone, at a late hour, and come to me. Oh, Madeline! By the memory of this first day's painful experience stop where you are. This is only the beginning of sorrows."

Madeline's lips quivered. Her eyes filled with tears. Her friend's reference to that one day's trials restored the memory of some things that gave pangs like dagger thrusts. Ah yes! There had been disappointments and humiliations that touched her to the very quick. Life had suddenly put on new aspects, fearful to contemplate.

"Dear friend!" she said weeping, "let me ask of you one favor. It shall not be very burdensome. I am in great extremity. One door is shut behind me, and another has not yet opened. Let me stay with you just one week. After that, I will go my way."

How eagerly would Mrs. Lawrence have given her consent, if she alone were to be considered. Mrs. Jansen saw the shade that crept into her eyes, and noted the hesitation that lingered over the sentence that was to constitute her friend's reply.

"O Madeline! Madeline!" So came the answer. "If you could look into my heart — if you could see how it yearns over you — if you could know all my love, all my present anxiety on your account! Dear friend! Let me again entreat you to go home. There is a mist before your eyes — you do not see clearly; you have lost your way, and every step in advance will carry you in the wrong direction. Get back, and quickly into the old, safe regions, where you know the landmarks; where your strong tower stands — where your walled gardens are safe from intruders; where enemies cannot find you."

Mrs. Lawrence was affectionate in her manner — she spoke with loving ardor. But, she had not answered the plain request of Madeline — "Let me stay just one week."

The tears dried up in the eyes of Madeline. Her face grew pale. With a thick huskiness of voice, she said —

"I thank you for your interest, Jessie, and for your well meant advice. But, it is useless to argue with, or persuade me. It is not with the past that I am struggling. The leaf that I have turned my hand shall not put back again. It is with the present and the future that I have now to deal."

She said no more. How was Mrs. Lawrence to reply? If she alone were interested, door as well as heart would open to her friend. But, to grant the request of Madeline would give cause of anger to her husband. And she knew him well enough to be certain, that his treatment of Mrs. Jansen, under the circumstances, would involve so much that was offensive, that she would not endure it for a single day.

"If I alone were concerned," she said, "the case would be different." Then paused.

"Say no more," quickly answered Madeline, the fire coming back to eyes that were dull an instant before. "It is the old inadequacy — the will behind your will. Ah well! Don't look sad about it, Jessie. I understand it all."

Something in the manner of Mrs. Jansen, touched a sensitive place in the feelings of Mrs. Lawrence.

"Pardon me," she answered, assuming an air of dignity; "but you are treading on forbidden ground. Whatever is personal to myself, must be held sacred by my friends."

This rebuke partially offended Mrs. Jansen. She made a cold apology, and in words not well chosen. It was not her habit to think twice on a sentence before giving it to speech.

It was in vain that Mrs. Lawrence, soon losing all unpleasant feeling towards Madeline, sought to come near her. By tacit consent, the thoughts just in their minds, were left unspoken — so there was no point of free intercourse — and so, they stood apart. Mrs. Lawrence, knowing her husband's state of feeling, did not think it right to ask Madeline to stay for the period mentioned.

"You are not going," she said to her, as she came down, about midday, with her bonnet on.

"Yes. If Carl replies to my letter, I must get his answer."

"You will return, if the answer fails, or is unsatisfactory, and spend at least one more night with me."

"No, Jessie; it would not be agreeable to your husband, and might disturb pleasant relations."

This was unkindly said — nay, worse, in a tone meant to wound. It was a thrust.

But, Mrs. Lawrence did not feel the slightest pain. Her heart was too full of pity for her friend — too heavily burdened with anxiety on her account. She kissed her at the door, saying —

"If it does not go well with you to-day, Madeline, come back in the evening. You know my heart. May God teach you the right lesson of duty, and lead your feet in the right paths. Oh, Madeline! Ask Him to enlighten your eyes, and show you the way. Look to Him, and not to yourself."

Their hands were clasped for a moment, in a tight pressure — tightest on the part of Mrs. Lawrence — and then, not looking back, Madeline went out blindly and desperately, to go she knew not whither.

CHAPTER XIV.

"IS that woman here?" It was the question of Mr. Lawrence as he came in at evening.

"No," was the simple answer of his wife.

"Thank fortune for that!"

"She may come back and stay all night," said Mrs. Lawrence.

"You asked her to do so, of course!"

"Yes; but the chances are against her returning. I scarcely think we shall see her."

"The affair is town-talk already," remarked Mr. Lawrence.

"What?"

"Mrs. Jansen's quarrel with, and abandonment of her husband. I heard it in half a dozen places."

"What was said? What cause was assigned?" asked Mrs. Lawrence.

"Oh, forty reasons were given."

"Of which thirty-nine were sheer fabrications," said Mrs. Lawrence.

"I don't know anything about that. The most plausible, to my mind, was this: — That Mr. Jansen had positively forbidden any further association with certain men and women of doubtful reputation; and that her ladyship had gone off in a huff, expecting him to repent, humble himself, and entreat of her to return and do just as she pleased. But, it is pretty generally held by those who know Jansen, that she will find it harder to get back than she imagined; and that 'the only door will be through a humiliation of herself, a confession of wrong, and a promise to do better. Jansen doesn't say much — don't throw his arms about, bluster, and talk large; but he is steady to any purpose as a steel spring. There was too much at stake when my lady hazarded that throw of the dice!"

"What other reasons were given?" asked Mrs. Lawrence.

"Oh, I can't remember a third of them. One was, that she wished to make a trip to Europe in company with a gentleman and his wife, not on the best terms with each other, who will go in the next steamer. Jansen demurred, and thence came a fierce quarrel. Another, that she wanted him to buy a house in Fifth Avenue, to which he positively objected. Another report connects her name with that of Mr. Guyton. It is said, that they are often seen on the street, and are altogether too intimate. The fact is, Jessie, that woman must have been very imprudent; if not, why so many stories about her? I trust she will not show her face here again! I don't want your name mentioned in the same breath with hers."

Mrs. Lawrence did not reply. Her thought was following, yearningly, after Madeline, and questioning as to her future, over which hung a dark and threatning cloud. The evening passed, but Madeline returned not to the house of her friend. Two or three times during the evening, as Mr. and Mrs. Lawrence sat, the one reading to himself, and the other sewing — the former, letting his book drop from his eyes, indulged in hard sentences against Mrs. Jansen, to which his wife made no other response than simply to look at him in her grave, quiet way, with as much reproof in her glances as she felt might be given without irritation.

All the next day passed without word of her unhappy friend reaching Mrs. Lawrence. When her husband came home in the evening, he brought no news of her. He had met Mr. Jansen on the street twice, each time receiving a polite, but rather stiff bow. There was nothing unusual in his manner — nothing from which he could infer the continued absence of his wife.

"It's my opinion," said Mr. Lawrence, "that one day's experience has been enough for our high-strung friend, and that she is safely at home again. It's all very fine for the bird to escape from its cage, and strike free wings upon the sunny air. But, in night and storm, in cold and hunger, in presence of the hawk, how gladly would it get back into its prison again."

"I pray that you may be right in your opinion, and that Madeline is with her husband," remarked Mrs. Lawrence, but not in a tone that expressed confidence.

Days passed, and still no certain intelligence about Madeline was received. To end this suspense, Mrs. Lawrence called at Mr. Jansen's house, and asked for her, as if she believed her to be at home.

"She's not here, ma'am," replied the servant, who had opened the door. Mrs. Lawrence stepped into the vestibule, in order to question the servant, and get from her all about her friend that she might be induced to communicate.

"When do you expect her to return?" she asked.

"I don't know ma'am,"

A chill of disappointment ran along the nerves of Mrs. Lawrence.

"Has she been back since she went away last week?"

"No, ma'am."

"Have you heard from her?"

"No, ma'am."

The servant answered these questions with evident reluctance. Mrs. Lawrence had closed the street door.

"Can't I sit down and rest for a few minutes?" she said. "I have come over from Brooklyn, and feel very tired."

"Oh, certainly ma'am," answered the servant, showing her into the parlor. She sat down, and the servant stood near.

"You can't tell me any thing about Mrs. Jansen?" said Mrs. Lawrence.

"No, ma'am." Still with a reserve that was almost embarrassing.

"I am not asking you these questions from simple curiosity. I am an old friend, and a warm friend of Mrs. Jansen; and I want to know something certain about her. She was at my house on Wednesday and staid all night."

"At your house!" a flash of interest swept across the servant's face.

"Yes, she came to my house in the evening, long after it was dark, and staid all night. In the morning she went away."

"Did she say where she was going, ma'am?"

"No."

The troubled look, which Mrs. Lawrence had noticed from the first, deepened.

"Oh, I wish I knew where she was!" exclaimed the servant, breaking out of her reserve, and wringing her hands together.

"Doesn't Mr. Jansen know?" inquired Mrs. Lawrence.

"I'm afraid not. If he does, he wont tell us anything."

"You have asked him?"

"Oh, yes. I ask him every time he comes home; but, he answers me short. He don't like us to question him, ma'am."

"He's very much troubled?"

"Yes ma'am; of course he's troubled. But, he don't show it as some men would."

Mrs. Lawrence did not feel that it would be honorable to press the servant any farther, though a crowd of questions were in her thoughts. The main facts were learned — that Mrs. Jansen had not returned home, and that the servants at least, were in ignorance as to where she had gone. She went away, feeling sadder than when she called.

Weeks passed, and still no word came to Mrs. Lawrence about her friend. She enquired of her husband, every day, if he had learned anything about her, but the answer was always the same. Madeline had dropped out of sight, like a foundering vessel, and there remained no sign upon the surface to say where she had gone down.

The weeks gathered into months, and yet the mystery that hung over Mrs. Jansen was not solved. Her husband remained as ignorant in regard to her as the small circle of interested friends, who, like Mrs. Lawrence, kept her in troubled remembrance. He need not have remained in such ignorance. Had he bent just a little from his cold, proud impassiveness — just far enough to have placed, through proper agencies, a follower on her path — he might have kept himself advised as to all her movements. But, this would have been felt as yielding or conceding something. The fact might, in some way, come to her knowledge, and be wrongly construed. She had gone of her own will; and when she came back, she must come of her own will. That was the position he had assumed and which he resolved to maintain. Suffer what he might, he would yield nothing. That would be to lower the dignity of his manhood.

This much must be said for Carl Jansen, he suffered intensely. He had loved his wife deeply — still loved her. For the words spoken so imperatively on that fatal morning, he had repented many times — and many times wished they had never been uttered. But, once said, they might not be recalled without humiliation such as pride would never brook. How many times had he come home, during the first few weeks of separation, fondly hoping to find his wife in her old place. He would not have welcomed her with any show of gladness. She would not have known of the sunlight and warmth that swept into his heart. But he would have been kind and gentle — perhaps tender. He would have been more guarded in the future, and less inclined to put hindrances in her way. Her liberty would have been larger. Alas for her! — alas for him! — that she did not return.

CHAPTER XV.

ET us follow the proud, sensitive young creature who dropped so suddenly beneath the surface of society, and see how it has fared with her. On leaving the house of Mrs. Lawrence, Madeline crossed the river, and went to Mrs. Woodbine's. Her reception was not with the old cordiality. The false friend who had first led her mind astray, could not forgive the independent action that went adverse to her judgment. While claiming for herself the largest liberty she chose to assume, she was always impatient of freedom in others when it touched her will, be it ever so lightly.

"Have you a letter for me?" asked Madeline. She was not able to conceal the suspense that was in her mind.

"No." How like a verdict of "guilty," to a waiting prisoner, fell the word upon her ears! The brave heart drooped. The courage failed.

"You expected a letter?" said Mrs. Woodbine, who noticed the disappointment her answer had produced.

"I thought there might be one," returned Mrs. Jansen, rallying herself.

"You did not take my advice," remarked Mrs. Woodbine, with a distant air.

"No. I could not."

"You are wrong my young friend; wrong!" Mrs. Woodbine spoke with emphasis. "And you will see it one of these days. I never dreamed of your carrying things, on so trifling a provocation, to this extremity. Pray, be advised by one who has seen a great deal more of the world than you have. Return to your husband—"

"Never!" exclaimed Madeline, interrupting Mrs. Woodbine. "Never, unless he says 'Come back.'"

"Which he may never say!"

The color receded from Madeline's face; but her eyes grew hard, and her lips rigid.

"So be it," she answered, huskily. "I have counted the cost."

Mrs. Woodbine drew herself up coldly, but made no reply. Madeline sat for a short time, and then arose, with an embarrassed air.

"You're not going," said Mrs. Woodbine, in such an unsympathizing voice that it was as if she had said, "go, and go quickly!"

"Yes."

They stood facing each other for a few moments.

"Good morning." Madeline did not extend a hand.

"Why are you in such a hurry? Where are you going?" asked Mrs. Woodbine. The interest was only a pretence, and Madeline was not deceived.

"Good morning." She repeated the words.

'Good morning. When shall I see you again?"

"I will call to-morrow, or the next day, to see if there is anything for me."

"Do, I shall be glad to see you. Oh, by the way, Mrs. Windall was here last evening."

Madeline could not help a start. Mrs. Woodbine's eyes were upon her, reading the expression of her countenance.

"Was she?" Mrs. Jansen tried to seem indifferent.

"Yes, and she was very anxious about you. It seems from what she intimated, that you gave her the slip. I was glad to hear it! Take my advice, and keep out of her way. She is a dangerous woman, and may lead you into harm."

"Dangerous in what respect?" asked Madeline.

"Oh, as to that, I can't speak definitely. I've never thought her a person of well based principles."

"Do you know any wrong of Mrs. Windall?"

"Well, no, I can't say that I do; but people are in the habit of speaking lightly of her. Situated as you are, Mrs. Jansen, carefulness in regard to those with whom you associate is a thing of the first moment. We are judged by the company we keep. Your life may be as pure as that of an angel; yet the breath of slander will be on your name. You cannot escape, in the way you are now walking, no matter with what circumspection you move. The most innocent act may be tortured into crime."

"How long have you known Mrs. Windall?" asked Madeline.

"Not over six months."

"Who, or what, is she?"

"That question, I find it difficult to answer. The fact is, I know little, if anything about her; except that she has no sensibility, and intrudes herself whenever she can find opportunity, whether she be welcome or not. Her presence has always been disagreeable to me. If you asked me why, I might not be able to give a satisfactory reason; but such is the case. I repeat the advice, keep away from her; and if she seeks you out, and tries to fasten herself upon you, push her off."

"You cannot dislike her more than I do."

The door bell rung, and a servant passed down the hall.

"If that should be her!" said Mrs. Jansen, with a look of real apprehension.

"Most likely it is," returned Mrs. Woodbine. "I saw yesterday, that she was determined to find you. She knew that any letter you might receive would be directed to my care, and asked if one had come."

"I cannot meet her! Oh, Mrs. Woodbine, let me hide away somewhere!" Madeline trembled like one in affright.

"Pass into the back parlor, and stand near the door," replied Mrs. Woodbine. "You will know her voice. If it is Mrs. Windall, slip out into the hall and go up stairs. I will not let her know that you are here."

Madeline had scarcely left the room before Mrs. Windall entered.

"Good morning!" she said, fixing her large weird eyes on the face of Mrs. Woodbine.

"Good morning," was returned with a smile not over warm, yet sufficiently cordial to put a woman like Mrs. Windall at her ease.

"Have you seen our young friend?" That was the

7

uppermost thing in her mind, and she could not hold it back.

"Yes."

The face of Mrs. Windall brightened.

"When?" she asked.

"She was here this morning."

"Ah! Did she get a letter?"

"No."

"There's hard stuff in her husband," said Mrs. Windall.

"She ought to have known him well enough never to have risked all she has done."

"How long since she was here?"

"Not a great while."

"Did she say where she was going?"

"No."

Mrs. Windall, who had taken a seat, arose almost immediately.

"How long since she left?"

"She was here not ten minutes ago."

"Oh! so late? How unfortunate that I did not arrive sooner! And you have no idea which way she went?"

"She said nothing of her intentions. I did not question her."

"Poor, unhappy young creature!" Mrs. Windall spoke with feeling. "I am deeply interested in her case. What will she do?"

"The best thing you, or any friend can do for her," replied Mrs. Woodbine, "is to persuade her to go back to her husband, and hold her own where she has rights to maintain. This cutting adrift is bad — always bad. But, you know my opinion on the subject."

"And you know mine," returned Mrs. Windall, tossing her head in a kind of defiant way. "Good morning!" she added, turning off. I think I know where Mrs. Jansen has gone, and I particularly desire to see her."

Mrs. Woodbine made no effort to detain the little woman. She simply responded to her good morning, and they separated. As Mrs. Windall passed into the street, Madeline came down stairs into the hall.

"I will remain for a quarter of an hour if agreeable," she said, in a subdued manner, like one who asks a favor.

"Stay by all means," returned Mrs. Woodbine, with a cordiality that partially atoned for her previous coldness. "I don't want you to meet that woman again. She is after you with the keen scent of a hound; not for your good, I am persuaded, but to serve some end of her own, Madeline. Out from your husband's protection, there is danger for one so young, so inexperienced, so personally attractive as you are! Pardon my earnestness; but I am deeply concerned for the result of all this."

"I thank you for this interest," returned Mrs. Jansen. "I believe it to be sincere. But I cannot go back, as I have before said, and live in strife with my husband. Anything but that! You know my views and feelings. I have spoken to you freely. There can be no change. If my husband says 'Come back,' I will go back. If he keep silence, the separation is eternal!"

"To argue the case farther, is useless," said Mrs. Woodbine.

"Useless!" echoed Madeline.

Mrs. Jansen did not remain longer than the quarter of an hour for which she had asked. Their intercourse during the time was marked by restraint on both sides.

Then she went away. But whither. Ah, how much does this question involve! Moved only by feeling, and throwing aside all prudential considerations as something below the heroic from which she believed herself acting, Madeline had taken no care to fill her purse — it contained only a few dollars — nor to provide for the transfer of clothing. She had simply dressed herself for the street, and so gone out, leaving everything behind. Her disappointment in regard to Mrs. Woodbine had alarmed and bewildered her — though it did not change her purpose. In fancy, she had pictured herself in the refuge of her elegant home, finding a world of sympathy in one heart at least. Counsel for the future — aid as it might be needed — wisdom from Mrs. Woodbine's large experience in the world, had all been taken for granted. Alas! How miserably had these expectations failed! How, almost instantly, in her death-like extremity, had this friend dropped away! Where next was she to turn? The first day's unhappy experience has shown how wildly she had calculated the future.

On leaving the house of Mrs. Woodbine, parting coldly with her at the door, Mrs. Jansen crossed the city towards the East River. There lived on Eighth street, near the Third Avenue, a lady whom she had often met at Mrs. Woodbine's. Her name was Mrs. Cairne. This lady had a kind and gentle way with her that had always pleased Madeline. She was one of the progressive school of women, but not so radical in her sentiments as were many who visited at Mrs. Woodbine's. Mrs. Cairne had, once or twice, called on Mrs. Jansen, and the latter promised to return her visits, but had not yet done so. From some cause, of which she was in ignorance, Mrs. Cairne's reception with several of Mrs. Woodbine's visitors was not of the most cordial nature. Madeline had noticed this, and wondered as to its meaning. The woman was gentle, cultivated, and of lady-like demeanor; and yet she did not seem to attract her own sex strongly. But, the men who happened at any time to be present when she was at Mrs. Woodbine's, were generally marked in their attentions. It had not escaped the observation of Madeline, that in conversation with men, Mrs. Cairne was always more animated than when in conversation with women. At such times, her face would light up with feeling, and her eyes dance and sparkle in a way that made her really fascinating. Something which then appeared in the expression of her face, was not pleasant to Mrs. Jansen. What its meaning was, she could not say; but it impressed her unfavorably.

Of all her friends — after Mrs. Woodbine and Mrs. Lawrence — on whom she felt inclined to call in this painful episode of her life, Mrs. Cairne came next. A dozen were thought of and passed by. Here there seemed the best chance for sympathy and temporary refuge.

As Mrs. Jansen stood at Mrs. Cairne's door, with her hand on the bell, a sudden shadow fell upon her spirit, accompanied by an inward fear, as if in the presence of evil and hurtful things. A strong impulse pressed her back; she let her grasp unloose itself from the bell-handle, and moving away, descended to the street. Five minutes afterwards she returned, walked firmly up to the door, and pulled the bell.

"My dear Mrs. Jansen! How glad I am to see you!" Cordially, and with an air of sincerity not to be mistaken, this welcome to the already heart-sick and almost fainting wanderer was given.

"I have heard of your trouble," added Mrs. Cairne, as she led Madeline back to the sofa from which she had arisen, and sitting beside her, still held her hand tightly, looking with questioning earnestness into her face.

Madeline could not keep back the tears from her eyes. Here was genuine sympathy, for which her heart was longing. Unable to control herself, she laid her face down upon Mrs. Cairne, and sobbed.

"For one so young! For one whose sky was so warm and bright! Oh, it is hard — very hard!" said Mrs. Cairne, in her tender, loving way.

The whole frame of Madeline quivered with sobs; but, she had a strong will, and self-control, and quickly regained her lost equipoise. To the pressing enquiries of Mrs. Cairne, made with such an affectionate interest, she opened all her heart — confided in her as completely as if she had been a beloved sister, older and wiser than herself. During the time, Mrs. Cairne sat with one arm drawn around Madeline, and a hand tightly holding one of her hands. Madeline's bonnet and shawl she had already, with kindly officiousness, removed.

No coldness, no shrinking back, or reserve on the part of Mrs. Cairne, followed. Instead, she drew closer to Madeline with a kind of motherly tenderness.

"I have a place for you both in my heart and my house," she said. "Come in and occupy as long as you will. I marvel at Mrs. Woodbine! I knew she was a selfish, and a worldly-wise woman in some things: but I saw, also, so many good points in her character that I gave her credit for more than she was worth. Trouble proves our friends. In blossomy spring and summer, and in the fruitful autumn of our lives, they gather around us thickly; but, the evergreens of friendship are few. You are passing amid your first fiery trials. I trust you have a strong will, a brave heart, and power of endurance. You will need them all."

"I have gone out alone," replied Mrs. Jansen, finding strength in the warm sympathy of Mrs. Cairne; "and if need be, I shall walk alone, straightforward to the end. I may be faint and weary — my feet may bleed — I may be in terror of the evil that meets me on the way; but there is one thing certain — I shall not turn back."

Up to this time, since leaving her home, Mrs. Jansen had been in a state of strong internal excitement. Nothing had gone tranquilly. The currents of feeling had been seething amid rocks, or dashing down rapids. Now they smoothed themselves out into a calm lake, and a slumbrous quiet, sweet as peace, fell gently over her spirit. Mrs. Cairne gave her a room, neatly furnished, and supplied with books.

"Stay as long as you will," she said, in her sweet, winning way. "I will be your friend, your companion, and your counsellor."

When left alone in her room, Mrs. Jansen, on taking note of her sensations, perceived a heaviness that weighed down her limbs, as though after great fatigue. Accompanying this, was a fullness about the head, and a dull, deep, aching of the brain — not severe, yet defining itself with steadily increasing throbs. As one aweary, she threw herself on the bed, and was soon lost in a heavy sleep. When she awoke, Mrs. Cairne was sitting by her side.

"Are you not well, dear?" was asked, with evident concern of manner.

An attempt to rise was accompanied by strong painful throbs in the forehead, and a sense of bewilderment. Madeline sunk back on the pillow with a low moan.

"You are sick, child!" said Mrs. Cairne, who saw that her face was flushed. Touching her skin, she perceived that it was hot with fever. "Do you often have spells of sudden illness?"

"No." The answer was dull, as if Madeline had only partly understood the question.

"You are sick, Mrs. Jansen." Mrs. Cairne spoke with an earnestness meant to rouse her guest.

Madeline opened her eyes, and looked about her in a disturbed way.

"I'm afraid I am," she answered.

"What can I do for you?" asked Mrs. Cairne.

"Oh, nothing at all. It will pass off. I've been worried and fatigued. Rest and quiet will do all that is needed."

"Your head aches," said Mrs. Cairne, who saw deep lines cutting down her forehead.

"Very badly."

"Shall I bathe it?"

"If you please."

But, something beyond simple bathing of the hot forehead was needed. Before night, it was deemed best, by Mrs. Cairne, to call in a physician. What he thought of the case, Madeline did not perceive. She was too sick to take much note of what passed around her.

CHAPTER XVI.

MRS. Jansen did not leave her bed for several days, nor her room for over a week. Every day, the physician who had been called in by Mrs. Cairne, came to see her. He was a man of about forty, with a frank, cheerful address, and an air of familiarity from which Mrs. Jansen, as fever subsided, and her mind grew clear, shrunk with instinctive delicacy. Something in the touch of his hand, moist and velvety, as he laid it upon hers, sent a faint shiver along her nerves; and the instant his fingers left her pulse, she would draw her hand away. His eyes, dark and with a mystery in them that she could not read, hurt her as she felt them going down into her very consciousness. She could not bear his look, and turned from him, always, with an uneasy feeling, as if there were harm in his very glances.

The doctor did not intermit his daily calls, even after

Mrs. Jansen could sit up in her room. Mrs. Cairne usually came in with him, but almost always made some excuse to leave them alone. He was an intelligent, cheerful talker, full of anecdote, and, as we have intimated, very frank and familiar. But, the repulsion felt by Mrs. Jansen in the beginning, did not wear off; and she invariably declined to let him take her hand, at the close of his visits, though he never omitted the attempt.

"It is unnecessary to call again, doctor," she said to him one day, a week after the beginning of her illness. "I am quite well again."

"Not so well as you think," he answered, smiling in his frank way. "There is some fever in your system yet." And before she could draw back her hand, he had taken it, and was searching for the artery that lay along the fair wrist. "Too quick and hard yet," he said. "You are not entirely safe, madam. The merest trifle may throw you off from this returning healthy balance; and you know that relapses are always bad. Don't be too weary of the sick room. An impatient convalescence is never a sure one."

He had risen to retire; but sat down again, and taking out his pencil, wrote a prescription. Mrs. Jansen remained standing.

"Send for that," he said, handing his patient the slip of paper on which he had been writing. He remained seated, but with his eyes fixed intently on Mrs. Jansen's face. Never had she been so affected, as at this moment, by gaze from human eyes. They seemed to hold her spell-bound. She felt in thrall. Intense, clear, pulsating in light, full of eager intelligence, like something alive, they seemed to draw, hold, consume. A vague, weak terror seized her.

She wished to fly, but had no conscious power of motion. A few moments elapsed, the doctor not once removing his gaze. Then rising slowly, his eyes not wavering, he reached forth a hand to take one of hers. The touch of that hand was like an electric spark, firing the passive will. Madeline started, and sprang back, her face deadly pale.

"Go, sir!" she said, sternly and imperatively.

He did not move. The eager, hungry light went out of his eyes; and a pleasant smile broke softly over his countenance.

"Don't be excited, my dear madam," he said, in a calm, persuasive voice. "This fever still lingers in your system, and presses on your brain. I only wished to examine your pulse before retiring. The giving of offence was the last thing in my thought. Good day! I will call in the morning and ask if the medicine has done its right work. You need not see me, unless you desire it. Good day."

And bowing in complete self-possession, and with undiminished blandness of manner, the doctor retired.

Weak and trembling, Mrs. Jansen sunk into a chair. All the little strength she had gained in her brief convalescence, seemed to have departed. "Fever still lingers in your system, and presses on your brain." The doctor had said this so earnestly, and looked, as he spoke, so kind and calm, that she was already beginning to feel a doubt as to her own clear perception of things. Might she not have altogether mistaken him?

Mrs. Cairne did not come to her room for nearly half an hour after the doctor retired. Mrs. Jansen was lying down, but arose as she entered, fixing her eyes so searchingly on the face of Mrs. Cairne, that she partly turned it aside, as if she feared more might be revealed there than she wished her guest to know.

"The doctor says that fever still lurks in your system, and that you must not think of leaving your room."

Mrs. Jansen did not reply — only looked more keenly at Mrs. Cairne.

"I have known Doctor B —— for several years, and have great confidence in him. His practice lies among the best families in New York; and he is much esteemed everywhere, not only as a skilful physician, but as a true and honorable man. It would be imprudent to disregard his injunction in anything."

"If he should call to-morrow," Mrs. Jansen replied, in a serious tone, "say that I am better, and do not wish to see him."

The expression of Mrs. Cairne's face changed, instantly. She looked both surprised and concerned.

"Why do you say that?" she asked. "I hope you have not misunderstood the doctor in anything. He's very plain and outspoken, sometimes. In what has he offended you?"

"I did not say that he had offended me in anything — only, that I did not wish to see him. I am better, and do not need his further attentions."

"You have fever." Mrs. Cairne took one of Mrs. Jansen's hands, meaning to offer its unnatural warmth in proof of her declaration. But she found it cold and moist.

"Your hand is hot in mine," returned Madeline.

The two women looked at each other with doubt and questioning in their eyes, and then mutually turned their eyes away, as if each had something in her thought that she wished to conceal.

"I will do as you desire, of course," said Mrs. Cairne, but not with her usual free and kindly way. "I am so warm a friend of Doctor B———," she added, as if in apology for her manner, " and know so well his excellence of mind and heart — his skill, his honor, his high professional worth — that it hurts me to know that one so near to me as you are; one whom I so truly love, should feel towards him the slightest repugnance, or misapprehend him in the smallest degree."

"We are not all alike," was the answer of Madeline. There was more in her thought that she intended to say; but she paused with this sentence. Mrs. Cairne waited for her to go on, but she kept silent.

"I'm pained," said Mrs. Cairne, " that anything in the slightest degree unpleasant should have occurred in my house with friends whom I so highly regard. Pray be frank with me, dear Mrs. Jansen! Tell me exactly what appeared in the doctor's manner?"

Something whispered Mrs. Jansen to be on her guard.

"I have nothing to tell," she replied. "We cannot always trace our impressions to their causes. It is enough, that I do not consider myself in further need of visits from a physician. We all have our peculiarities, you know. Set this down as one of mine; but do not, I pray, let it stand as anything between us."

"No — no, not for an instant!" warmly and frankly returned Mrs. Cairne, and she kissed her friend. To Mrs. Jansen, the kiss had a strange feeling, as if it were a kiss of betrayal.

On the next day, Doctor B——— called at the usual hour. Mrs. Jansen heard the bell, and going to her room door, opened it and listened. She knew the doctor's step as he entered the hall. Mrs. Cairne was in the parlor, and came out to meet him. For some time they talked in low voice. Madeline stood in the upper passage, and leaned over the baluster, hearkening intently; but she could not make out a word. From the hall they presently retired into the parlors, and with a sense of relief, Madeline returned to her room and shut the door. She did not feel at ease in her mind. An impression of insecurity lay heavily upon her heart. Many doubts had oppressed her in the last twenty-four hours, many questions perplexed her that were still as far from being solved as ever.

From this state, as she sat musing she was aroused by hearing the sound of a man's feet on the stairs. The doctor, in spite of her request that his visits should cease, was coming to her chamber! A feeling of indignation flashed through her soul. Her first thought was to confront him at the door, and sternly order him to retire; but a sense of loneliness and weakness quickly brought another resolution. She turned the key in the lock, and then, feeling secure, retired across the chamber, and sat down. A light tap announced the doctor's presence.

"Who is it?" Madeline asked.

"The doctor," was replied.

"I do not wish to see you." There was an angry impulse in the tones of Mrs. Jansen, as she made this abrupt response.

A moment after, and a hand was laid upon the door knob; but the sprung bolt proved an interdict. All was still for the space of a minute. Madeline sat with half suspended breath, listening anxiously. At length her ears detected a movement, and she fancied that whispers were in the air. The sound of retiring feet came distinctly — a muffled and diminishing sound, that soon fell away into silence. More than an hour elapsed before Mrs. Cairne came to her room.

"You are a foolish thing," she said, half chidingly, yet with her usual frank and pleasant manner — "I'm sorry you didn't see the doctor. But, no matter. He thought strangely of you — how could it be otherwise?"

"*I* thought strangely of *him*," was Madeline's answer, speaking with slight signs of anger. "He may be gentle, manly, and all that; but when a patient says she does not wish to be seen, both gentlemanly feeling and professional sensitiveness would prompt a physician to regard her will."

"Oh, well, let it pass, dear," said Mrs. Cairne. "The doctor was over-anxious about you, and in trying to see you, even against your wishes, only obeyed a sense of duty. But while he thought strangely of you, I said, he was not offended. He is used to these idosyncracies of patients, and can make allowance for them."

In the eyes of Madeline there had come over Mrs. Cairne a strange transformation. She had noticed something of this from the moment she entered her house — it had progressed day by day, and now as she looked upon her, she did not appear like the same woman she had known. Beneath the courteous manner, the open, free-hearted smile and voice, was revealed another personality — selfish sinister, false and cruel. Mrs. Jansen felt a chill of repulsion steal along her nerves as she looked at her. To the last remark of Mrs. Cairne, no reply was made.

"I am going out for an hour or two this morning," she said, after remaining with Mrs. Jansen for a short time — "is there anything that you would like me to get for you?"

"Nothing, thank you," was replied, "and don't hurry yourself about returning; I shall find company in a book."

But no book had interest enough for Mrs. Jansen on that morning. Soon after Mrs. Cairne went out, she changed her dress, and descended to the parlor, for the first time in many days. She felt weak but not sick. Fever had relinquished its hold upon her system. She had been in the parlor scarcely half an hour, when a visitor came in. So absorbed were her thoughts that she had not heard the bell. Rising quickly as a lady entered the parlor, she found herself face to face with Mrs. Windall!

"My dear, dear child!" ejaculated the latter, coming quickly forwards, and grasping her reluctant hand — "what on earth are you doing here?" She spoke in an excited manner, yet in an undertone, very low and mysterious. Her whole manner expressed concern, as well as surprise.

"Why not here?" inquired Madeline, relaxing just a little from her coldness.

"That you should ask such a question, standing as you are in the very gates of death and the jaws of hell!" said Mrs. Windall, with painful solemnity of manner.

Madeline's face grew white.

"Explain yourself. What does this language mean?" demanded Mrs. Jansen.

Mrs. Windall bent to her ear, and whispered a few words. Mrs. Jansen started as if a serpent had stung her, ejaculating —

"No! — no! that is impossible!"

"It is as true as the sun shines, and every moment you linger here is a moment of shame and peril. Should the fact of your having been in this house reach your husband's ears, the barrier between you will become eternal. He will look upon you as one of the vilest."

"And pray what are *you* doing here?" asked Mrs Jansen, her pale, trembling lips growing firm.

"Ten minutes ago I met Mrs. Cairne, and learned to my astonishment that you were in her house. That is why I am here. Could I hesitate an instant, when I knew that you were on enchanted ground, full of snares and pitfalls? I am here to warn you of danger, and to aid you in escape. Ah, my dear young friend! the way in which you have elected to walk is a difficult and a dangerous one. Not Christian, on his journey to the Promised Land, was more beset or in more peril than you will be."

"I shall leave instantly," said Mrs. Jansen. She was pale and distressed, and shivered with a nervous chill.

"Have you been sick?" asked Mrs. Windall, observing her more closely.

"Yes; this is the first time I've been out of my room for several days; I've been quite ill with fever."

"Shall I get a carriage?" asked Mrs. Windall.

"Oh, no, no!" replied Mrs. Jansen, "I wouldn't be seen going from here in a carriage for the world. How near do the stages run?"

"Very near."

"I will put on my things and leave immediately. You'll wait until I come down?"

"Yes; but don't be long; Mrs. Cairne may return at any moment, or you may be confronted with some caller, who will bruit the fact of your being here, and blast your good name."

A little while afterwards, and the two women went out together. Madeline's steps were feeble. She clung to the arm of Mrs. Windall, moving slowly away, her veil drawn tightly over her face. There were many persons in the street as they emerged from the house of Mrs. Cairne, and, from some cause, they attracted attention, two or three individuals stopping and turning to look after them, as they passed along the street.

"Who was that man?" asked Mrs. Windall. They were only the distance of three or four houses away from Mrs. Cairne's. A man, a few steps in advance of them, had paused suddenly, as if to speak, or in surprise. It was plain to Mrs. Windall from the start and shrinking against her of Mrs. Jansen, that she knew him. But Madeline did not meet the sign of recognition — only drew her veil closer, looking down, and passing on.

"Did you know him?" Mrs. Windall repeated her question, but in another form.

"Yes."

"Who was it?"

But the question received no answer.

"He recognized you."

The only response to this was a nervous pressure against the arm on which she was leaning.

Yes, he had recognized her, and she knew it — he, of all men living, the last she would have met of her own will just in that place! Had he seen her leaving the house of Mrs. Cairne? Did he know the reputation it bore? These questions seemed as if they would kill her. Suddenly, there seemed to rise between her and her husband a barrier high as Heaven. She was shut away from him forever. It was no longer by her own will that she stood apart. A wall of separation, impossible to scale, had been erected in an instant, and she was now a hopeless wanderer on the other side.

CHAPTER XVII.

ONCE more fairly in her power, Mrs. Windall used all the subtle art she possessed, in order to hold Mrs. Jansen passive to her will. She had, within a day or two, changed her home, and was now residing in Jersey City, occupying a pleasant room in a suburban residence that overlooked the bay. Not in a boarding-house, but as the guest at will of a lady in good circumstances, a recent acquaintance, between whom and herself a sudden and close intimacy had been formed. This lady's name was Barling. She was a widow, with only one child, a boy six years old.

Mrs. Barling was a woman of some cultivation and taste, and enjoyed intercourse with intellectual people, though not very intellectual herself. In the sphere of other and stronger minds, her thought was quickened to higher activity, and so dwelt in regions which she could not have attained alone. There was sufficient pleasure in this to lead her much into the society of men and women of superior minds. Mrs. Windall, slightly repelling her at the first meeting, had, subsequently, attracted her strongly. She noted peculiarities — some of them in opposition to her good taste — but set them down as eccentricities of genius. These she soon ceased to observe. Flowing in with the even current of Mrs. Barling's life, Mrs. Windall had pleased her with flatteries skilfully applied, and so won upon her affection and confidence. An invitation to spend a few weeks at her house was given with such an earnest cordiality, that a person of far less independence of feelings than Mrs. Windall, would scarcely have hesitated on the question of acceptance.

By the time Mrs. Jansen reached the residence of Mrs. Barling, she was so exhausted that she could scarcely bear up the weight of her body. Assisted by Mrs. Windall and a servant, she was just able to ascend to one of the chambers, where she sunk, half fainting, on a bed. A little wine gave artificial stimulus to the weak and palpitating nerves. In the repose that followed she slept.

During this interval of sleep, Mrs. Windall had opportunity to explain fully to her friend the circumstances under which she had found Mrs. Jansen, and to awaken a strong interest in her favor. A cordial welcome to her house, and an invitation to remain as long as she felt inclined to do so, were given by Mrs. Barling, and thankfully accepted.

"Do not apprehend," said Mrs. Jansen, her eyes full of grateful tears, "that I will become a burdensome intruder. Give me a brief time to recover my strength, and to determine my steps for the future, and I will pass on. The way before me is shrouded in darkness. I cannot see in what direction it runs, but I know that it is a difficult and dangerous way. I need a little pause, and in a place where I can stand firm, that I may gird myself for the struggles that await me."

The effort and excitement which had attended Madeline's escape from the house of Mrs. Cairne, left her very weak, and with symptoms of fever. Two or three days passed before she was able to leave her room. During the time she was scarcely ever alone, Mrs. Windall was her constant companion. The strong repugnance she had felt towards this woman gradually subsided, and while she felt no attraction towards her, she almost unconsciously yielded up her will, and suffered her thoughts and future plans to take the direction that she pointed out.

Mrs. Windall was a thoroughly selfish and unscrupulous woman. Every thought was limited by considerations of a personal nature, and ministered to sinister ends. Under the guise of philanthropic profession, she concealed an unwavering devotion to selfish ends. Her first thought, on meeting Mrs. Jansen at the house of Mrs. Woodbine, after the separation, was — "How can I turn this circumstance to account?" And, almost instantly, a suggestion of the means came. It was for this reason that she was so prompt to invite Mrs. Jansen to go home with her, and that she was so basely unscrupulous about the ways in which she sought to obtain control over the tried and unhappy woman.

Too indolent or proud, for ordinary useful work, whereby to secure an income, Mrs. Windall lacked the genius for higher efforts. A few times she had tried public readings, but miserably failed, the receipts for tickets not covering half of the expenses. Once pressed for the means of living, after exhausting the patience of temporary friends, who gradually receded the more intimately they knew her, she tried, under an assumed address, the game of a public swindler. In this she was more successful in a pecuniary way; but ran such a narrow risk of arrest and exposure, that she had never since-felt easy in mind.

The swindling operation we have mentioned was in this wise. Mrs. Windall, under a false name, and with forged letters of credence and introduction, purporting to be from well known persons in the Southern States, visited Buffalo, where she advertised for twenty-five teachers, young women, to go South, promising immediate engagements in seminaries and families, with liberal compensation. Applications, many, came in to her, and she found little difficulty in making arrangements with twenty-five young ladies to accompany her to Charleston. A time was appointed for the journey to begin, and on the day previous, each of the girls placed in the hands of Mrs. Windall the sum of thirty dollars, for the payment of expenses. She was to procure tickets for the company, and to meet them at the railroad depot in the morning. But, on their assembling at the depot at the appointed time, Mrs. Windall was not there. She had departed in a midnight train, with over seven hundred dollars in her pocket, and was never again seen or heard of in Buffalo.

The swindle was published, and some efforts made to find and punish the swindler. But, as the cheated girls were poor, and without influential friends, there was but little to stimulate police efforts, and Mrs. Windall, though seriously alarmed for her safety, managed to run clear. She did not think it prudent to try other schemes of a like nature. The risk was to plainly before her eyes.

The manner in which she proposed too use Mrs. Jansen to her own advantage was this. The suggestion had come to her at the house of Mrs. Woodbine, and the more she dwelt upon it, the more assured of success did she feel. Mrs. Jansen was young, and attractive in person. Dressed for effect in the flash and glare of evening lights, she would appear brilliant. She had talent of a certain order. In some of the companies which met at Mrs. Woodbine's there had been readings, and Madeline, on these occasions, had several times taken part, and acquitted herself to the admiration of all. Enthusiastic, and apt to enter with her whole soul into whatever she might be doing, she had, in some of her efforts, reached a singular perfection, holding her little audiences almost spell-bound. All this Mrs. Windall remembered; and when she saw this beautiful young creature breaking away from her home, instead of pain and pity for the grief and trouble that were before her, came a thrill of pleasure in the thought, that she might turn her talents to account for her own benefit. It was this dimly shadowed purpose that led her so promptly to encourage Madeline, in opposition to Mrs. Woodbine; and that induced her to take her home, as we have seen.

The plan of using Mrs. Jansen's personal attractions and talents as here indicated, once conceived by Mrs. Windall, was not to be relinquished. She saw an easy way of improving her rather desperate circumstances opening before her, and it was worth an effort to remove the obstructions that kept her feet back from entrance.

The first thing done by Mrs. Windall towards accomplishing her end, now that she had her victim in her power, and full time to plot and plan at leisure, was to win over Mrs. Barling to her views. Mrs. Barling was a weak, as well as a confiding woman; and where she trusted another of stronger mind than herself, could easily be led to see with that other one's eyes. The first intimation of what was in the mind of Mrs. Windall, rather shocked her feelings than elicited approval. But, Mrs. Windall not only understood human nature in general, but the particular human nature of her friend, and with the skill of an accomplished tactician, soon managed to lead her into the position she considered it most desirable for her to occupy.

To Mrs. Jansen, the subject was at first introduced in remote hints; but she did not understand them. Nothing could have been farther from her thoughts. When, at last, the suggestion came to her mind in a definite form, she shrunk back from the idea with a shiver of reluctance. In pondering the future, and scanning the ways and means by which she was to live, this had not once occurred to her. Most emphatically did she answer, "No, no! I will never think of that."

But Mrs. Windall was not the woman to relinquish any well digested scheme in which she was to derive benefit. First bringing Mrs. Barling entirely over to her views of the case, which was easily done, she commenced her insidious work upon Mrs. Jansen. With a most painful vividness did she bring before her mind the difficulties that would beset her way. She must live self-sustained, but how?

"Now is the time to look this question clearly in the face," she said, "and to determine your course for the future. How will you live? If I were less your friend than I am, I would not pain you by thrusting the subject into view; but, as your friend, deeply interested in your well being, I cannot shrink from the way of duty. How are you to live? In breaking away from the tyranny of your husband, you left empty-handed, and you are too proud and independent to ask of him anything. You have no income in your own right. So the question of living is resolved into self-dependence. You must earn your bread. Here is the naked truth; and the question repeats itself — How? There are only two ways; by skill of hands or skill of head. Which will you choose? For women, as you are too well advised, the avenues to remunerative positions are few. You cannot get a clerkship in a bank or counting-house, nor secure the secretaryship of an insurance company. The doors of all public offices are closed against us. You might find a place in some fancy dry goods' or mantilla store. Perhaps Brodie would accept your services at four or five dollars a week as a lay figure, on which to exhibit cloaks. But, I dont know. Then there is teaching. What are your gifts and qualifications, looking to this line of employment?"

Mrs. Jansen shook her head gloomily.

"You are not fit for a teacher. That is clear," said Mrs. Windall, emphatically. "What then? There is needlework; or, in other words, suicide. But, one possessing your gifts and education, would hardly go down to enter into competition with poor, half starved needle women. No — no. You were made for something higher and better — for a broader and nobler sphere — for the exercise of talents such as only the few possess. You have dramatic powers of no ordinary kind."

"You are mistaken," replied Mrs. Jansen, warmly, yet with a troubled tone and manner. "And even if I did possess dramatic talents, one thing is certain, I will never go on the stage. Teaching, the needle, store-attendance — anything but that!"

"I did not suggest the stage," said Mrs. Windall. "You misunderstood me. I only referred to your dramatic power as an important element in public reading. That is the guarantee of your high success; a success that will make you independent in the world. A little earnest training of your voice — and a few lessons from a good elocutionist — and you are as certain as the day to succeed. I know your delicacy of feeling — your sensitiveness about coming before the public; but there is a way of self-protection entirely justifiable. You may come out as a public reader, and yet avoid all unpleasant notoriety."

"How?"

"By doing as others have done. Assume a name for public use. No one is hurt thereby. No wrong is intended. The act will be, as I have intimated, simply one of self-protection. A writer has the option of concealing his personality under a *nom de plume;* and may not a speaker do the same? It is clear enough to my mind; and a little reflection will make it clear enough to yours."

But, against both a public appearance and an assumed name, the feelings of Madeline strongly revolted; and it required all the subtlety and management of the woman in whose power she had fallen, to overcome the delicacy and high sense of honor that were shocked by the proposal. Of all the means used to reduce Madeline to her will, we will not speak. The reader has already seen the dangerous power that Mrs. Windall had gained over her; a power not likely to be relinquished, when its use would serve the purpose she had in view. It was on her side, and against her victim, that with every submission of will to the exercise of that demoniac influence which had laid passive the volition of Madeline, susceptibility increased. Of causes, and the philosophy explanatory of these causes, it is not for us here to speak. We have to do only with a fact that is full of significance and warning.

CHAPTER XVIII.

RS. Barling was a kind, generous, hospitable woman; and it went hard with her, after Mrs. Jansen had been in her house for a month, to let an intimation drop, on the presence of a fitting occasion, to the effect, that it was time she was beginning to try her strength in the world. Of herself, she could not have done this. It was Mrs. Windall who spoke through her.

That hint was sufficient, and Mrs. Jansen, stung to the quick, made almost immediate preparation to leave. It was in vain that Mrs. Barling remonstrated, and in all sincerity urged her to remain longer. The native pride and independence of Mrs. Jansen was hurt and nothing could reconcile her to stay. The question of going clearly settled, that of when and whither was fairly opened, and grave discussions followed that only showed Madeline how dark and difficult was the path lying before her, and left her mind deeper in labarynthine doubts. Half maddened by the pain of her situation, the unhappy woman at last gave up, and dropped, passively, into the hands of Mrs. Windall. A few months of training for the new work upon which she had so reluctantly consented to begin, was considered necessary both by Mrs. Windall and Mrs. Barling, and after strong persuasion and repeated apologies and explanations from the latter, Mrs. Jansen consented to remain her guest during this time of preparation.

In Philadelphia the first trial was made by Mrs. Jansen, just six months after the fatal day of separation from her husband. The newspapers, jointly with posters displayed all over the city, announced that a Mrs. Aberdeen would give dramatic readings at the Musical Fund Hall, on a certain evening. The programme embraced a few well known passages from Shakspeare; the "Lady Geraldine's Courtship," by Mrs. Browning; "Horatius," from Macaulay's Lays of ancient Rome; "The Raven," and "The Bells," of Poe; with humorous pieces interspersed.

Mrs. Windall had many old acquaintances in Philadelphia, and she did not hesitate about calling on them, notwithstanding her collapse in that city some years before. She trusted to a weakness of memory, the softening influence of time, and her own assurance, for a re-establishment of former friendly relations. Some, who did not easily forget, and others who could not renew a confidence once betrayed, kept her at a distance; but she found enough ready to forget and forgive the past, and through them was able to create a warm interest in her young and attractive friend, and secure for her a fair audience.

As the hour for Madeline's first appearance in public

drew near, a nervous anxiety about the result took possession of her. An active imagination kept the scene in which she was about to participate too vividly before her mind. She saw herself standing alone before a large concourse of people, and felt herself dumb in their presence. How could she lift her voice in calm assurance? How could she lose self-consciousness, and dwell in the ideas and characters she was to represent? It seemed to her impossible. Mrs. Windall, who saw, with deep concern, the state into which she was falling, used all the means of reassurance that were suggested to her thoughts, but without apparent success. The paleness of Madeline's face, its anxiety, and the expression of dread or fear that was settling over it, alarmed her for the result of the evening's experiments.

"This will never do," she said, half kindly, half chidingly, as the evening approached. "Confidence creates success, even where ability is small. In your case, where there is so much talent, all that is needed for triumph is self-assurance. Throw all this timidity to the winds. You are standing at the threshold of a brilliant career; do not, by any unwomanly weakness, put the result in jeopardy."

"I have no faith in myself," Madeline replied gloomily.

"While I have all faith. Forget yourself; and be, for the time, the character you assume."

"I cannot forget myself." Some irritation appeared in Mrs. Jansen's manner. "What I am — where I am — and what I am about doing, hold my thoughts in bondage. I see myself shrinking, trembling, dumb in the presence of a multitude. Oh that I could fly away to some desert, and escape this fiery trial!"

Mrs. Windall was alarmed. She had given Madeline

credit for more strength of nerve; had built confidently on success. What was to be done? Madeline's nerves were excited — she must tranquilize them if possible. She took one of her hands. Its coldness struck her with surprise.

"I'm afraid you are not well," she said.

"My head is aching badly," Madeline answered.

"How long has this been?"

"It has been aching all day. Slightly during the forenoon — intensely for the last two hours."

"Why didn't you tell me of this?" said Mrs. Windall, a little sharply. They had been sitting close together, facing each other. Mrs. Windall arose, and standing near Madeline, drew her head against her side. There was a feeble effort on the part of Madeline to remove herself from this contact, but Mrs. Windall smoothed her hair softly with one hand, while she used some force with the other to retain the head where she had placed it. In a few moments, Mrs. Jansen was entirely passive.

"Is your head easier?" asked Mrs. Windall.

"Yes."

"You should have mentioned this before. There is magic in my touch. I have the gift of healing."

Mrs. Jansen made no reply, but sat with her head leaning heavily against Mrs. Windall, like one who had abandoned herself to the enjoyment of that easeful rest which follows pain. A dull kind of stupor followed, from which it required some effort on the part of Mrs. Windall to arouse her. Slowly the mind of Mrs. Jansen came back to a realization of the actual. The audience, in presence of which she had, in imagination, stood weak and shivering, had faded from her eyes. She had forgotten everything external in the dreamy quiet which this syren had thrown around her spirit. Now, as thought was released from bonds, and imagination went wandering again in the mazes from which it had been withdrawn, the old quiver shook her nerves — the old throb beat in her temples — the old fear took possession of her heart.

"I shall fail!" she said, with visible agitation. "Miserably fail! What folly! Oh, that there were time to recall the announcement."

"If there was one quality above all others for which I gave you credit," replied Mrs. Windall, "it was courage. I never imagined, for an instant, that the woman who could face the issues you have faced alone, standing up so bravely in your own strength, could be coward in so small a thing as this. Think of what is to follow success or failure! If you succeed, you are independent of the world. If you fail, what then? Forget whatever may seem unpleasant in the means, for the sake of the end. Look to the end — to the end my dear Mrs. Jansen! Away to the goal, and not down to your feet, dreading lest you stumble and fall. The confident command success; the timid and hesitating are sure to fail. Summon the native strength of your character. Let pride come to your aid. Spurn, as unworthy, all that is man-pleasing or man-fearing. Stand up strong, heroic, daring. Confidence is inspiration."

Madeline turned her face away. There was no power in all these sentences to help her. She felt herself growing weaker and weaker. She was frightened at the prospect before her.

The afternoon had worn away until five o'clock. At eight, Mrs. Jansen was announced to appear at the Musical Fund Hall. Only three hours intervened.

"If you could fall asleep," said Mrs. Windall, who had become alarmed for the result.

"Sleep calms the mind, and restores its lost equipoise. Lie down. I will close the blinds. Perhaps you may lose yourself. Even a few minutes of forgetfulness will do much good."

"Sleep!" returned Madeline, almost passionately, "you might as well ask the martyr on his bed of coals to sleep!"

"All this is unworthy of you," said Mrs. Windall, in a rebuking voice. "You are a woman, equipped for life's battle; not a half-grown child. Will you cower and skulk in face of an enemy? Run at the first encounter? For shame!"

The spur went pricking into the sensitive flank, and the dull blood leaped along in fuller currents. The heart of Madeline was a little stronger. She struggled with weakness, and grew brave.

"All this is unwomanly," she said. "I must rise above it."

"Spoken like your own self," answered Mrs. Windall. "Yes, you must rise above all these petty weaknesses. Strength comes of will. Look onward to achievement; not aside at difficulties. If there be lions in the way, the brave heart shall find them chained."

Evening came. At eight o'clock Madeline passed up from one of the small ante-rooms on the first floor, to the platform, and stood facing the audience, a vision of beauty that sent admiring murmurs throughout the hall. She was not dressed according to her own taste and sense of propriety; nor yet in a manner to satisfy Mrs. Windall. There had been a compromise on this head between manager and debutante. The former contended for low neck, short sleeves, and pink satin; the latter for plain black and a modest arrangment of her dress. A dove-colored silk, rather profusely trimmed, with some hair ornaments, and a gay sash, exhibited this compromise. As there was not much in Madeline's attire to draw attention from her face, which was almost colorless as she advanced in front of the audience, all eyes scanned it with curious interest.

This was the critical moment. Mrs. Windall, who had accompanied her on the stage, held her breath in painful suspense. Madeline, as she stood thus confronting a sea of upturned, curious, expectant faces, felt the old sense of weakness and terror stealing over her. But, rallying herself with a desperate effort of will, she threw out her voice in the opening piece of the entertainment. It was low and unsteady at first, causing a hush throughout the assembly; but soon gained firmness and volume. There were some faults in the elocution; but so much in the whole rendering of the scene she had chosen which took the audience by surprise, that she was greeted with an electric outburst of applause as she turned from the reading desk, and disappeared from the platform. Her second and third pieces were more enthusiastically cheered than the first. In a humorous effort that followed, she was not successful. Her mind was not strung to anything like this. "The Raven" that came afterwards was a surprise, and had to be repeated. Grandly she gave "Horatius," stirring all hearts with a battle scene. Tenderly, and with almost unequalled pathos, she read "the Lady Geraldine's Courtship." Mrs. Browning herself, had she been present, must have felt some passages quite as deeply as when they thrilled her soul in the first fervors of poetic inspiration.

It was a triumph. Rarely has it occurred that such

complete success attended a first appearance in public. One thing was noticeable. The paleness did not leave the face of Madeline. Her beautiful eyes flashed and changed, and her countenance was mobile to every passion and sentiment; but the whiteness remained. A few friends, made during her brief sojourn in Philadelphia, came into the ante-room below after the performance, to offer their congratulations. They found her in an exhausted condition, like one whose strength had been greatly overtasked. She manifested no pleasure when they spoke enthusiastically of her success; and seemed only desirous to get away.

On reaching her room at the hotel, Madeline, who had remained wholly irresponsive to Mrs. Windall, (that person was in a kind of ecstacy over the evening's triumph) asked to be let alone.

"You will have something," said Mrs. Windall, lingering.

"Nothing," replied Madeline coldly.

"You are exhausted by so unusual an effort. Let me send for a glass of wine." Mrs. Windall made a movement as if about to pull the bell.

"No — no!" said Madeline, in a quick, impatient voice. "I said that I wished to be alone," she added, with an assertion of will that took Mrs. Windall by surprise.

The latter withdrew; as she shut the door after her, Madeline turned the key, that she might be safe from further intrusion. Then disrobing herself, she got into bed, and shrinking down among the clothes and pillows, lay as still as if sleep had fallen upon her instantly. But sleep was very far from her eyelids. Every faculty of mind was awake and in action. She had succeeded in her first public reading, far beyond even Mrs. Windall's anticipations. As for herself, she had counted on failure. A nervous fear had, almost up to the last moment, oppressed her. How she overcame the weakness was not clear. She had lost the chain of mental action. A link was missing that she could not find. Blindly she had stepped over a chasm into which she had expected to fall — blindly, and so the way across that chasm was lost, and she could not approach it again in any hope of a safe passage.

As the case stood with Mrs. Jansen, there was no assurance in the future from this night's success. The triumph was only an accident; not a sequence. It was the question of advancing or receding which now fully occupied her thoughts; a question that she meant to determine before the next day dawn. How she determined will appear in the following chapter.

CHAPTER XIX.

THREE days after Madeline's debut at the Musical Fund Hall, Mrs. Barling received the following letter from Mrs. Windall.

"MY DEAR MRS. BARLING:—I promised to write you fully about Mrs. Jansen's first appearance. After a magnificent debut everything has failed. I write in chagrin and disappointment beyond what I can express. It has turned out as I feared. She has talent, genius, power; but, no faith in herself—nothing of that tenacity of character so essential to high achievement. But, let me come down to the plain facts, and tell the story as it occurred. On arriving in Philadelphia, we took rooms at the United States Hotel on Chestnut street, and I immediately renewed my acquaintance with several dear old friends, of high social position and much influence. The warmest kind of interest was taken in Mrs. Jansen or rather in Mrs Aberdeen, the name by which she was introduced. I am sorry to say, that she did not respond with anything of her natural grace, vivacity, and sweetness of temper to the generous interest that every one manifested. She was distant and cold towards all who approached her. The change that became apparent from the time of our arrival in Philadelphia was remarkable. From the beginning of my acquaintance with Mrs. Jansen, I possessed great influence over her; but that influence was strangely broken on our coming here. It seemed as though a new spirit had taken possession of her, which I had no power to exorcise.

"To be brief, Mrs. Jansen lost all faith in herself. She had no confidence in the approaching trial, and persistently talked of failure. Up to the last moment, she held back, and could she have met a single person injudicious enough to utter a doubting word, would have refused to confront the waiting audience. All this I saw, and you may be sure I was in an agony of suspense and fear.

"I took her hand as we ascended from the waiting-room below. It was like ice, and had a low, quick shiver, that sent a chill along my nerves. 'Courage!' I whispered —'you stand on the threshold of a grand success!' She made no response. I walked out with her upon the stage, holding my breath. The decisive moment had come; I saw her shrink in the presence of an eagerly expectant assembly, and my heart stood still. Another moment, and her voice swept out low and clear, but with slight faltering. My heart went on again. I was assured. Two or three sentences, her voice steadily rising, and then she was in full command of herself. I never saw, in any of our most successful actors, a more perfect absorption of self in the impersonation of a character than was shown by Mrs. Jansen. It was simple inspiration and wonderful! When she retired, at the close of her first piece, the whole house thundered with applause. I caught her hand and wrung it enthusiastically—I filled her ears with praises and congratulations—but she was cold and dumb as a stone. The paleness had not left her face—the thrilling shiver was in her icy hand. She sat down, her lips dropping apart, and remained like a statue until the waiting audience gave signs of impatience; and even then, I had to arouse her for the new effort. As at first she advanced in the face of the audience in a spiritless, hesitating manner; but she was all life and energy when the work, from which she held back with such a strange reluctance, began. Her second effort was better than the first.

"'Glorious!' I said, as I put my arms around her on receiving her again from the platform. But I might as well have spoken to an image. She sat down as before, in a dull, despairing kind of way, wholly irresponsive. So it continued throughout the evening. Before the audience she was inspired, electric, passionate, wonderful! Out of their presence, a weak, shivering, frightened child.

"'No matter,' I said to myself, as we rode home after her triumph, reviewing in thought the strange contrast of state I have mentioned—'she can do the work, and that is the great desideratum—how she does it is a thing of minor importance. She will get over this intense nervousness in time. The wonderful success of to-night, when she comes to review it, will give her a large measure of confidence. All is well! Her future is safe.

"But, alas! it was not safe! Arrived at the hotel, she went immediately to her room, whither I accompanied her. I saw that she was much exhausted, and urged her to take a glass of wine; but she refused all refreshment, and desired me to leave her at once alone. I did not think this well, seeing in what a nervous condition the performance had left her, and determined to remain for a time. But, recognizing my purpose, she turned on me with an imperious manner, such as I had never seen her put on before, and pushed me, by will and words stronger than hands, out of her room. I had a glimpse of her character in that moment not seen before. Her husband in their late quarrel, which led to a separation, was not, I now fancy, all in the wrong. There is a slumbering volcano in her heart, and all volcanos have their periods of irruption.

"My room adjoined Mrs. Jansen's. For two whole hours, I sat close to the partition which separated her chamber from mine, listening intently. Not a sound reached my ears. In the stillness of night, the respiration of a sleeper may be heard at a considerable distance. I hearkened for the sighing breath of Mrs. Jansen, with my ear against the partition; but all was still as death. About twelve o'clock I became so nervously anxious, that I went out into the passage, and going to her door, knocked gently. 'Who's there?' was instantly called out, in the clear tones of one who was evidently wide awake. 'Are you sick?' I asked. 'No,' was returned. That 'No,' was as full of repulsion as any word flung at me two hours before. I returned to my room and went to bed. It was a long time before I slept. During my wakeful hours I still listened towards Mrs. Jansen's apartment; but the silence there remained unbroken.

"In the morning when I awoke, the sun was shining brightly. Looking at my watch, I found that it was past seven o'clock. Hastily dressing myself, listening all the while for sounds in the next room, but hearing no movement, I went out in the passage. The door of Mrs. Jansen's room stood ajar; I pushed it open and went in. Mrs. Jansen was dressed, and sitting by the window. She turned towards me as I entered, and I saw that her face was still quite pale. Her eyes had a look of purpose in them that in no way lessened the uneasiness I felt.

"'How are you, dear?' I asked, with all the affectionate interest I could throw into my voice and manner, advancing quickly towards her, and grasping one of her hands. I stooped to kiss her, but she turned her head, and refused the salutation. Her hand gave back no pressure.

"'Very well,' she replied, coldly.

"'Have you slept soundly?'

"'No,' she said, without change in the dead level of her voice.

"'You are refreshed. The exhaustion of last night has passed away,' I continued.

"'In a measure,' she returned, with the same indifference of manner.

"'Let me repeat my congratulations at your triumphant success last night,'.I said, coming to what was nearest my heart.

"'Rather,' she replied, 'at my escape from failure and humiliation.' She spoke calmly — I might say, coldly, turning towards me, and looking at me in full self-possession. 'The success was not anything of mine.'

"'Whose was it, pray?' I asked, in surprise at her appearance and language.

"'I know not,' she answered, 'but this I know, that it was not Madeline Jansen who held that audience as in a spell, and extorted admiration and applause. In outward person she stood in face of the assembly, and her tongue, voice and body were instrumentalities, but not her conscious soul.'

"'What folly to talk thus,' I said, interrupting her— 'you are giving yourself to a wild fancy.'

"'No.' How cool and self-poised she was! 'No, not this morning. I have left the region of wild fancies, and possess my reason. All night I have pondered this matter, and my conclusion is reached.'

"'What is your conclusion?' I inquired, in painful suspense, for both her manner and her language were troubling me.

"'Never again to appear before an audience,' she answered, and I saw and felt that her decision was final. There are occasions when the purpose so writes itself in the face that mistake is impossible. I was too much confounded to speak, and she went on. 'It is due to you, after all the trouble and expense to which you have been subjected, that I give plain reasons for what I have declared. The chief reason, I have already intimated. To proceed is to fail. Last night's success came from unknown and intangible causes. I was like one seized by a superior being, and made to act from his strength and volition. In nothing that occurred can I recall myself—can I recognize my own skill, perception, indentity. I was lost—passive—possessed—anything that you will; but not myself. To venture on this ground again would be folly, and I have as the result of a night's reflection determined not to venture again. It will be useless for you to argue the point with me; I have resolved, and my resolution is final.'

"I made no attempt to move her from the purpose she had expressed; I felt that it would be useless. Our relation to each other had undergone a sudden and remarkable change. A little while before, and I was conscious of an almost complete influence over her — she was passive to my will. Now she stood like one afar off, whom I tried vainly to reach and influence. She seemed lifted out of my sphere of action — removed to a distance — set in a way wherein my feet were not to walk.

"What do you purpose doing?" I asked.

"'I have no settled purpose beyond the one expressed just now. Time will show the ways wherein I must go. There are paths for all feet.'

"I left her and went back to my own room, that I might consider the case, and arrive at some conclusion. I am not one to abandon a line of conduct because difficulties rise up in the way. If I cannot climb over a hill, I generally manage to get around it. But I did not get over nor around this obstructing mountain. When I looked again into Mrs. Jansen's room she was not there. Going down, I found her in the ladies' parlor. Approaching, I sat down near her — near her as to person; but in my soul I felt that she was at an immeasurable distance from me — that a gulf had fallen between us which it was impossible to bridge. I wished to refer again to the last night's success — to feel on that subject once more into her mind. But I could not utter a word bearing on this theme. The sentences formed in my thought were scattered like clouds in the wind ere expression could take them, instead, an inward voice uttered for me the words — 'Our ways part here!'

"And there, my friend, they parted. We held only a brief and distant communication, as if we were two strangers sojourning at the hotel. After breakfast she went out alone, and did not return for some hours. In the afternoon she went out again. I noticed, when she came back towards evening, a troubled and disappointed look in her face; but I asked her no questions, for I felt that it would be useless.

"The actual result of the evening's entertainment was a loss. At least one-third of the audience came on complimentary tickets, which were freely distributed, in order to get the prestige of a good house. Much was thrown away at the beginning in order to reach a final success. There are printing bills to pay, and other expenses to meet, for which I am, unfortunately, not in funds. To-morrow I shall leave Philadelphia, and return to your house for a brief season. I have a hundred things I wish to say. Mrs. Jansen's conduct in the matter is bad, consider it as you will. She has caused me to waste a great deal of time, and now involves me in pecuniary embarrassment among strangers. I am distressed and mortified at the result. But she doesn't seem to care a farthing. She is responsible for nothing.

"But I will be with you in a day or two; so adieu for the present.

"AGNES WINDALL."

"P. S.— Since writing last evening, Mrs. Jansen has disappeared from the hotel. She paid her bill early this morning, and left in a carriage before I was up. No one in the office or about the hotel could give me any information in regard to her. After breakfast, through the assistance of a porter in the establishment, I discovered the hackman with whom she went away; I learned from him that he had taken her to the landing at Walnut-street wharf in time for the six o'clock New York train. I have changed my mind about returning at once to Jersey City. Some friends here are very anxious that I shall remain with them for a few weeks, and I am inclined to yield to their importunities. But I trust to see you very shortly. Meantime, I will write you often.

"A. W."

CHAPTER XX.

RS. Woodbine was entertaining some friends in her parlor, when a servant came in and said there was a lady in the hall who wished to speak to her. It was Mrs. Jansen. She stood, shrinking near the vestibule door. Mrs. Woodbine met her with a coldly polite air, very much as she would have met a stranger who had called to ask a servant's character. She did not even offer her hand to Madeline, on whose part there was as reserved and distant a manner.

"Have you a letter for me?" A sadness crept into the speaker's voice in spite of her effort to seem calmly indifferent.

Mrs. Woodbine shook her head.

"No communication of any kind?"

"None."

In a half hesitating, half lingering way, Mrs. Jansen

stood for some moments, then moving back into the vestibule, she said —

"Good morning."

"Good morning," returned Mrs. Woodbine; and the vestibule door shut on the retiring visitor.

This was on the day after Mrs. Jansen left Philadelphia.

"Who do you think it was?" said Mrs. Woodbine, on returning to the parlor.

"Who?" asked two or three ladies at once.

"Mrs. Jansen."

"No!"

"Yes."

"Why didn't you ask her in?"

Mrs. Woodbine shut her lips, looked painfully mysterious, and shook her head slowly.

"Anything wrong about her?"

"I'm afraid so."

"What have you heard?"

"Nothing that you can just put your hands on. But, I've had hints and intimations; a word here and a word there which, all put together, have an unpleasant look. She hasn't fallen into the right kind of company — whether this be her fault or her misfortune, I cannot say. The fact is so far against her. We judge of people, you know, by their companions."

"What did she want?"

Mrs. Woodbine lifted her eyebrows

"A letter from her husband."

"You are jesting."

"No. 'Have you a letter for me?' That was her question. I will explain. Six months ago, as you are aware, she left her husband. I was her friend, and opposed her in every possible way; but she was stubborn and self-willed, and would listen to no reason. In going away from her husband, she wrote him a letter, in which she said, that unless he sent for her to come back, she would never return. My house was given as the place where any communication would reach her. She had, I can't understand why, counted on making it her head quarters! But she was doomed to disappointment in that. Her call to-day shows, that she still clings to the hope of hearing from her husband. But, her hope is vain. He is just as strong-willed as Mrs. Jansen. I warned her that she was playing a desperate game, with all the chances against her It has come out as I expected."

"When was she here last?"

"About three months ago."

"Where has she been, during the time?"

"Can't say."

"Away from the city?"

"Possible." Mrs. Woodbine affected to know more than she cared to divulge.

"How did she look?"

"Badly."

"In what respect?"

"Her face was much thinner than I had ever seen it, and had an anxious expression. She looked ten years older than she appeared on the day she left her husband. She always dressed elegantly, as you are aware. The contrast in her appearance to-day was painful. She had on a dark straw bonnet, with plain brown trimming; a merino dress, and a cloth mantle that had seen considerable service. Almost any one would have passed her in the street for a servant."

"How has the mighty fallen! And yet, I pity her from

my heart," said one of the ladies. Her husband is a brute, I am told."

"No," answered Mrs. Woodbine. "Not a brute. That word expresses to much. He is, like most men, a self-sufficient tyrant, and looks down upon a woman as an inferior being. If his wife had not been a silly, self-willed little fool, she might have got along with him. But, she was too proud to bend the tenth part of a degree out of her fine perpendicularity. She would not stoop to manage him — O no! Home, happiness, reputation before the world, were nothing in her eyes when set in opposition to her pride. No bending for her. She would stand erect or break, and so she broke. Well, I have no patience with such people. Faithfully, as in duty bound, I warned and remonstrated; but she let my words pass as the idle winds. Now she must go her own way; and I fancy she will find it rougher than was imagined."

Slowly Mrs. Jansen descended the steps, up which she had gone a few moments before, with a faint hope glimmering in her mind. That hope was dead! Slowly she moved away, her veil drawn closely about her face. At the next corner she found herself face to face with her husband. Suddenly her feet stood still. The power of motion was gone. But, her dress and thick veil proved a complete disguise. He passed her, without a pause. His name was on her lips. Under a wild impulse she tried to call after him. But her tongue was, for the instant, paralyzed. Standing, moveless as an image, she gazed after his receding form, until it was lost to sight; then, with hard shut mouth, deathly pale face, and hands clenched so tightly that the nails almost cut the flesh, she passed on her indeterminate way.

CHAPTER XXI.

"I WILL give her one year to repent and return."

On the third day after Madeline's departure, Carl Jansen had reached this decision. It meant, that he would not break up their home until twelve months had expired.

"The door shall not be fastened against her; but, if it opens to let her in, her own hand must give the pressure. She went out of her own will; and of her own will she must return."

To this purpose, feeling and thought had crystallized.

The year had closed. It found Jansen with clearly visible pain-marks on his face. Cold, resolute, self-approving, he had kept to his decision without wavering until the full period given to his wife had expired; but it was not in human nature to go through such a year without intense suffering. He had taken many draughts from a bitter cup, and the drugged portion had fevered his blood in heart and brain. The loneliness, the desolation of hope, the restless disquietude, the doubt, the questionings, the uncertainty of this period, would have left disfiguring signs on one of sterner stuff than Carl Jansen.

The year had closed. Nothing had been changed, as to the external order of things, in the household, during all that time. Not a drawer or wardrobe belonging to Madeline had been meddled with. If she had returned, on any day of the year, she would have found everything that was personally her own, just where she had left it. But, the fixed time had closed. No matter what change of feeling had taken place with Jansen towards his wife; no matter as to what evil-hearted rumor had reported; no matter as to how far belief had accepted slander; up to the last day and hour, he remained true to his first intention — " I will give her one year to repent and return."

The year had closed, and now there must come a change. This state of things was no longer possible. He must destroy this marred and desecrated temple which had been erected to the household gods — must pull down these altars from which the holy fires had long ago departed. Through the last night of the last day, nothing was disturbed. A vague, restless pause in Jansen's life, seemed like the shadow of that coming presence for which through a long year he had waited. Up to the final instant of grace, he would keep the door of entrance unfastened. But, all was at last over. A new day in the new year of his fate began; and the door was barred!

Three large trunks, locked and strapped down, contained at the close of this day all the clothing and personal effects of Madeline, once the beloved wife of Carl Jansen, now self-repudiated, and a wanderer out in the world;

where, and under what circumstances, the husband knew not. Upon their contents, he had gazed for the last time. Nothing would ever induce him again to touch or look upon the garments in which she had often appeared so beautiful in his eyes. He had shivered with many sudden ague-fits, as one article after another, passing under his hands, had quickened bright memories of the past, and set the beautiful being he had once clasped with such tender joy to his heart against a back ground of all things pure and lovely.

The purpose of Jansen was, to send these trunks to Madeline; and now, for the first time since her abandonment of home, he began making inquiries in regard to her. With an almost business-like coldness of purpose, he settled in his mind the proper methods of procedure, and then went to work systematically. First, he called on Mrs. Woodbine. That lady gave him a courteous reception, and freely answered all his inquiries; but could give no information as to Madeline's present abode.

"When did you last see or hear from her?" asked Jansen.

"I have neither seen her, nor heard from her in six months. In fact, sir, she has kept away from me ever since she took that fatal step. Before, her visits were frequent. But, I did not approve the course she was taking, and urged her so strongly to go back, that she became offended."

"You saw her six months ago?"

"Yes."

"Where?"

"She called here one day about that time."

"Ah! For what purpose?"

"To ask if there was a letter for her."

"A letter! Did she receive letters directed to your care?"

"None ever came here for her."

"From whom did she expect a letter?"

"From you."

"From me!" The surprise on Mr. Jansen's part was not feigned.

"Yes, sir. When she went away from home, she left a letter, so she told me, in which she informed you, that if you would write to her and say 'Come back,' she would return. She fully counted, I think, on your taking her at her word. She expected a letter, and the invitation to come back. For full six months, as is plain from her calling here, did she cherish this hope."

A deep, irrepressible sigh, struggled up from the breast of Carl Jansen. He sat very still and silent for some moments, his face turned partly away from Mrs. Woodbine, who was observing him with the keen eye of a curious woman.

"In which she was doomed to disappointment," he said, in a low, husky voice, speaking as if to himself.

"Bitter, heart-aching disappointment," said Mrs. Woodbine.

"You think so?" Jansen looked up almost with a start.

"I know it. Nothing but pride kept her from going back. If you had opened the door for her, even so much as an inch, she would have crowded through. You were too hard and unyielding, Mr. Jansen. You did not understand the woman you had asked, in her tender, confiding girlhood to become your wife. She was loving and true, but proud and self-willed. You should have considered the whole of her character — should have let the good overbalance defect. It was a hard thing in you as her husband, to drive her as you did to desperation. Before heaven, sir, you are not guiltless in this matter! If she suffer harm, a cast-out and a wanderer in this hard and evil world, something of the sin will lie at your door. Pardon this plain speech, Mr. Jansen; but I am an outspoken woman; and it may be well for you to know what others think of your conduct."

"By my own act I am willing to stand or fall," replied Mr. Jansen, with slight signs of displeasure. "A husband may, surely, have freedom to approve or disapprove of his wife's conduct; and even to speak strongly if she set herself defiantly against him. I did no more than this — and simply for this she went away, thinking to force me into concession which no man with a true, manly character will ever make. Of her own will she left her home. The door was not locked against her. At any time within the last twelve months she could have returned. She had only to push open the door she had closed herself. But, not choosing to do so — not willing to bend the neck of her self-will — she remained on the outside. Who is to blame? Not Carl Jansen! His conscience is clear on that head. But, excuse me, Mrs. Woodbine, I had rather not go on with this discussion. The argument will be fruitless on either side. Madeline called here, you say, about six months ago?"

"Yes, sir."

"And asked for a letter?"

"Yes, sir."

"Had you any conversation with her at the time?"

"None. The interview was brief. She did not come in."

"Do you know where she went, after leaving your house?"

"No, sir."

"Have you heard of her since?"

"Nothing directly."

"What indirectly?"

Mrs. Woodbine thought for a little while

"It must be over three months ago, that I heard a lady say that she met her, or a person singularly like her, on one of the Albany boats going up the river."

"And beyond this, you know nothing?"

"Nothing at all, Mr. Jansen."

"Perhaps you know of some one who might be able to give me the clue for which I am seeking."

"She was, for a while, very intimate with a woman named Mrs. Windall; and, I am told, went away from the city with her seven or eight months ago."

"Who is Mrs. Windall?"

"Not a very good kind of person, I regret to say. She is an adventurer, and, I think, attached herself to your wife in the hope of using her in some way to her own advantage. It was intimated, at one time, that she was training Mrs. Jansen for a public reader, or to go on the stage. Indeed, the story runs, that a public reading was given in Boston or Philadelphia. But, I cannot vouch for this."

"How can I find Mrs. Windall?"

"She has not been seen in New York for a long time."

"Is there any one who is likely to know her address?"

"She staid for awhile, I believe, with a Mrs. Barling, in

Jersey City. Your wife was there also, now that I remember. Mrs. Windall and Mrs. Barling trained her, so I have heard, for elocutionary readings."

"Do you know Mrs. Barling's exact location in Jersey City?"

"I do not."

Mr. Jansen went away, feeling less comfortable in mind than when he called. Some things said by Mrs. Woodbine went down to sore places and hurt; and some things disturbed the self-approving states which he had formed. He was not so well satisfied with himself — not so sure that he had been altogether right in his dealings with Madeline.

His interview with Mrs. Barling did not help his state of mind. She corroborated what Mrs. Woodbine had suggested, and gave him the particulars of Madeline's appearance at the Musical Fund Hall in Philadelphia. In fact, read to him the letter of Mrs. Windall, in which she gave a description of Madeline's brilliant success, and subsequent disappearance. As Mrs. Jansen did not return to her house, nor communicate with her, Mrs. Barling could not furnish any present information in regard to Madeline. Nor was she able to give the address of Mrs. Windall.

Next he called upon Mrs. Lawrence, in Brooklyn. To his inquiry as to when she had seen his wife, he received the answer —

"She was here in the Spring."

"How long did she remain?"

"Only an hour or two."

"Have you met with her since?"

"No, sir."

"Do you know where she is at this present time?"

Mrs. Lawrence answered in the negative, further remarking, that she believed it was her intention to leave the city. "She was not communicative," Mrs. Lawrence said. "I pressed her with questions as to her future; but all her answers were vague. I do not think she had any settled plans. She was very unhappy. My heart ached for her. What have you heard, Mr. Jansen?"

"Nothing! She has never had any communication with me since she went away. I am entirely ignorant of her condition or locality. My present desire is, to get her address, in order to send her three trunks containing her clothing and personal effects. If you should learn anything about her, will you be kind enough to let me know?"

"If I hear of her, you shall know it immediately," said Mrs. Lawrence.

Observing a certain sternness in Mr. Jansen, amounting almost to anger towards his wife, this kind, true friend, of the unhappy woman felt called upon to say a word for her early and beloved companion.

"I do not wish to intrude upon you," she said, "in a matter so painful and delicate; but you must permit me to speak in favor of one whom I have known intimately and loved tenderly."

Mr. Jansen knit his cold brows, but Mrs. Lawrence went on.

"There is among most men and women, a bad inclination to suppose evil instead of good,— to give to each other's acts the worst instead of the best interpretation. I trust you are keeping this in mind. A woman standing to society in Mrs. Jansen's unfortunate relation, would be evil spoken of, were she as pure as an angel. Don't forget this, and if any evil surmise, or positive assertion of wrong, comes to your ears, do not give credence. She erred sadly in leaving her home. As to the extent of mutual blame, I know nothing; but I will not believe her to have been all wrong and you all right. I must say this in cause of my friend, and of my sex. A woman of her pure, true and loving nature, would never have broken away so madly from a home in which all material good abounded, if there had not been laid upon her some things intolerable to be borne."

"Excuse me," said Mr. Jansen, rising. "The past is past, and we will not uncover it. I understand my own position thoroughly, and, of course, better than you or any one else can understand it. My conscience is clear in the matter."

"Nay, excuse me, sir! Sit down again, and hear me for my friend," answered Mrs. Lawrence, with that mild resolution which subdues quicker than anger. "I will not be rude nor insulting. What I desire is, to speak for her on the side of kindness and charity. There will be enough to whisper detraction — to suggest evil — to assert as facts the mere creations of a vile fancy. For a night and a day she was with me after leaving your house. I looked away down in her heart, and scanned it with a jealous fear that something evil might be lurking there, — something disloyal to her husband, I mean, and to her marriage vows. I found pride and self-will, but not impurity — not disloyalty. These were her words. I shall not soon forget them. She said, 'As a wife and equal, I will cling to my husband through good and evil report — in sickness, poverty, disgrace — under any and all circumstances of outside wrong and oppression. His love would bind me by cords impossible to be broken.' Again she said, 'If my husband writes to me, and says, simply, Come back, I will accept it *gladly* as an evidence that I am to live with him as an equal. If he does not ask my return — will not concede anything — then the die is cast — we stand apart forever.' Ah, sir, not to many men are given a woman of her high quality. Alas! that you did not comprehend her. As your loving equal, she would have stood up by your side, brave and strong, amid the direst calamities — a wife of whom the proudest might be proud. If you could have had faith in her — if you could have understood her, and wisely forborne where opposition could only blind! She was not perfect. Are you and I? But she was loving, and pure, and true. Let evil tongues speak what they may; all are liars who touch her name with a vile word! I who knew her as girl and woman; I who have looked down deeper into her heart, as to some of its hidden chambers, than even her husband, say this boldly in the face of all. Ah, sir! she has taken up a heavy burden; and, in all your thought of her in the time to come, Mr. Jansen, do not forget that your hands helped to make that burden, nor that a single word from your lips would have lifted it from her shoulders. My heart so aches for her, that I say boldly under the excitement of pain what otherwise could not have pased my lips. O, sir! Let me conjure you to bend a little from your high position. Will you not say to her those two little words for which I know she has been all the time thirsting in this desert of her life — 'Come back?' They would thrill through her desolate soul! By all that is sacred in life, I implore you to speak those words!"

"It is too late!" answered Carl Jansen; the sternness of manner he strove to assume broken and veiled by conflicting emotions. For several painful moments the husband and friend of Madeline stood gazing into each other's eyes. Then the interview closed. Silently bowing Jansen retired. He had not felt so miserable since the day of Madeline's departure.

CHAPTER XXII.

EEKS gathered themselves into months, but no tidings of his wife came to Carl Jansen. All inquiry proved fruitless. She had dropped away from public observation, like a pebble in the sea, and not even a ripple was left to guide the searcher.

Jansen did not hesitate in the work of dismembering his home. At a public sale, everything was dispersed, not an article being left to remind him of a desolated paradise. Madeline's three trunks were stored, in order to be sent whenever the place of her retirement was discovered. Previous to this, no very marked change had appeared in Jansen. He was only a little graver in manner. The excitement always attendant on a state of uncertainty, had kept him up. But, now that all this waiting and uncertainty were over, — now that he had taken down the household altar, and dispersed its broken fragments—he experienced a sense of desolation that was almost intolerable. The foundation upon which he had builded his temple of earthly happiness was removed; the temple was gone; and he was out in the sun and storm, shelterless. Every one noticed a change in Carl Jansen after this. Inward working pain cut its signs upon his features. He was reserved beyond his wont—absent minded — shy of company. This state continued for over a year, during which period no intelligence came to him of Madeline. He had long ceased to make any inquiries in regard to her.

About this time he caused notice of a suit for divorce to be given. The plea was desertion. No response came; and in due legal course the marriage contract was annulled. So far as external bonds were concerned, Carl Jansen stood free again. But was he conscious of interior freedom? Did all stand with him as it had stood before his promise in the sight of heaven, to love and cherish Madeline so long as life should last? Was she really nothing to him now, more than any other woman? Could he think of her as indifferently as he could think of others? No! that was impossible! The divorce had not made him free — could not make him free. It was not in the power of legislatures nor courts to break inward bonds — to satisfy conscience — to put a man right with God and his own spirit, when he was wrong interiorly.

Carl Jansen had intended to put all the former things of his life behind him. This act of legal separation was to restore the status which existed prior to marriage. Alas! for his peace of mind; it wrought no such magical result. There lived a woman, where he did not know, with whom he had stood at the altar, and exchanged vows of lasting fidelity. He knew of nothing against her purity of life; of nothing that could work a plenary separation, and so an interior divorce. There had been incompatibilities; jarrings and alienations, — but all flowing from lack of self-discipline on one side or the other. It was the evil things of the unregenerate mind that were to be separated — divorced — not the living souls. Somewhere, in teachings by pulpit or press, this truth had found its way into his mind, and it proved troublesome. It was a sword flashing before his eyes, or cutting down into his life. It would not let him be at peace.

It took all of another year for the crust to harden over this new state of feeling. In the meantime he had gone more into society; and as he was a man of good personal appearance, known integrity of character, and in excellent circumstances, many fair lips smiled upon him, and many bright eyes sought to win him by their magic. But, he was not of easy fascination. There was ever a disturbing inner consciousness of a woman's claim upon him, yet uncancelled, that sat itself against all these allurements.

The time came when all the past was so hidden from view, that Carl Jansen could look upon another woman with loving eyes, and draw near to her with loving words. From among the fair beings who crossed his way, he selected Margaret Williams as the best and worthiest to hold the high relation of a wife. He chose with a keen perception of womanly qualities; but sought to mate with one who had loftier views of marriage than he possessed. His offer was declined. Now, Jansen was not of that class of persons who, when they make up their minds to attain a certain end, are easily baffled. He was not over sensitive, and the denial of his suit did not, therefore, wound his pride very deeply. He saw in Miss Williams a woman above all others desirable for a wife; and he meant to gain her for himself if that were possible. "Faint heart never won fair lady," he said to himself, and pressed his suit again. This time, Margaret Williams gave him something more than a simple refusal.

"Sir," she answered, sternly, "have I not once said no! Mr. Jansen, others may think as they please, but I regard an offer of marriage from *you* as little better than an insult! Do you understand me?"

Her eyes flashed with unwonted fire.

"An insult! No, I do not understand you."

"You have a wife, sir!"

Carl Jansen turned pale.

"God's law is above all human law," said Miss Williams. "What God joins, it is not for man to put asunder until divine law works a separation. I have not heard that this is so in your case. You gave in no plea but that of desertion; and this works to no annulling of the marriage bond in the sight of heaven. Sir, your offer of marriage sent a shudder through my soul! And, now that you have presumed on its repetition, I make bold to say what another might hesitate to declare."

Jansen essayed a feeble argument, but Miss Williams waved her hand that he might keep silence, and then turned from him with a cold dignity of manner that scarcely veiled her contempt and aversion. He never troubled her again.

But all the women he met did not possess the pure instincts and high principle of Margaret Williams. There were plenty who fixing their eyes on lower and more worldly things than she made primary in marriage, were ready to meet him in exchange of vows and obligations the most sacred and the most vital to the soul's well being and peace of any that are made. Jansen did not lack discrimination — was no dull reader of character. He saw the wide difference between this class of women and the class represented by Margaret Williams; and for a time held himself away from the sphere of their attractions. Moreover, the outspoken rebuke which she had administered did not die upon his ears like murmurs of the idle wind; but quickened his thought into perceptions that troubled his peace.

Time moved on. Jansen, standing lonely in the world, strongly desired companionship. Because of an unhappy experience in marriage — because of one sad shipwreck — must there be no further venture? He did not believe in this necessity of the case. His nature rose against it in protest. He wanted a home — domestic associations — a family in which he might embosom himself. Once more in his life, all the beautiful ideals of marriage and its felicities crowded his imagination. Ardor of feeling began to obscure his judgment; and, finally, he made an offer of his hand to one who, contrasted at first in his thought with Margaret Williams, dropped below the line of even respectful consideration. She was but a woman of the world, beside whom, as to fine instincts and capacities for womanly development, Madeline was a being of higher order.

How it fared with him in this new relation, we shall see.

CHAPTER XXIII.

HERE was nothing coarse or sensual about Carl Jansen. If he was not very sensitive, he yet had a refinement of character that gave delicate perceptions and which, but for his mistaken notions about marital prerogative, and his cold, self-will, would have lifted him into a just appreciation of Madeline's pure and sweet quality of mind. If he had not been so foolish and blind, he would have looked through all exterior veils, and recognized in her his own ideal of woman. This was seen in the beginning; but pride and passion had dimmed his sight.

We shall not dwell on the incidents attending his second alliance. Women of the class represented by Margaret Williams, could not stoop to one holding his questionable relation to the sex. They recognized in marriage something more than a good external arrangement. They wanted the man as seen by interior light; and not the man as he stood before the world. And so, Carl Jansen was compelled to choose from among the meaner natures — to take into the closest of all human relations a woman of inferior quality; one without pure instincts or noble impulses; one who smiled on him because he was rich and respectable; and married him to secure ease, luxury, and a position.

It did not take Jansen long to discover his mistake; and with the discovery came a sense of weakness never felt before. In the case of Madeline, he knew that he had a being of sensitive spirit to deal with, and therefore had encouragement to act against her when she stood in his way; but, it soon became apparent that his new wife was of a different organization. Not less self-willed, but of such coarse quality, that he found himself bruised in the first conflict. The relation of sensitiveness was transferred. While in proof armor against most of the weapons he might bring, every thrust she made penetrated the quivering flesh.

There were periods during the first year of this incongruous union, when Jansen's repulsion towards his wife was so strong, that he felt impelled to disregard all bonds, and shake off the dust from his garments against her. But, many worldly and selfish motives came in to restrain him. Once in this time she was attacked by a dangerous illness, when there came into his heart the wish that she might die. As this desire took form in his mind, Jansen was startled, and sought to drive it away. But it would not be cast out; and when the crisis was past, and she began to recover, he stood face to face with an irrepressible regret, the existence of which showed him the magnitude of his error.

The spirit moulds the flesh. A coarse nature takes of the coarser elements to build its earthly tabernacle, and builds after the pattern of its meaner ideals. In the spring-time of life, when the active forces lie near the age of innocence and purity, a finer selection is made, and so we have beauties of the flesh that are not in correspondence with the mind's true quality. But, after the early days of manhood and womanhood, when the age of freedom and reason comes into fullness, a new order prevails, and then we begin to see changes that often bring surprise, disappointment and pain.

Such changes began with Jansen's second wife soon after their marriage. The body undergoes perpetual recreations. There is decay and new formation daily. Old things are being all the while put off and new things taken on. But in the spirit we have all that is real and substantial; and according to its quality will be the earthly garment it assumes. If we see men and women growing coarse, vulgar, and sensual-looking as they grow older, we shall scarcely err in our estimate of their quality, should we conclude that coarseness and sensuality appertain to the spirit. If they become more refined; if we see the original, harder textures of their flesh growing translucent with revelations of inner life and beauty, shall we be less in error if we say that with all such the spirit is growing purer and more truly human?

The new wife of Carl Jansen did not thus grow beautiful in his eyes; but changed, as the years progressed, into a grosser and grosser image of selfishness and sensuality. It was remarked by those who observed Jansen closely, that while his wife's face grew coarser, his grew more refined; yet with a blending of sadness and disappointment in all the lineaments. He was graver, quieter, more abstracted. No wonder; for he stood daily confronted with a great life-error, and knew that the time for its correction was gone beyond recall. If he could have forgotten the past — forgotten Madeline — the case would have been lighter for him. But, memory, as the years crept on, seemed to grow more distinct.

Children were born of this union — three sons and two daughters. It is not often that either men or women, in approaching marriage, think about mental and moral qualities as reproduced in offspring. If this were soberly considered in the light of reason, many would draw back, and re-consider the whole question involved, before taking a step so fraught with good or evil consequences. In Coventry Patmore's, "Faithful Forever," Mrs. Graham, in writing to Frederick, touches the key note to this subject, when she says —

> "Nor would she bring you up a brood
> Of strangers, bound to you by blood,
> Boys of a meaner moral race,
> Girls with their mother's evil grace."

The brood in Carl Jansen's home partook largely of the mother's meaner quality and evil grace. As she had never governed herself from any principle of honor or high breeding — had never put mental rein on appetite, impulse, or passion — her nature manifested itself, strongly at first, in the children. The father's character showed scarcely a sign of reproduction. But, that lay in the beginning out of sight. It was a hidden and more interior life, to become active in later years.

The beauty, the grace, the sweetness of childhood, as

they appear in some homes, were not seen in that of Mr. Jansen. When his babes first lifted their soft blue eyes, so full of light from heaven, and smiled at him, the father's heart leaped in its gladness, and overflowed with promise. Alas! that the promise was never fulfilled. Too soon the mother's evil grace appeared — the taint of coarseness — the sensuality — the mean and low proclivities, that, under disorderly conditions at home, it was found impossible to repress.

Mrs. Jansen had no system or government with her children; and so they grew up like "wild asses' colts." All attempts at restraint on the father's part, when at home, were in some way thwarted, or set at naught by the mother. If he attempted punishment, she was almost certain to interfere; if he laid down laws, she permitted their infraction. Her very manner of treating him before the children, diminished their respect for his authority. It was a common thing for her to scout his opinions, and make light of his suggestions. If he became angry, and spoke with firmness or passion, she never failed of coarse retort. If he assumed an attitude of command, she either defied him or laughed in his face.

Alas for Carl Jansen! He had driven from him a woman moulded of finest material — a woman of tender and true impulses — a woman who held the sweetness of love in her heart as a rose holds its perfume — and in her place had consorted with a clod from a human valley!

CHAPTER XXIV.

TEN years of such a life, separating itself daily more and more from all true sources of enjoyment — from all the satisfactions and delights after which the soul thirsts — wrought severely upon the bodily and mental health of Carl Jansen. A too intense absorption of his thoughts in business was added to the undermining forces. At thirty-six, he found himself failing; at forty, he was an invalid — broken in spirit as well as broken in health.

Now it was that his heart began to yearn intensely for that care and tender consideration which was denied. The strong, exacting, self-willed man felt himself growing weaker daily, and less and less able to compel the service which love failed to give. Hearty, coarse and strong, Mrs. Jansen had a kind of animal contempt for the weakness of her husband. Physical superiority gave her a sense of mental and moral superiority. Daily, he seemed dwarfing at her side; and she soon came to regard him as of little more consequence than a sickly boy, full of whims, wants, and petty exactions, that were to be treated more by the rule of denial than favor.

At this period of his life, when its bitterness was fresh to his revolting taste, Jansen often dreamed of Madeline. She came to him, in vision, always as his wife — young, beautiful, and lovingly ministrant. Her hand smoothed and softened his pillow, and held refreshing draughts to his thirsty lips. She comforted him in weakness and pain with tender words and heart-warm kisses. What sad, hopeless, self-accusing awakenings followed these sweet dreams, that so mocked the painful reality?

Steadily disease kept on, sapping the foundations of life. Physicians enjoined entire withdrawal from business, and change of air. During the milder seasons, travel was recommended as of more avail than medicine. So trade was relinquished, and Mr. Jansen devoted himself to the work of acquiring health. In this, partial success would have been gained, if Mrs. Jansen had given to her husband's case the just consideration it demanded. But, he was not first in her thoughts. A lover of self and a lover of the world, she had gained the position and the wealth for which she had married him; and, as a natural result, the man through whom these most desirable things were reached, fell into the back ground as of minor consideration.

Mrs. Jansen was pleased with the idea of travelling about and seeing the world. She had always expressed a desire to visit Europe — to see Paris — "Dear, delightful Paris!" as she said. But, in giving way to professional advice, and closing up his business, Jansen had not contemplated the excitement and fatigue of a tour in Europe. A quiet residence of weeks by the sea shore, alternating with weeks among the mountains — rest of body and mind — these were, in his thought, the limitations of at least the first season of leisure. The sole end in view with him was health. But Mrs. Jansen scarcely thought of this. Her husband's failing health brought the opportunity she had long desired, and she was eager to embrace it.

There are occasions when the will of the weakest stands as a wall of iron against all opposition, and cannot be borne down. It was so with Mr. Jansen in this case — at least during the first year or two after giving up business. His wife was resolved on a trip across the Atlantic, and he was just as resolute in his purpose not to go. The power was in his hands, and he maintained it, in spite of the bitterest and most persevering assaults. But, the contest robbed him of that mental repose so essential to his bodily condition. The days were all either stormy or cloudy. No tranquillity; no sunshine. If the selfish, willful wife could not have her way, she could at least have her revenge, and there was no intermission of her evil work, for there was no softness nor pity in her heart towards any who crossed her purposes. There are a thousand ways in which an unfeeling wife may torture a husband whose strength of mind and body is waning. Mrs. Jansen never failed in this cruel work. To neglect and indifference, she added the chafings of ill temper, and a systematic opposition to whatever he might desire or suggest. Their children were growing up undisciplined, self-willed, and spoiled by indulgence; yet, in every attempt at correction he was baffled by his wife, and his authority set at naught through her persistent interference. She was perpetually degrading him in their eyes; and they were daily learning to regard him with indifference, if not contempt. A part of this result was due to his own peevish and fretful states. If he had been a strong man interiorily, there would have been, in reserve, powers of mind ready to adapt themselves to this new condition of things. An unselfish love for his children would have manifested itself in forms that were attractive instead of repellant. He would have gained a power over them for good, that must have largely counterbalanced their mother's evil influence. But, he had not gained that moral wisdom which is born of self-denial. He had not the sweetness of ripened fruit. If you tasted him, it was to find him yet bitter and sour.

Mr. Jansen wished to spend the first summer after his emancipation from business, in Minnesota and the northwest. His physician strongly recommended the pure, invigorating air of the Upper Mississippi. But, Mrs. Jansen would hear to no such thing.

"If you go," she said, positively, "you go alone."

Going alone did not suit Mr. Jansen. He was weak and depressed in spirits. Two or three slight hemorrhages from the lungs had not only alarmed him, but made him unwilling to leave home unaccompanied by his wife. Saratoga and Newport, if not the Continent,— Mrs. Jansen would hear to nothing else. Mr. Jansen pleaded for a quiet sea shore season at a less fashionable watering place than Newport, but his wife was immovable. To Saratoga, accompanied by their two oldest children, coarse, hoydenish girls of fourteen and sixteen, they went and passed a few weeks. Then they migrated to Newport, where Mrs. Jansen displaying herself in rich attire and flashing jewels, excited contempt and criticism, which she fancied to be envy and admiration. Poor Jansen was treated with the most shameless neglect and indifference by his wife. Saratoga water and sea-bathing had not helped in any way. Their hygienic virtues were not strong enough to overcome the depressing effects of fatigue, excitement, and the perpetual exasperation of mind consequent on the behavior of his wife and daughters in public. They were all the while shocking his more delicate sense of proprieties. The red spots that stained his cheeks were as much symptomatic of mental as physical irritation.

One day, Mr. Jansen was sitting alone on the porch of the hotel — he was alone for most of his time, neither wife nor daughters finding in his society the companionship that pleased them — when he was seized with a more than usually violent fit of coughing which continued for a considerable time in spite of all his efforts to control it. A tough mucus had collected on the lining membrane along the bronchial tubes, that he found it difficult to dislodge; and as he was feeling unusually weak, this cough seriously exhausted him. He was near a window that opened into one of the parlors, and, before this paroxysm had been listening to the prattle of a child within; unseen because the blind was down. In the pauses of his cough, he noticed that the sweet young voice which had fallen so pleasantly on his ears, was silent. He had been coughing for several minutes, when a beautiful little girl, not more than two years old, came timidly upon the porch, holding a small box in her hand, which, with that artless, yet shrinking grace so lovely in children, she held out for his reception. The instant he took the box, she turned and flew back with the swiftness of a bird, vanishing through the door by which she had come upon the porch.

Glancing down at the small, round paper box left in his hand, Mr. Jansen saw, by the label, that it contained cough lozenges. Surprise mingled with a feeling of pleasure at this delicately offered relief. He placed one of the lozenges in his mouth, and in a little while the irritating mucus was dissolved, and the cough abated. When Mr. Jansen went into the parlor soon afterwards, the child and her attendant — mother or nurse — were gone. A gentleman with whom he had some acquaintance was there, with three or four other guests. Taking a seat beside this person, Mr. Jansen said—

"Did you notice a beautiful child here a few minutes ago?"

"Yes," was answered.

"Who was with her?"

"No one but her nurse."

"Are you certain?"

"Yes."

Mr. Jansen felt disappointed, he hardly knew why. It was on his lips to ask if the incident of sending out the box of lozenges had been observed; but on second thought, he remained silent on that head.

"Whose child was it?" he inquired, after a pause.

"I do not know."

No farther questions were asked by Mr. Jansen. An hour afterwards, as he sat in one of the piazzas, gazing out upon the sea, a sudden burst of musical child-laughter near at hand, caused him to look round quickly. Only a few paces from him was the sweet little fairy, whose image had not yet faded from his mind. She was struggling, merrily, with her nurse, a slender girl or woman, from whom she had escaped. The face of the nurse being turned from Mr. Jansen, he could not see her features. She caught up the child in her arms, and ran back through the door from which it had come, disappearing from sight. The scene passed in a moment. Soon after, a lady of refined and graceful appearance came out, leading the child, who walked quietly at her side. They moved down the piazza, through its whole length of two hundred feet, and then back again, passing Mr. Jansen, but not seeming to observe him. The lady then withdrew into the house.

On the evening of the same day, near sundown, Mrs. Jansen took a walk accompanied by her husband. She was tricked out in an abundance of finery, that acted as a foil to her coarse face and vulgar figure. As she moved amid the promenaders, she talked loudly, attracting a kind of notice that was mortifying to her husband. Many turned and looked after her, smiling at her vanity, or sneering at her vulgarity. If Mr. Jansen did not see this, he knew, from perception and his knowledge of human nature, that it was so.

"The air feels chilly this evening. Let us go back," said Mr. Jansen, after walking for half an hour. He paused as he spoke. Mrs. Jansen replied, speaking in the elevated tone of voice common to people of small refinement —

"Indeed and I'm not going back! You're as 'fraid of pure air as if it were poison. Come along, Mr. Jansen!"

She spoke the last sentence quite imperatively.

The child, from whose hand Mr. Jansen had received the lozenges, ran, at this instant, frolicking against him. He stooped and caught her in his arms to prevent her from falling. Then he stood face to face with her nurse; a pale, slender woman, of not less than thirty-five. She had clear, brown eyes; exquisitely cut features; and a mouth full of tender sadness. Reaching out her arms for the child, she gazed steadily, but only for an instant, into the face of Mr. Jansen; then vanished in the crowd. It was Madeline! The recognition had been mutual.

CHAPTER XXV.

THIS scene passed, later in the evening.

"Can I speak a few words with you?" The lady to whom this was addressed glanced up at the speaker, who was standing, and then at her husband, who was reading at a centre-table.

"Yes," she answered, in a kind voice, yet with a certain dignified sense of superiority, that was quite apparent in her manner; and then waited for the communication about to be made.

"Can I see you alone?"

"Oh, certainly!" said the lady, evincing slight annoyance, yet rising promptly.

"What is it, Madeline?" she asked, as soon as they were in the adjoining bed-chamber — lady and nurse; the one sitting and the other standing.

"You will think strangely of me ma'am, but —" The nurse stopped in the middle of her sentence, and caught her breath with a half sob, like one under the influence of strong feeling.

"Strangely, Madeline! On what account? Speak out plainly." The lady's brow grew a little severe.

"I must leave you in the morning," said the nurse, quietly, in a very low voice.

"Leave me! I don't understand you, Madeline. Leave me for what?"

"I came here very reluctantly, ma'am. If it hadn't been for Netty —" The voice choked again.

"You don't mean that you are going from Newport tomorrow morning!"

"Yes, ma'am."

"Leaving me, away from home, without a nurse! Impossible, Madeline! I shall consent to no such thing."

The nurse dropped her eyes from the lady's half angry face, and stood, looking quite pale and agitated, for some moments. Then she replied, with a steadiness of voice that left her auditor in no doubt touching her resolution to do as she had intimated.

"I cannot explain, ma'am; but I must go. No inducement in your power to offer would keep me here another day. I shall leave in the early boat. If I did not know," she added, "that you would object to any such arrangement, I would propose taking Netty with me. I could go home with her, and remain there until you returned."

The lady shook her head and said, "No," emphatically.

"But what is the meaning of this? I cannot understand it, Madeline. Sit down," she added, in a gentler voice, seeing how white the face of her nurse was growing.

Madeline sat down, leaning heavily against her chair, like one oppressed with faintness.

"What is your reason for going?"

Madeline did not reply.

"Will you not confide in me? I am your friend."

"It would avail nothing, ma'am," answered Madeline.

"It might avail much. Who and what are you? There is a mystery about your life. I have seen this from the beginning. Give me your confidence. It will be better for you, Madeline; I know it will be better. There has been some sad error. Tell me the story frankly, so that I may know how to be your true friend."

"There are few lives without error," replied Madeline, sadly. "Mine has not escaped. But, as in too many instances, the error is past correction, and I must still eat the bitter fruit. I feel your kindness, but the confidence you ask cannot be given."

A long silence followed. The lady was surprised and perplexed. Madeline, who had been in her family as a nurse for over a year, going quietly and faithfully through her duties, taking her place with the servants in the family as a servant, came all at once into a different aspect. The mistress felt a new impression of her character — felt, from her language, manner and bearing, the presence of an equal mind with equal culture.

"Let it be as you will, Madeline," she said, breaking the oppressive silence. "There must be painful, and I will believe, imperative reasons, for the course you are taking. It will leave me embarrassed here. I cannot hope to supply your place; and shall be obliged, failing in the effort, to return home."

Tears fell over Madeline's face as she answered —

"The reason, dear madam, is indeed painful and imperative. If it were not so I could not leave you. Oh, if you will but consent to my taking Netty home! That would relieve you from all embarrassment, and you could remain here through the season. I will be very careful of her."

"No — no, Madeline. I cannot think of that, and I know that Mr. B—— will object, positively. I am afraid, too, that, when he hears of your sudden purpose to go, he will be very angry."

Madeline sighed heavily.

"Can't you put off your departure for a day or two. The time is so short,"

Madeline shivered, as she replied —

"I cannot remain a day longer. If you knew—" She stopped, showing much agitation.

"Knew what, Madeline? My dear woman, why not trust me?"

For a few moments there was struggle and hesitation with Madeline. Out of it she came resolved and firm Her answer closed the interview. Rising, she said, with a quiet dignity of manner that left Mrs. B—— no further plea for remonstrance —

"I shall never forget your kindness, and never cease to regret the necessity that compels me to leave you now. In every life, madam, there are things too sacred to be uncovered, even for the eyes of those nearest and dearest. There are burdens which we must bear alone, even though they become so heavy upon our weak shoulders that we fall fainting by the way. Mine is such a burden; and I shall only lay it down, when my feet stand at an open grave."

Turning away, she left the room, going out quickly. The lady made no effort to detain her. Madeline's room was on the next floor above. As she came along the passage, near the main stairway, she encountered Mrs. Jansen, accompanied by her two daughters, gayly dressed in ball attire. There was to be dancing in the great parlor on that evening, and the music was already echoing through the house. Madeline shrunk aside, turning her face to the wall. She feared to meet the husband and father. But, he had no heart for music and dancing, as she found soon after. She stood still for a little while, and then passed up stairs. In her confusion, she turned to the right hand instead of the left, and did not perceive her mistake until she commenced examining the numbers, in order to determine her own room. This increased her bewilderment. As she stood, trying to get her mind clear, a deep, jarring cough sounded from one of the rooms. She knew from whom it came but too well! For some moments her feet seemed bound to the floor. The cough rattled on, painfully intense; ceasing with a heavy moan. In the pause she was about moving back along the passage, when there came from the room an exclamation of alarm, and the door was thrown open. Mr. Jansen stepped out a pace or so. His eyes was starting with a look of fear. He held to his mouth a white handkerchief, that was stained with blood.

"Oh! Oh! Call somebody!" he cried out, in a half smothered voice. Then coughed, raising large mouthfuls of blood.

Madeline did not hesitate for an instant. It was no time to consider questions of propriety. The case before her stood as for life or death.

"Go in and lie down quickly!" she said, as she sprung

across the passage, and almost forced him back into the room. "Lie down quickly!" she repeated.

Jansen obeyed, passively. Madeline jerked the bell, and then asked —

"Is there any salt in the room?"

Mr. Jansen shook his head.

The blood still came up in large mouthfuls. Madeline held a basin, and wiped off the red stains from his lips at each expectoration. She was preternaturally calm — calm from the pressure of intense excitement — and pale as marble.

"Bring some salt, a tumbler, and water! Quickly! And call a doctor!" said Madeline, to a servant who answered the bell. The servant comprehending what he saw, ran down stairs, and soon reappeared with the desired articles.

"Did you find a doctor?" asked Madeline, as she mixed the salt and water.

"Yes. He will be here in a moment."

Madeline raised the head of Mr. Jansen, and held the saline draught to his lips. The servant went out, and she was again alone with him. The blood still came up freely, but the intervals were longer. She was wiping the blood and mucus away from his lips when the doctor came in, accompanied by the servant who had just left the chamber. Madeline moved back from the bed, giving place to the doctor. Her face was pale as death. She staggered a little, and caught herself against the wall; then went groping towards the door, like one who saw but imperfectly.

"Your nurse has fainted, ma'am," said one of the waiters, coming into Mrs. B———'s room hastily. "She's fainted, and lying on the floor.

"Where is she?" asked Mrs. B———, as she started up.

"She's lying in the passage, up stairs, ma'am."

When Mrs. B——— reached the upper passage, she found that Madeline had been carried to her own chamber She was lying on the bed, white and insensible.

"What does this mean? What happened to her?" she asked; but no one could answer her question.

It was nearly an hour before signs of life appeared. During this time, Mrs. B——— heard something about Mr. Jansen's hemorrhage, and the assistance which Madeline had rendered. The doctor had found her in the sick man's room, looking ghastly and frightened, yet doing all that was best to be done in the alarming emergency.

"This woman puzzles me," said Mrs. B———, as she sat with her husband, after Madeline had come to herself, and was considered well enough to be left alone for the night. "What was she doing at the other end of the house, where Mr. and Mrs. Jansen's rooms are situated? Her chamber is at the extreme east, and their apartments at the extreme west."

"Jansen?— Jansen?" Mr. B——— uttered the name in a tone of curious inquiry. "Oh, he's the man that had such a time with his first wife. Don't you remember? He married a gay, spirited, beautiful girl — her name was Spencer, I believe — "

"Why, that is Madeline's name!" exclaimed Mrs. B———

"Madeline Spencer! The very name! I remember it perfectly!"

Husband and wife looked at each other in silent surprise.

"Can it be possible that Madeline is the former wife of Mr. Jansen?" said Mrs. B——

"I shouldn't wonder. She's always seemed to me above her position."

"No one could have been more faithful," replied Mrs. B——

"I did not mean that she assumed airs above her position; but, that she was fitted for a superior place."

"In my interview with her this evening," said Mrs. B——, "she put off the relation of a domestic, and talked with me as one of equal condition. Heretofore, few words have passed between us. She has not been communicative nor chatty, like girls who usually fill the place she held with us. To-night, her language was that of an educated woman, who had thought, and felt, and suffered; of a woman of character and purpose — strong to bear, and resolute to do, what her convictions showed to be right."

"Depend upon it," said Mr. B——, "she is Jansen's first wife."

"And if so, how infinitely superior to the coarse, vulgar woman who now claims him for her husband. Why, she disgusts every one! She's the laughing stock of the house. And such forward, hoydenish girls! They've been here only two days, and yet everybody is remarking on their rudeness and want of good manners. I noticed Madeline looking at them yesterday, as they ran screaming up and down the piazza. And I now remember that she caught up Netty suddenly, and ran with her into the house, as if to escape from their annoyance. I do not wonder that she decided to leave here immediately."

"She will not be well enough to go in the morning,' said Mr. B———. "The shock of this evening's encounter with Mr. Jansen will probably make her ill."

"Her case assumes a new aspect," remarked the lady. "Did you ever hear anything ill against her?— anything touching her character, I mean?"

"Well, there was some hard talk— there always will be in such cases. People are very prone to imagine evil. But, I fancy, she kept her garments free from stain. The separation was her own act. They had a quarrel, it was said, about something. He was overbearing and tyrannical; and she strong-willed and independent. In a fit of passion, she went away, declaring her purpose never to return unless he promised a different line of conduct. He would not promise, and she would not humble herself. So they stood apart, year after year; and, finally, on the plea of desertion, her husband obtained a divorce. So the case stands, I think. This is the head and front of the offending— nothing more."

"Taking it for granted," said Mrs. B———, "that Madeline is the person we suppose, can we blame her for going away?"

"Not fairly. I do not see how she can remain a day longer."

"Is she not entitled to consideration on our part," asked Mrs. B———.

"I think so."

"She has been in our family for over a year, and has been faithful to Netty. I do not like to see her going away from here alone; going out into the world friendless and homeless, it may be. Her case touches me."

"What have you to suggest?"

"That we leave here to-morrow afternoon."

"And go home?"

"Yes. I cannot remain without a nurse; and the chances are all against my obtaining one. Beyond this, I am impressed with the conviction that we cannot disregard Madeline and be blameless. In the order of that Providence which gives no respect to persons, she is now in our hands. Her situation, if what we suppose in regard to her be true, is one of peculiar interest. Let us take her home. It may involve a little self-denial. But, good is born of self-denial."

"The matter is in your hands," said Mr. B———. "I shall make no objection, decide as you will."

"Then I decide to go home to-morrow."

"So let it be."

In the morning, Madeline did not come as usual, for Netty.

"I'm afraid she's sick. The agitation of last evening has been too much for her," said Mrs. B ———, on rising to attend to her early awaking child.

"It may be well to see how she is," suggested the husband.

It was nearly seven o'clock. After dressing Netty Mrs. B ——— went up to Madeline's room. She found the door open, but no one in the apartment. Glancing around hurriedly, she saw that Madeline's trunk had been taken away; and on examining the closet and case of drawers, discovered that everything had been removed from them. Inquiry at the office, settled all doubts. The nurse had left Newport by the early morning line.

CHAPTER XXVI.

A YEAR afterwards.

"She owes for three months now," said a hard, impatient voice.

"Not quite three months," was answered by a woman. The tones were mild and deprecating.

"Is she doing any work?"

"Yes. But not much."

"Send her adrift. She can't pay the rent."

"She will pay," said the woman. "I'll trust her. She's honest."

"Honest? Pho! What's the good of being honest, if you haven't anything to be honest with."

The woman did not answer.

"She must go; unless she settles up. I wont have her in the house a day beyond this quarter." The man spoke angrily.

"If she goes, we lose all," replied the woman. "But, if we let her stay, she will make every dollar of the rent good. I'll trust her for that."

"Why do we lose all if she goes?" asked the man, turning abruptly to his wife."

"She has nothing to pay with now."

"She has a bed and a bureau."

"But you'll not take them!"

"I'll have my rent. You may trust me for that."

The man, after saying this, went out. The wasted, shrinking figure of a woman, in years not beyond the prime of life, stood in the door of a small room, on the second story, listening to this conversation. At its close, she went back again, noiselessly, into the apartment from which the voices below had attracted her, and sitting down, with a weak, weary air, hid her face among the folds of some coarse muslin that was lying on a small work-table. One hand was held closely against her left side. She had remained thus, almost motionless, for several minutes, when the opening of her door caused her to look up. The visitor was her landlady, who came in with a serious face.

"Arn't you so well to-day, Mrs. Spencer?" inquired the landlady, as she looked into the woman's exhausted and suffering countenance.

"About as usual," was replied. The woman was struggling for self-possession; for the moral strength by which she could be calm and rightly adjusted in the presence of an inferior who had power over her. Her success in this was only partial.

"You don't look so well," said the other, kindly.

A silence, embarrassing to both, followed.

"I didn't sleep soundly last night," said the woman, breaking through this silence.

"Were you sick, or in pain?"

"No; my thoughts kept me awake." Then she added, with that abruptness which is sometimes born of sudden resolution, "It's getting worse and worse, Mrs. Jackman. My rent is nearly three months behind, and the prospects do not grow brighter. I stint myself in every way; but earn so little that it seems impossible to get all right again. How would it suit you to take my bureau? It cost me sixteen dollars, and is as good as it was the day I bought it. You shall have it for twelve dollars, and then we shall be even again. I think, maybe, I can keep up in the future. After two or three weeks' trial, if I can't get along, I will leave your room for a better tenant."

"I shouldn't like to take your bureau," said the landlady, in no feigned reluctance at the thought of accepting this proposal.

"It is my own offer," replied Mrs. Spencer; "and if you can accept of it, the obligation will be on my side."

"I will talk with my husband. If he doesn't object."

"Why should he object, Mrs. Jackman? He can send the bureau to auction and get the money for it whenever he pleases."

"He might not think so. Still I'll do my best with him. But, Mrs. Spencer, suppose you can't get along any better? What then?"

"I'll go away. You shall not be troubled with me any longer." She spoke in a tone of irrepressible sadness.

"Go away where? What will you do?"

"He knows." The eyes of Mrs. Spencer glanced upwards.

"Have you no friends, ma'am? You're not fit to be alone. If you've any friends, you'd better go to them. You're sick and can't work."

Mrs. Spencer did not respond to this. On the table near which she sat, some partly made unbleached muslin drawers were lying. She reached her hand for the work which she had laid down a little while before.

"Take my advice," said the landlady, "and go to bed. You're pale as a sheet this blessed minute! My!" She started towards Mrs. Spencer as she made this exclamation. A faintness had come over the exhausted woman, and she would have fallen had not Mrs. Jackman been at her side. Large drops of perspiration covered her forehead, and stood beaded around her mouth. The faintness passed off in a few minutes, but not until Mrs. Spencer had been supported to her bed.

"It wont do no how!" said Mrs. Jackman, continuing her remonstrance. "You must stop and take rest. You'll be down with fever, or something worse; and then what'll become of you?"

"If I could only die!" was the answer, made, passionately, through a gushing flood of tears. "If God would only take me now!"

Mrs. Jackman stood over her, full of pity, but helpless for comfort.

"Isn't there somebody that I can see for you, ma'am?" she asked. "Some friend who would not let you want, now that you are too sick to help yourself? I'll go anywhere for you?"

Mrs. Spencer made no answer.

"Now do think, ma'am," urged the sympathizing landlady. "I'm sure you can get help if you will only ask for it. We can't always let our pride have its way; and, maybe, it wouldn't be best for us in the end. I've had to humble myself a great many times, though it did go hard."

"You are kind and good, Mrs. Jackman," replied Mrs. Spencer, with recovering self-possession. "I'll think about what you say, though I'm afraid nothing will come of it."

"That, maybe, will depend on yourself."

There was no reply to this.

"You wont try to do anything this morning. You'll just lie still in bed," urged Mrs. Jackman.

Mrs. Spencer shut her eyes and turned her face away. The landlady stood over her for a little while, and then went down stairs.

Not very far from the poor tenement in which this scene occurred, stood a large dwelling, crowded in every part with modern appliances of comfort. In one of the chambers a man sat alone. His form was stooping and wasted; his eyes sunken far back in the hollow orbits; his lips thin and white; his face of an ashen paleness. He sat alone, as we have said, in a back chamber. There was a book-case and secretary in the room, which was used as a kind of private office, or library. The man occupied a large easy chair, which had been drawn up to the secretary. He was engaged in looking over some papers. Pausing in this work, he reached his hand for a bell-cord that hung near, and pulled it. A servant answered the call.

"Tell Mrs. Jansen that I would like to see her," he said.

"She's gone out sir," replied the servant.

"Gone out!" He spoke in a tone of fretful disappointment.

"Yes, sir. She went out more than an hour ago. Is there anything that I can do for you?"

"No — no. I wished to see Mrs. Jansen. But no matter — no matter."

The servant withdrew. Again the reader has Mr. Jansen before him. A year has gone by since the exciting events at Newport. He was very ill there, and not well enough to be removed with safety to New York for nearly three weeks after the attack we have described. During this year, he has wasted gradually, growing sensibly weaker from day to day. There has been no return of the exhausting hemorrhages.

It had been a year of painful experience and retrospection. The neglect and indifference of his wife had become, to one in Mr. Jansen's condition, positive cruelty. There did not exist, in the breast of Mrs. Jansen, a single spark of affection for her husband; and she had ceased to make a pretence of what she did not feel. His wealth gave her the means of self gratification; beyond that, she did not consider him. As to tying herself down to a fretful, unreasoning sick man, she would do no such thing! If he wanted special attendance, let him get a nurse. He was able enough to employ one. So she thought, and her actions were in agreement with her thoughts.

After the servant went down stairs, Mr. Jansen resumed his work of examining certain papers taken from a drawer which had not been disturbed for a long time. Among them he came upon a letter enclosed in an envelop that bore his address. The hand writing he knew but too well, and the sight of it made his heart leap with a sudden throb. For a few moments, he sat holding this letter, his eyes fixed on the superscription, then he made a motion to put it away out of sight, but paused ere this was half done. A good while he sat very still, communing with himself. Then, slowly, but with firm hands, like one who had made up his mind, he withdrew the letter from its envelop, unfolded it, and read —

"My Husband — I fear that we have come to a place in life where our paths must diverge : not however through my desire or my election. As I look out into the world, and dimly realize what I must be, and do, and suffer, living apart from my husband, I faint in spirit — I shudder at the prospect. My heart turns back, fain to linger in the sheltered home where it took up two years ago its rest in peace and joy. But, you have dictated the only terms on which I can remain in this home. I must be inferior and obedient. You must be lord, and I serf. The free will that God gave me, I must lay at your feet. Alas for me! I cannot thus submit. As your equal, I can walk by your side, true as steel to honor, virtue, purity, and love ; as your inferior there can be no dwelling together for us in the same house.

"To-day, you have laid on me a command, and, deliberately, in face of all consequences, I resolve to act as freely as though it had not been spoken. At the same time, I shall give you credit for being in earnest, and refrain from coming back, after I leave your house, until you send me word that you desire my return. I go, because I will not live with you in strife; and the terms you dictate render concord impossible. I pray you not to misunderstand me! Too much for both of us is involved. I do not go away from you, because I desire to repudiate our marriage contract, nor because there lives on this earth a man whom my heart prefers before you. I go, because you will not let me live with you in the freedom to which every soul is entitled, and in the equality that I claim as right. Here is the simple issue, as Heaven is my witness! In whatever you elect to do, keep this in mind, Carl! Your wife asks for love, and will give love in return; but if you command obedience, love dies. She cannot dwell with you as a slave, and will not dwell with you in open contention.

"My heart is full, Carl, and my eyes so dim with tears, that I can scarcely see the page on which I am writing. If I were to let my feelings have sway, there would go to you such a wild, such an impassioned appeal, as no man living, whose heart was not of stone, could resist. The words are pressing, nay, almost imploring, for utterance. But, I press them back, and keep silence, for I will not be a beggar for the love you promised, nor a craven to submit. Equal, Carl! We must stand side by side as equals, or remain forever apart.

"It is vain to write more. If you cannot comprehend the stern necessity that is on me, after what I have said, further sentences will be idle. I go, because you have declared terms that make it impossible for me to remain. I will return, if you write a single line of invitation. If you say 'come back,' I will take it as a hopeful assurance for the future. If you keep silence, this separation is eternal! If you wish to see me, or write to me, call or send to number 560 ——— street.

MADELINE."

Two or three times, as Carl Jansen bent over this letter, he caught his breath, and repressed a choking sob. Two or three times he wiped away the tears that made his eyes too dim to read the sentences. Once, under the pressure of uncontrollable emotion, he laid his face down on the writing-desk before him and wept, actually moaning in his weakness from mental pain.

And this was the letter he had read, years before, in blind anger, and put away coldly and unrelentingly! — this letter, throbbing in every sentence with a love that could not die, though wronged, repressed, and trampled on. The true spirit and meaning of it were felt and comprehended now; but it was too late!

Carl Jansen folded the letter carefully, handling it like some precious thing; but, ere returning it to the envelop, re-opened and read it through again. With every muscle of his face quivering in lines of anguish and remorse, he lifted his eyes upwards, and sobbed out, "God forgive me!"

Not long afterwards, Mr. Jansen rung for a servant.

"Tell Edward to bring the carriage 'round," he said, when the servant appeared.

"Mrs. Jansen has the carriage," was replied.

"She has!" In a quick fretting voice.

"Yes, sir."

"Oh, very well. Then go and order me a carriage. I wish to ride out."

"No —— Fourteenth street," was the order given by Mr. Jansen as he took his seat.

A ride of fifteen minutes brought him to the number designated.

"Is Mrs. Lawrence at home?" he asked.

The answer being affirmative, he entered, handing his card for the lady. Mr. Jansen tried to be calm and self-possessed. But this was impossible. When Mrs. Lawrence met him in the parlor, she found him so agitated, that he spoke with difficulty. She was shocked at his wan and wasted appearance.

"Why, Mr. Jansen!" she exclaimed, in her surprise. "I should not have known you."

"I'm but a wreck," he answered sadly. Then recovering himself, as they sat down, he added — "You are of course, a little surprised at my visit. It concerns Madeline."

He spoke the name with a slight falling of the voice, in which Mrs. Lawrence was surprised to detect a quality of tenderness.

"The past is past," he added, "and cannot be recalled. We can only act in the present. Do you know where she is?"

Mrs. Lawrence shook her head.

"How long is it since you heard of her?"

"Not for several years."

"I saw her a year ago."

"You did! Where?"

"At Newport. I am going to talk with you very frankly — very plainly, Mrs. Lawrence. It may hurt and humble me; but I want your assistance, and I must lay off disguise. You are Madeline's true friend; I know that. You tried to save us from the misery we dragged down upon our heads; but we were blind and mad, both of us — I, the blindest, the maddest, the most to blame! I saw Madeline at Newport a year ago."

"What was she doing there?"

"She was in the family of Mr. B——, of Hyde Park."

"In what relation?"

Mr. Jansen did not reply immediately. The answer, when made, seemed to hurt him —

"As a nurse to his child."

"Poor Madeline!" The voice of Mrs. Lawrence trembled, and her eyes filled with tears.

"We met, for a few minutes, in a strangely agitating interview; one that I cannot describe. I did not see her again; in fact, I was ill and confined to my room for two or three weeks afterwards."

"How did she look?" asked Mrs. Lawrence, in the pause that followed.

"Pale, patient, saintly."

The face of Mrs. Lawrence brightened.

"She is still pure — still true to honor and virtue?"

"Pure as an angel!" said Mr. Jansen, with much feeling. He then bowed his head, and sat mute for awhile.

"What of her since?" asked Mrs. Lawrence.

"I know nothing. But, I can no longer remain idle in regard to her. She must be removed from this state of dependence. Madeline a servant! The thought torments me like a ghost with bloody hands. I have an abundance, which she is justly entitled to share. I wish to dispense a portion of it for her benefit — to settle upon her a liberal income. Will you help me to accomplish this?"

"All that is in my power to do, shall be done," replied Mrs. Lawrence.

"First we must ascertain where she is."

"Yes."

"Will you write to Mr. or Mrs. B———, and ascertain if she is still in their family?"

"Yes; immediately. But, I'm afraid, Mr. Jansen, that she will not feel at liberty to accept of anything at your hands."

"Oh, she must! She must! Not at my hands as a gift,

or gratuity. But, as an equitable transfer of what is her own. Her going away from me — our separation by divorce — was only a personal event. In all fairness it did not touch her right of property — gives me no honest claim to keep back what was justly her own. I now propose restitution. Personal matters are one thing. Rights in property another."

"Where man and wife are concerned, law and custom decide differently," said Mrs. Lawrence.

"I know; but that doesn't touch abstract rights. If custom and the courts decide unjustly and oppressively, it is no reason why my conscience should be bound. I wish to do justly. You see my stand point."

"Oh yes."

"And you will do all in your power for Madeline?"

"As if she were my own sister."

"You will write at once."

"To-day."

"The mail will go up this afternoon. There should be an answer by the day after to-morrow."

"Yes."

"This is Wednesday. I will call on Friday." And Mr. Jansen went away.

CHAPTER XXVII.

"AVE you any response?" eagerly asked Mr. Jansen. Friday had come, and he was at the residence of Mrs. Lawrence.

"Yes."

"What is it?"

"Madeline is not there."

"Not there!"

"No. Here is Mrs. B———'s letter."

Mr. Jansen read — "It is just one year since the person about whom you inquire left us under peculiar circumstances, suddenly. We have not, since, been able to learn anything in regard to her, though we have made considerable inquiry. Two months of her wages remain in our hands. If you succeed in discovering her, we should like to be informed of the fact, so that we can send her the amount due."

Mr. Jansen, after reading this letter, sat, with drooping head and an air of deep disappointment for a considerable time.

"The search cannot be given up, Mrs. Lawrence," he said, at length, in a husky voice.

"I am weak. I cannot bear fatigue or excitement. But, if it cost me my life, I will find Madeline — that is," he added, with a dropping of his voice, "if she be still living in this world."

"If we had any clue," said Mrs. Lawrence.

"We must find a clue."

"An advertisement might reach her," suggested Mrs. Lawrence.

"I will think about that."

"It might be so worded as not to attract the attention of curious or meddlesome people, and yet indicate Madeline in a way to make her understand it. Turn the suggestion over in your mind. Perhaps you will see it more clearly."

The suggestion was turned over in the mind of Mr. Jansen and acted upon. He could see no other way of discovering Madeline. The advertisement was in these terms : — "An old school friend of Madeline Spencer (Jansen) desires to see her. A line to 'Jessie,' at this office, giving address, will have immediate attention."

Some controversy passed between Mrs. Lawrence and Mr. Jansen as to the exact terms of this advertisement. The delicate part was the name. There was no knowing under whose eyes it might fall. Mr. Jansen had reasons of his own for not desiring his wife's attention in any way attracted. For all her selfish indifference towards him, she had, on more than one occasion, evinced a jealous alertness, that surprised and annoyed him. It had not escaped her notice, that a woman had been found in his room at Newport on the occasion of his sudden illness.

This woman left immediately on her appearance from the ball-room, whence she had been summoned.

"Who is that?" she had asked, as Madeline, retiring from the bedside, went quickly out of the chamber. The alarm occasioned by her husband's dangerous state, was not strong enough to repress something more than curiosity.

"One of the nurses," was replied by the waiter who had called the physician.

"Whose nurse?"

"I don't know," was replied.

On the next day, Mrs. Jansen pursued the subject, and ascertained that the woman she had found in attendance on her husband, was Mrs. B———'s nurse. Singularly enough, as it appeared to her, this nurse was nowhere to be seen. Two or three times, during the morning, she saw Mrs. B———, and always in attendance on her child. Suspense with coarse minds is intolerable. They will break through all delicate reserves or decent proprieties for relief. So Mrs. Jansen accosted Mrs. B——— with the question—

"Where is your nurse, ma'am?"

"She was taken ill, and went away this morning," replied Mrs. B———, who knew her questioner, and felt that she might entertain a suspicion of Madeline's true identity.

"Taken ill! Why, what ailed her? She was well enough last evening." There was a rude abruptness about Mrs. Jansen that Mrs. B——— did not feel inclined to tolerate.

"All are subject to sudden illness," she answered, quietly, yet with a studied reserve that was meant and felt as a rebuke.

"Who is this nurse?" asked Mrs. Jansen, in a more subdued and respectful manner.

"She was my nurse. I can answer in regard to her no farther, except it be to speak of her kind and dutiful conduct in my family, and to regret the circumstance that deprives me of her services."

"What is her name?"

"I trust the sickness is only temporary, and that I shall find her at home when I leave here," said Mrs. B———, not answering the question.

"What did you call her?"

Mrs. B——— stooped to give some attention to little Netty, whom she was holding by the hand. The child drew upon her, and wished to go in from the piazza where they were standing. This afforded a plea for getting rid of Mrs. Jansen. So, with a polite inclination of the head and body, Mrs. B——— said—

"Good morning, ma'am," and withdrew into the house.

Curiosity, baffled, is only increased. Mrs. Jansen made another attempt to gain from Mrs. B——— the information she so much desired, but was no more successful than at first. Piqued, annoyed, and rendered more suspicious from this appearance of mystery, Mrs. Jansen tried, by inquiries among the servants, to learn something about Madeline. But none of them knew anything about her.

"Did you know that woman I found here on the night you were taken sick?" she asked, abruptly, of Mr. Jansen, as she stood at his bedside on the second day after the serious attack we have described, and while he was yet in a very weak and dangerous condition. The question made him start.

"Which?" he inquired, with an effort to seem indifferent that was not entirely successful. Suspicion gives keenness of perception. Mrs. Jansen saw down through this veil.

"Why, the woman who was holding your head, and putting the salt and water to your lips! You know who I mean."

"Oh, yes. She was in the passage when I ran to the door in alarm. I might have died but for her prompt assistance," Mr. Jansen replied, feebly, shutting his eyes and turning his face to the wall.

"You knew her!" said his wife, sharply, with accusation and reproach blending in her voice.

"How should I know?" Mr. Jansen did not lift his eyelids, nor turn his head. Taking the case as it stood, he felt the necessity of concealment and circumspection; and so, even in his weakness, exercised strength of will. His condition was his refuge.

"How should *you* know her? This is just the question. Of course, you *did* know her! That is plain!"

So she probed him; but he kept silent — and ever after kept silent when she touched the subject.

From this it will be seen upon what delicate ground Mr. Jansen was treading. He understood the dfficulties by which he was environed, yet did not hesitate. The object in view raised him above all hindering questions. He did not wish the advertisement to fail, and so, after much debate with himself, resolved to give it the wording we have seen. He knew, of course, that if it met his wife's eyes, it would subject him to sharp and suspicious interrogation. But, he trusted in his power to veil everything under an habitual cold and unemotional exterior

He did not know that his wife's suspicions were aroused in advance, and that she was already on his track.

It so happened, that Mrs. Jansen was riding past the house of Mrs. Lawrence at the very time her husband was entering it, on the day he first went there to make inquiries about Madeline. She had seen him standing at the door, but with his face turned from her. The form seemed so like his, that she was startled by the resemblance. She drove home immediately, and found that he had gone out in a hired carriage. A host of wild suspicions was born instantly in her breast. Her first thought was to order the coachman to drive her back into the neighborhood where she had seen her husband; but this, on reflection, was deemed imprudent. The house she had seen him enter was one in a row of six or eight, precisely alike in external appearance. She had failed to note it so particularly as to insure identification. Mrs. Jansen was annoyed at this impediment.

"I'll catch him," she said to herself. "I'll find him out. I'll know just where he has been, and who he visits."

"Oh! So you've been taking a ride to yourself," she said, in a half querulous, half bantering tone, when Mr. Jansen returned. "Why didn't you say that you wanted the carriage? I could have walked."

"I didn't think of going until you were away. But, no matter. The carriage I had was very easy."

"Where have you been?" The woman's keen eyes were fixed on his face, and he knew it.

"I only took a short ride," was answered. "The day being fine, I knew the air would refresh me."

"Did you stop anywhere?"

"Yes."

"Where?" Very imperatively.

Mr. Jansen turned and looked at his wife steadily for some moments. Then answered coldly, and without taking his eyes from her face —

"Pray" when did you acquire the right to question me in regard to my outgoings and my incomings?"

He still kept his eyes upon her. Mrs. Jansen's face grew livid, and then very pale. A storm gathered swiftly in her breast; but she held it back from bursting.

"Oh, just as you like!" she answered, a gurgling laugh in her throat. It did not fall upon her husband's ears like a human laugh.

Each was willing to retire from the conflict, but for different reasons.

Under this aspect of affairs, it was risking something to let the name "Jansen" appear in the advertisement for Madeline. But, after weighing every consideration that presented itself, Mr. Jansen decided as we have seen.

A very intimate acquaintance called to see Mrs. Jansen on the day this advertisement appeared. She had encountered it in looking over the "Times," and could not rest until she had brought it to the notice of her friend.

"Have you seen that?" she said, on meeting Mrs. Jansen, handing her, with a look of mystery, the advertisement she had cut from the morning paper.

Mrs. Jansen devoured it with her eyes greedily.

"Madeline Spencer (Jansen)! What does it mean?" She looked at her friend in blank astonishment.

"That's just it! What does it mean? I thought, maybe, you hadn't seen it, and so I put on my things and ran right around here."

"It was considerate of you. Madeline Spencer (Jan-

sen)! An old school friend desires to see her. 'Jessie:
Who's 'Jessie,' I wonder?"

"And who's Madeline Spencer (Jansen) asked the friend.

"I know!" A strong, red light flashing into Mrs. Jansen's face. "I know!" And she gripped her hands, and shut her teeth firmly.

"Who?"

Mrs. Jansen bent towards her friend, and whispered huskily —

"His first wife!"

"Who's? Mr. Jansen's?"

"Yes — yes. I've had a suspicion that something was brewing. Of course, I talk to you as if you were my own sister; and you'll be as close as death."

"His first wife!"

"That was her name — Madeline Spencer."

"Goodness! I thought she died years ago. But, what do you make of this effort to find her by some old friend? You've had suspicions, you say. About what?"

"I don't know. Something's in the wind — that's sure. It was thoughtful in you to bring me this advertisement."

"Suppose *you* answer it?"

Mrs. Jansen turned this suggestion over in her mind before responding.

"'A line, giving address, will have immediate attention. I'm not Madeline Spencer Jansen, and can't give the required address.'"

"That doesn't signify," returned the friend. "Send a note to the office, asking for this 'Jessie's' address. You'll get a reply, and so find out who 'Jessie' is."

"Maybe yes, and maybe no. Some people are mighty

cute. 'Jessie' wants Madeline's address; and until she gets that, will hardly give her own. I'll tell you what's come into my mind. You'll help me all you can?"

"Dont fear for that. Say on, Mrs. Jansen."

"You answer the advertisement."

"How?"

"Pretend to be this Madeline."

"But, I must give an address."

"That may be managed, I think."

"I don't see the way."

"Of course, you can't see her at your own house. Somewhere else must be found. I'll tell you who might be trusted. She's under obligations and will do anything for you."

"Jane Bradley, the dressmaker?"

"Yes," replied Mrs. Jansen. "Jane has over half a dozen workwomen, and you might personate one of them as 'Madeline.' You need'nt go very far, you know. All we are after, is to find out who this 'Jessie' is, and what she wants."

"Do you think Jane Bradley can be trusted?" asked the friend.

"I've not a doubt of it."

The dressmaker was approached by the friend of Mrs. Jansen, and found pliable. She was a thoughtless woman, fond of excitement or adventure, and not apt to consider consequences. A note was sent to the "Times" office by the pretended "Madeline," asking for an interview at the dressmaker's. The first impulse of Mrs. Lawrence was to go; but, on reflection, she concluded to wait until Mr. Jansen called, and submit the note to him.

"Not our Madeline," said Mr. Jansen, in a tone of disappointment, on reading the note.

"Why do you think so?" asked Mrs. Lawrence.

"This is written by an uneducated person. You see the bad spelling, and the cramped, heavy hand."

"True. I hadn't considered that."

"And yet," said Mr. Jansen, in a thoughtful, perplexed way, "there is something familiar about the writing. It isn't Madeline's I know."

"Perhaps she is ill. This may have been written at her dictation," suggested Mrs. Lawrence.

"Then she would have had the fact stated." Mr. Jansen lifted the note and read it over once more.

"At Jane Bradley's!" he exclaimed, his whole manner putting on a new aspect.

"Who is Jane Bradley?" inquired Mrs. Lawrence.

"My wife's dressmaker!" There was a look of blank discomfiture in his countenance. "And now I recognize the hand-writing of this note. It is my wife's penmanship."

The face of Mrs. Lawrence showed alarm.

"I have made a narrow escape," she said. "This ground is not safe for me."

Mrs. Lawrence glanced through the closed Venetian shutters as she spoke. She had turned her head so that the expression of her countenance might not be seen by Mr. Jansen.

"Do you know that woman?" She spoke quickly, with concern in her voice.

Mr. Jansen arose, and looked out from behind the shutters.

"There she is, walking slowly down on the other side. I've seen her about here three or four times in the last two days. Once she came up our steps and examined the door, evidently searching for an address. I saw her do the same thing next door. . There! She has stopped and is looking round. You see her face. Do you know her?"

Mr. Jansen moved quickly back from the window, and sat down.

"Do you know her?" repeated Mrs Lawrence, moving back also, and confronting Mr. Jansen.

"Yes."

"Who is she?"

"A woman I detest. One of my wife's particular friends."

They were silent for some time, Mrs. Lawrence standing and her visitor sitting. The latter spoke first.

"One thing is plain," he said, "It will not do for me to come here any more."

"Not on any consideration," replied Mrs. Lawrence.

"And yet I cannot give up this search for Madeline — I cannot, and I will not!" Mr. Jansen spoke with decision.

"Some other means must be adopted. You see in what a questionable position I am standing," said Mrs. Lawrence. "My husband would be angry if he knew what I had done. He has, like all of us, his peculiar ways of thinking; and is particularly sensitive about getting mixed up, as he calls it, with other people's affairs. I wanted to talk with him about this matter, and get his approval of what I was doing, but I feared an opposition so decided that I could not act against it. My heart was with Madeline, and for her sake, I have done what would seriously displease my husband if it should come to his ears, even without bias or exaggeration. But, now that your wife's suspicions are aroused; now that she answers my advertisement, and sets a watch upon my house, it is full time that I retraced the steps I have taken."

"Will you not send to the Times office again? Madeline may see the advertisement and answer it."

"I'm afraid to take another step forward, Mr. Jansen, as things now are. The imprudence of letting my Christian name appear in the advertisement, was very great. I was so intent on having Madeline recognize the hand of a friend, that I did not consider its personal bearing on myself. My husband is as likely to see it as any one else."

"Perhaps," suggested Mr. Jansen, "it will be safest, all things considered, to tell your husband the whole story from beginning to end."

The rattle of a key was heard that moment in the front door. Mrs. Lawrence started, changed color, and looked frightened.

"My husband!" she ejaculated. But instantly regained her composure.

"All must now be told," she said. "Manifest no disturbance, and leave all to me."

There was a heavy frown on the face of Mr. Lawrence, as a moment afterwards, he stood in the parlor door. His wife went towards him, smiling, and said, introducing her visitor —

"Mr. Jansen."

The latter, with more self-possession than he had hoped to assume, arose, and took the hand which Mr. Lawrence could not help offering.

"We are secret plotters," said Mrs. Lawrence, with an ease of manner that took Mr. Jansen by surprise; "and now that you have come in so opportunely, or, inopportunely as the sequel may prove we must take you into our counsels. I know that you are not good at working underground; still, in the multitude of counsellors there is said to be wisdom, and you may be of signal service."

"No, I am not good at working in the dark," replied Mr. Lawrence, scarcely relaxing in anything his severe manner. "Above board is my motto, always. More harm than good comes of these secret doings."

"All rules have their exceptions," said Mrs. Lawrence. "Where the end is pure and humane, and it cannot be reached, through the interference of wrong-minded people, if pursued in common observation, it is right to work in secret. And this is just what we have been doing. The end has been good to one and harm to none. If any come in and try to make harm, the evil is with them. But this to you is unintelligible. Let me lift the veil and show you just what has been purposed, and what has been done."

Mrs. Lawrence then related, without concealment of anything, what the reader knows of their efforts to discover Madeline. With a womanly tact and eloquence, against which the most implacable natures are not always able to protect themselves, she managed to interest her husband's feelings. Suspicion was disarmed, when he knew the whole truth. We say suspicion, for that had been awakened by an anonymous letter, the receipt of which had brought him home at an unusual hour. The letter was from the hand of Mrs. Jansen.

"And now, Henry, that you know all about these secret doings, will you not give us the benefit of your clear judgment, your skill, and your prudence. We must find Madeline if she be living. Mr. Jansen's relation to the matter is delicate, and exceedingly embarrassing. He cannot move a step without exciting a jealous suspicion;

nor without danger of misjudgment. We might, in the cause of justice and humanity, take this work into our own hands, and do it in our own way. Acting with my husband, I should then be safe from unjust judgment. There is no danger, here, of getting mixed up with other people's affairs — your peculiar horror. It is a plain case. We have, simply, to find Madeline, and do for her what Mr. Jansen may request. He can see you at your store, and the business upon which he calls be your own affair, and out of the reach of meddlesome curiosity."

Mr. Lawrence dropped his eyes, and pondered the matter for a good while. All his natural inclinations and peculiar modes of thinking, were in opposition. He belonged to that class of men who consider the time lost that is occupied in other people's affairs. He asked no one to look after him or his — he was competent to take care of his own concerns — so he thought, and so he was in the habit of expressing himself. Trouble was involved in all this that he was called upon to do; trouble that brought no reward. But, how could he say no? It was a case from which he could not turn himself, and escape the charge of inhumanity. Moreover, something in his wife's appeal, and something in the grieving sadness of Mr. Jansen's wan and wasted countenance, touched his pity, and moved him to consent.

"If I can serve you, in this, Mr. Jansen," he said, with far more of sympathy in his manner than his wife had hoped for, "I will do so cheerfully."

Mr. Lawrence looked from Mr. Jansen to his wife, as he thus answered, and saw light gleam over her face; a light that made her look doubly beautiful. She turned upon him eyes full of gratitude and pleasure; eyes, in which he saw more of the old regard and tenderness than had been manifested for a long time.

"You have lifted a heavy weight that was bearing me down," said Mr. Jansen. "My heart is very grateful. Mrs. Lawrence knows my views about Madeline, and will communicate them. I leave all the means of finding her in your hands. Do for her, if found, all that your judgment and feelings warrant, and I will bear the cost. Oh, my friends!" — and his voice trembled — "let me beg of you to fail in no effort. I believe her to be pure and true. I saw her a year ago, and read her face. It was written all over with lines of suffering, of patience, and of resignation. She passed me, as a rebuking spirit; and yet, laid on me, tenderly and forgivingly, the hand of blessing as she passed. When I think of what she has suffered — of what she may now be suffering, I am so deeply pained that I can scarcely endure the anguish. I am wasting, as you see. My strength is gone. I am of but little more use in this world. But, this work of mercy my hands must do if I fail in everything else."

"Leave all to us," replied Mr. Lawrence, with an interest in Madeline's case that surprised even himself. "We will do all that lies in our power. If living, we will certainly find her."

" Thus assured, Mr. Jansen went away, Mr. Lawrence accompanying him to the door. As they stood talking just within the vestibule, the woman noticed by Mrs. Lawrence went past again, on the other side. She saw Mr. Jansen, and quickening her pace, hurried out of sight.

CHAPTER XXVIII.

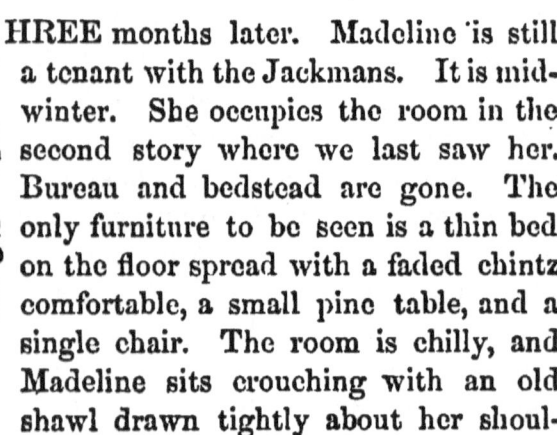

THREE months later. Madeline is still a tenant with the Jackmans. It is midwinter. She occupies the room in the second story where we last saw her. Bureau and bedstead are gone. The only furniture to be seen is a thin bed on the floor spread with a faded chintz comfortable, a small pine table, and a single chair. The room is chilly, and Madeline sits crouching with an old shawl drawn tightly about her shoulders, near the fire-place, where a few sticks are burning On the table, which has been drawn near the fire-place, lies some needlework.

Three months have done their wasting work on Madeline. She was sick when we saw her last; too sick to bear up and continue the work by which the wolf of starvation was to be kept from her door. After a week of mental and bodily prostration, she had rallied again, and gone on with her weary tasks. Mrs. Jackman acceded to her proposition about the bureau, and took it in the place of money, so cancelling the rent obligation. But as the weeks gathered themselves into months, the rent again accumulated, for Madeline's strength was little more than feebleness itself, and all she could earn was consumed in fuel, food and medicine. Then the landlord became restless again, and demanded of his wife the removal of their unprofitable tenant. He was pacified on the relinquishment by Madeline of her bedstead, two chairs, and a fine lace collar, which were sold for more than the sum actually due. Mrs. Jackman could not find it in her heart to turn the poor sick woman out of doors. She was so gentle, so patient, "just like a hurt lamb," she said, that she could'nt act towards her in the hard, selfish way she had been in the habit of acting towards people of her own class. And so she had continued to stand between between her tenant and her husband.

But, even Mrs. Jackman saw that there must come an end to this condition of things. Mrs. Spencer grew weaker as the days went on. Bureau, bedstead, and chairs were gone, and the earnings diminished instead of increasing. When the winter days came on, Mrs. Spencer found herself too thinly clad to go for her work. Pitying her condition, Mrs. Jackman took the work home for her, and brought back a new supply.

At Christmas, Madeline was again in debt for her room.

"It's no use, Kitty," said Jackman to his wife. "I'm going to put my foot down once for all. That woman'll have to leave."

"I wish she were in a better place," answered Mrs. Jackman. "And she will be, I'm thinking, before many months go over her head. D'you know, John, she talks about dying just as I'd talk about going on a visit somewhere. She isn't the least bit afraid of death. It makes me feel strange to hear her."

"Then, my advice to her is, to die at once," replied Jackman, roughly. "She can't be any worse off than she is here. And she must do it quickly, or she can't have the privilege in my house. But jesting aside, Kitty, I'm not going to fool with her any longer. She owes, now, more than her duds will sell for, and every day she keeps that room is money out of my pocket. If she has no friends to look after her, she must go to the poor-house, and the sooner you let her know what's to come, the more time she'll have to get ready. Next week she must be out of that room. On Monday I shall put up a bill."

"Don't say that, John!" replied his wife, with unusual sobriety of manner. "No good will come of hard treatment to this woman. I can't tell why it is; but I feel strangely about it. There's something in her that's uncommon, like."

"You always were a fool, Kitty!" retorted Jackman, half angrily. "I don't know what you mean by hard treatment. The city and county take care of the poor. That's what the alms-house is for. That's what I pay a tax for. Do you think I'm going to fill my house with paupers? Not I! John Jackman isn't quite a born fool. I don't see what's come over you, Kitty. Ever since this woman came into our house, you've acted as if you were afraid of her."

"No, John, not afraid of her. That isn't it at all. I've pitied her, poor weak thing! She isn't like the people I've been used to seeing, or she'd been sent adrift long and long ago. I can't just say what it is, but there's something about her that makes my heart soft. Just let her stay through the winter."

"No!" Jackman spoke with a strong impulse in his voice.

"It wont be anything out of our pockets, John."

"Of course not! She'll pay like a queen;" he answered with irony.

"It wont be in the long run, I mean. D'you know, John, that a verse in the Bible which I read when I was a little girl, keeps all the while coming into my mind. I haven't thought of it before for a dozen years. 'He that giveth to the poor, lendeth to the Lord, and He will repay him again.' That's it, as near as I can remember. It seems as if it was meant just for us."

"Pooh! Pooh! Stuff! I guess, if the truth were know, it would be found that Mrs. Spencer put this into your head. People like her are smart."

"No, John. Mrs. Spencer never repeated that verse in my hearing. It came up all of itself. I tried not to think of it, but the more I tried, the more it would come up. She's poor, and sick — dying I might say. Now, it wont be much for us, John, just to let her stay where she is 'till spring; or, maybe, not 'till longer than February. She isn't going to trouble anybody very long."

"I said no, and I mean no!" Mr. Jackman showed increasing irritation. "Next week she must go or pay her rent. 'Tisn't any use in you to bamboozle about her any longer. I've put my foot down and it shall stay down. The money due must be paid or she goes out. You'll tell her so at once."

"It's no use, John," replied Mrs Jackman, "I can't give her warning. You must do it yourself, if it's done at all."

The man grew very angry at this, swore bitterly, and stormed about in a fruitless rage. Twice he started for the stairway, asserting that he would make short work of it with Mrs. Spencer; but, some thing held him back.

"I'll call in a policeman and have her taken off," he said, at length, catching up his hat and going out. Mrs. Jackman understood her husband's character, and did not feel concerned at this threat.

A little while afterwards she went up to Mrs Spencer's room. She found Madeline crouching near a few burning sticks in the fire-place, a thin shawl clutched tightly around her shoulders — shivering. The air struck coldly on the face of Mrs. Jackman.

"Indeed, indeed, ma'am, this will never do!" said the landlord's wife. "Your room is as chilly as a barn. You'll get your death a cold." She stood for a few moments and then went out quickly; but soon returned with an armful of light wood.

"There," she said, when a bright blaze glowed on the hearth, "that will do some good. I'll bring you up two or three armfuls. You must keep warm, Mrs. Spencer. And now it just comes to me. There's a society that gives out small stoves and coal to poor people. Mrs. Blunt was speaking about it last week. I'll go right away and see if I can't get you a stove and half a ton of coal."

"Oh, if you could!" A faint light came into Madeline's wasted countenance. "How thankful I would be," she added, in a grateful voice.

"If it's to be done, I'm the one to do it," replied Mrs. Jackman. "Nothing stops me when I once get a thing into my head. As my husband says, I'll go through fire and water to gain my ends. So, you may count on the stove and coal if they are to be had."

Mrs. Jackman went out full of this new purpose. She found sundry impediments in her way; but a strong will removed them. In less than two hours from the time she set about her work it was accomplished, and a small, hot stove sent its genial warmth into every corner of Madeline's room.

"This is comfortable," she said, as she felt the pleasant heat, and saw Madeline lay off her shawl. But, even as she spoke, the nakedness of the room, and its comfortless aspect, struck her unpleasantly. At the same time, something like shame, or guilt, troubled her feelings. Why was this poor sick woman's room so naked? Who had taken bedstead, bureau, chairs, carpet? The smile of self-satisfaction died out of Mrs. Jackman's face. The little she had just done for this woman, seemed as nothing in view of what she and her husband had done against her. She felt as if she had been a robber and an oppressor. She turned her face away, as Madeline laid a hand on her arm, and said, gratefully — almost tearfully —

"God bless you, Mrs. Jackman! I cannot find words in which to speak my gratitude. If I never repay you, He will not fail."

"Oh, it's nothing — nothing!" answered Mrs. Jackman, not able to repress a disturbed feeling, and still keeping her face turned aside. "I'd not deserve the name of a woman, if I kept back from a trifle like this."

And Mrs. Jackman went down stairs, glad to escape from the presence of Madeline, in whose grateful expressions her heart found more of rebuke than blessing.

Mr. Jackman came home while a portion of Madeline's half ton of coal still lay on the side walk.

"What does that mean?" he demanded of his wife, referring to the coal.

"It means," she answered, that a charitable society has sent Mrs. Spencer a stove and some coal."

"Did they send money to pay her rent?"

"No."

"Then they can take them back again. No stove shall be put up in my house."

"The stove is up already," said Mrs. Jackman, quietly.

"And you permitted it to be done?"

"Yes."

"Well, I'll pitch it out of the window, and the woman after it!" Jackman was furious. His wife remained silent.

"Have you told her that she must go next week?" Jackman confronted his wife with a menacing look. His passions were, at times, uncontrollable. More than once he had struck her.

"I have not." Her calm voice and steady eyes mastered him. "That must be your work, as I have already said."

"It shall be my work!" exclamed Jackman, and he left the room, and went with a heavy, stumbling tread up stairs. His wife did not follow him; but sat down, folding her hands, to await the result.

A pale, startled face, met Jackman as he pushed open the door of Madeline's room — a pale, startled face, and large brown eyes, soft, tender, suffering, questioning. Madeline had drawn her single chair near the window, and was sewing. She arose on her landlord's entrance, and stood bending a little forward, with her eyes fixed upon him.

The raging beast was subdued; the man felt himself in a wrong position. The woman and her landlord stood looking at each other for some moments in silence.

"You have a stove, I see," said Jackman, breaking through the strange embarrassment which had fallen on him so suddenly.

"Yes, sir, thanks to the interest made for me by your kind-hearted wife." The tender sweetness of Madeline's voice penetrated his ears like music. The wild beast in his nature slunk still farther away and out of sight.

Jackman was dumb. He gazed in a bewildered, half fascinated way, at Madeline; then around the stripped, comfortless room; then out of the window; and then, like a baffled and rebuked dog, turned and retreated. It was the first time he had gone into his tenant's room; and he felt sure it would be his last adventure in that direction.

CHAPTER XXIX.

HE sudden appearance of Jackman had frightened Madeline. On his withdrawal, she sunk back into the chair from which she had arisen, feeling weak, and trembling inwardly. She knew him to be a violent man, and there had always rested on her mind a dread of encountering him. She attempted to resume her sewing, but her hand trembled so that she could not guide the needle. The air of the room felt close and stifling — her face was hot, as if she were, before a fire. She panted for breath. Seeking for relief she opened a window, and let the cold air fall over her. There came a sensation of ease, followed too soon by a shuddering chill that seized her without warning.

There was not now heat enough in the little stove, red in some parts, to remove the inward cold that made her vitals shiver. She gathered her shawl about her, but it gave no impression of warmth. Her head was confused —

her limbs heavy — weakness oppressed her. So, she crept into her poor bed on the floor, drawing the thick comfortable over her.

"Why, bless me! Are you sick?" Mrs. Jackman came in nearly an hour afterwards, and found Mrs. Spencer in bed.

Madeline roused herself from a dull stupor, and looked up without replying.

"What's the matter? Are you sick?" Mrs. Jackman repeated her question, bending over Mrs. Spencer as she spoke.

"I'm afraid so," was murmured.

"How do you feel! Where are you sick?" Mrs. Jackman was earnest, but very kind.

"I'm so tight here." Madeline laid her hand on her chest, and tried to take a long breath. Then she closed her eyes in a listless way.

Mrs. Jackman raised herself up, and stood thinking for some moments; then left the room and went down stairs, where she met her husband.

"Look here, John," she spoke with a will in her tones not to be mistaken, "I've got something to say to you."

"Say on," growled the beast in Jackman, not yet fully restored to brutal confidence.

"There's a sick woman up stairs! What did you do or say to her."

"I said nothing, and did nothing, that could harm a fly," he answered, putting himself on the defensive, just where his wife wished to get him.

"You frightened the poor thing by storming into her room as you did. I was afraid of it when you went up. You didn't consider how weak she was, poor creature!"

"I didn't storm into her room," returned Jackman, not yet entirely recovered from the sense of shame that overwhelmed him so suddenly when he found himself in the presence of Mrs. Spencer. "I didn't speak an unkind word."

"I'm glad you didn't, John," answered Mrs. Jackman, mollifying a little. "You'd never have forgiven yourself. And now, John," she continued, "there's only just one thing for us to do, and that is to put her room in a little decent order. She'll have to have a doctor, and I'll not stand the disgrace of having one come into my house to visit a woman like that, lying on the floor in a room without furniture. There's a bedstead in the garret, and I'm going to have it put up for her. I'm going to have a bureau moved in there, and some pieces of carpet spread down. She shall be made comfortable — she shall! Poor soul! It wont hurt us any."

Jackman's selfish spirit winced at this proposal, but, as the case stood, he had not the courage to demur. His wife was one of those prompt, in earnest persons, who never stop long between purpose and act. She saw that she could have her own way for the time, and did not pause for a change of feeling in her husband. Returning to Madeline's room, she said, kindly and cheerfully —

"Come, Mrs. Spencer; I want you to go into the next chamber for a little while. It's pleasanter, and maybe you'll feel better. Come!"

She stooped to the floor where Madeline was lying, and assisted her to rise from her pallet of straw, hard almost as the floor itself. The sick woman made no resistance, but suffered herself to be taken into an adjoining chamber and placed in a more comfortable bed. Her skin was hot with fever, and her breath quick and obstructed. She complained of a dull aching all through her chest.

Jackman growled to himself in an undertone, as he brought down the unused bedstead from the garret and put it up as directed by his wife in Mrs. Spencer's room; but did not rise into any overt opposition to the new condition of things about being inaugurated. The whole spirit of his life had been — "take, take" — never — "give, give." He had been eager to gather from all sources, to harvest in all fields whether his own or his neighbor's; but not to distribute for the good of another. But now, he felt strangely impelled in another direction. Now he was conscious of something like an inward pleasure in providing for the comfort of one whom, but a little while before, he would have cast into the street without a throb of compunction. He made no objection to helping in with a small bureau, and actually proposed the removal to Mrs. Spencer's room of a light dressing-table and glass.

When Madeline was taken back, she hardly knew her chamber. The transformation, so quickly made, touched her deeply. As Mrs. Jackman assisted her into the comfortable bed she had provided, Madeline's feelings gave way, and in tearful thanks she laid her head on her breast, sobbing — "May the Lord, who put this kindness into your heart, bless you a thousand fold!"

A new emotion thrilled the heart of Mrs. Jackman as this benediction fell upon her ears. She seemed to be lifted above the common influences of her life, and to be in association with something higher and purer.

"Say to your husband," Mrs. Spencer added, as she sank back with her head among the soft pillows, "that God will not let his good act go unrewarded. He is very near to us. He sees all our actions; he knows all our thoughts; he keeps for each one of us a book of remembrance."

She closed her eyes and was silent.

"Don't let anything trouble you," said Mrs. Jackman. "You're sick and can't help yourself. It shall all be right."

Mrs. Spencer opened her large eyes and fixed them on Mrs. Jackman. How full of grateful thanks they were! A soft smile gathered around her lips. A radiance from within lighted her countenance. Half entranced, and half in awe, Mrs. Jackman looked upon her, and felt that a beauty not of this earth was flooding her spirit.

"If you could have seen her face, John," she said to her husband, afterwards. "I've seen pictures of angels; but I never saw a face like hers. I've had a different feeling ever since. Wont you just go up and see her? She's afraid of you. Just go up and say a kind word, and so put her heart at ease."

But Jackman growled an emphatic "No!"

"Now do, John!" urged his wife. "I want you to see how nice and comfortable she is. You'll both feel better for it."

"If she's comfortable, I'm satisfied. You've had your own way about her, and I hope you're content. What are you bothering me for? I don't care for the woman."

But he did care for all that, as his wife saw plainly enough. Something had touched his feelings, and changed his sentiments in regard to her. He was puzzled at his own state.

"She ought to have a doctor," said Mrs. Jackman. "I don't like that fever and tightness of the breast, coming on so suddenly. She coughed when I was in her room just now."

"I'll go for a Dispensary doctor," replied Jackman.

"She ought to have a good doctor. She's a very sick woman."

"Who's to pay a doctor? She's got nothing." Jackman frowned. He understood his wife.

"See here, John"— Mrs. Jackman came close to her husband, speaking in a serious, coaxing way —" We haven't a chick or a child — no one to take care of but ourselves — while most of our neighbors have houses full to provide for. We're getting along, while dozens that I could name are standing still or going behind hand. Now it wont hurt us to do a little for somebody else once in our lifetimes. Let us think she's our child, and do for her, now that she is sick, just as if she were our own."

"If you arn't losing your senses, Kitty, then I wonder! What on earth is coming over you," exclaimed Jackman, trying to look the anger he could not feel.

"Just as you please, John," answered Mrs. Jackman, who did not think it prudent to press her husband any farther. "Get a doctor for her; — I leave that to you."

Jackman started out, and took his way to the nearest Dispensary. But his wife's suggestions were in his mind, and he could not push them aside. At the door of the Dispensary he paused, still undetermined; then kept on without entering. Not having had occasion to call in a doctor for some years, Jackman had no family physcian; so he was at a loss where to go. He walked on slowly, and with an irresolute manner; stopping now and then, as the old purpose to call in a Dispensary doctor returned. But, he did not retrace his steps. He never had been so undecided in his life. It was a new thing for a struggle

12*

to go on in his mind between a selfish and a generous feeling.

In one of these pauses, a carriage drew up at the sidewalk where he stood, and a man past the prime of life, with a grave but mild countenance, alighted, and crossing from the curbstone, went into a basement office. In the window of the office was a sign bearing the name of Doctor Wheatland. Jackman correctly inferred, that the person who had alighted from the carriage was Doctor Wheatland himself. Something in his face attracted him, and so, without taking time to consider and hesitate, he went in and asked if he would call and see Mrs. Spencer.

"She's very poor," he added, as a saving clause for himself, "but, maybe, if it isn't too much, it can be paid."

"What did you say her name was?" asked Doctor Wheatland, showing more interest in the case than Jackman had expected.

"Mrs. Spencer," was replied.

"Who is she?" inquired the doctor.

Jackman shook his head. "Don't know anything about her, sir. She took a room at my house six or seven months ago."

"How old is she?"

"She isn't young, sir. Maybe about forty; and maybe older."

The doctor mused for a little while.

"What has she been doing at your house?" He put the question with evident interest.

"She took in sewing."

"Does any one come to see her?"

"No, sir. She don't seem to have any friends."

"Spencer is the name?"

"Yes, sir. Mrs. Spencer."

"What kind of a woman is she?"

"I've not seen much of her," replied Jackman. "But, I guess, she's a nice kind of a woman. My wife thinks so."

"I'll call and see her." And the doctor wrote down the address in his memorandum book.

CHAPTER XXX.

"ERE'S the doctor."

Mrs. Jackman had entered Mrs. Spencer's room, followed by Doctor Wheatland. The instant the physician looked into Madeline's face, he took hold of Mrs. Jackman's arm, and drawing her back from the bed, whispered —

"I would like to see her alone for a few minutes, if you please."

Mrs. Jackman withdrew. The Doctor then sat down by the bedside. Madeline glanced into his face, and recognizing him, started up in bed, looking at him, from her large, fever glistening eyes, in a kind of blank bewilderment.

"My poor Madeline!" said the doctor, with an emotion he could not repress. "My poor Madeline!" he repeated, pressing her back upon the pillow from which she had arisen, and laying his hand softly on her temples, smoothing back the hair caressingly, tenderly, as if she had been his own child.

"Oh, doctor! doctor!" sobbed Madeline, surprise and hope in her voice. Then feeling overcame her and she wept passionately.

"My poor child!" murmured the doctor, his hand still resting on her head. "It must have gone hard with you since our last meeting! But you are sick. The physician first; the friend afterwards. How do you feel? What ails you?"

As soon as Madeline could get voice to speak, she explained how a sudden chill had seized her as she sat, overheated, by the window, followed by fever, tightness and pain in the chest. A cough interrupted her speech. It was dry and wheezing. The attack had been sudden, and she had grown worse rapidly. The doctor's countenance grew serious. He bent his ear down close against her chest, to get the sound of her respiration. He held her pulse, counting the beats. Examined her tongue; and then sat pondering the case, searching in the storehouse of thought for the remedy best suited to her case. After it was chosen and administered, he sat and watched for the effect, which was soon apparent in the lessening heat of her skin, and lighter breathing. The cough, which had begun to be troublesome, returned at more distant intervals, and with lessening force.

"You feel better?" whispered the doctor.

"Yes."

"Can breathe more freely?"

"Yes."

"How is the pain in your chest?"

"I scarcely feel it now."

"The attack was sudden; but we shall soon have the disease under control."

Madeline lay with her eyes fixed on the doctor; never moving them for an instant.

"It seems," she whispered, "as if God had sent you here."

"He is in all our ways," replied the doctor.

"Yes — yes," she murmured. "But His ways are not as our ways." Her eyes shut quickly, and there was a spasm of emotion in her face. "Nor," she added, recovering herself, "our ways as His ways. But all will come out right in the end. I have kept my faith in that, doctor."

"And your heart pure."

"My life pure," she answered. "At least, I have tried to keep it so. The pure heart is from God."

"Yes — yes. God only can change the perverse will. The external life is ours, and we may do good or evil But, over desire — over feeling — we have no inward power. God changes all this in the degree that we act from right principles. We must *do* right if we would *be* right."

Madeline's eyes closed heavily as the doctor ceased speaking. He saw this and remained silent. In a little while, she was in a gentle sleep. Rising, noiselessly, he went to the door, and opening it stepped out. Mrs. Jackman, who was in an adjoining chamber, met him in the passage and asked about Mrs. Spencer.

"She is more comfortable," replied the doctor, in a whisper, "and has fallen asleep."

"Is she a very sick woman, doctor?

"She is ill, ma'am, and will require careful attention."

"Oh, she shall have that!" replied Mrs. Jackman, showing much interest. "I'll nurse her as well as if she were one of my own flesh and blood."

"You know her to be a right kind of a woman?"

There came a flash of resentment into the eyes of Mrs. Jackman.

"Right kind of a woman! You'll not find many as good, if you travel the world over."

"Just my own impression, which I am glad to hear you confirm," replied the doctor. "And now, I want you to be careful in giving her the medicine I shall leave. Here are two powders. Dissolve them in about a wineglass of water each, and give a spoonful, alternately, every half hour."

"That is, first from one glass, and then from the other, half an hour apart," said Mrs. Jackman.

"Precisely. You understand the direction. Use two clean tumblers in which to dissolve the powders, and let there be two silver spoons, one for each medicine."

"It shall be just so, doctor. I'll see to it myself."

"She is sleeping now. When she wakes, say to her that I will call in again during the afternoon."

The doctor then retired, and Mrs. Jackman got the two tumblers and dissolved the powders. Mrs. Spencer was still asleep when she went back to her room. She moved about noiselessly, and then sat down near the bed to watch her patient; half wondering with herself at the interest she was feeling in one whose presence in the house had been for months a trouble and a concern.

Madeline slept for nearly half an hour. When she awoke, she started up and looked eagerly about the room; then turned to Mrs. Jackman, saying, in a disappointed voice —

"Oh, it was so real!"

"What?"

"The dream I had just now." She paused, and looked intently at Mrs. Jackman — then let her eyes move about the room.

"Has any one been here?" she asked.

"Yes."

"Who." She became agitated.

"The doctor."

"Doctor Wheatland?" Eagerly.

"I didn't know his name. He was an elderly man."

"Where is he?"

"Gone. He left you some medicine. There it is on the mantel-piece. You must take a spoonful now, and another in half an hour." And Mrs. Jackman crossed the room for one of the glasses in which the powders had been dissolved.

"Did he say he'd come back again?"

"O yes. He's coming back again this afternoon."

Madeline's heart beat violently; she was in a tremor of excitement.

"Do you know the doctor?" asked Mrs. Jackman, whose curiosity was aroused.

"I've seen him before."

"What is his name?"

"Doctor Wheatland. I knew him many years ago, when I was only a girl."

"He's one of the great doctors of the city," said Mrs. Jackman.

"He's always stood high as a physician. And then,' she added, after a pause, "he's such a good man."

Meantime, Doctor Wheatland was making his round of afternoon visits. In passing through Fourteenth street, he bowed to a lady who happened to be at the window.

After going half a block farther, he ordered his driver to turn and set him down at the house where he had recognized the lady.

"This is not a professional call, Mrs. Lawrence," said Doctor Wheatland, smiling, as he met the lady in her parlor.

"Which makes your visit none the less welcome," she replied, her countenance full of pleasure.

"I've had what might almost be called an adventure to-day," said the doctor, looking more serious.

"Ah? What was it?"

"I met an old, old friend of yours and mine."

"Who?"

"You remember Madeline Spencer — Mrs. Jansen, afterwards?"

"Oh, doctor!" Mrs. Lawrence became excited. "What of her? Where is she?"

"She is sick — very poor, and friendless."

"Friendless and poor no longer!" replied Mrs. Lawrence, with increasing excitement.

"Your old regard for her has not died," said Doctor Wheatland. "I'm glad it came into my thought to see you."

"It is in Providence that you called," answered Mrs. Lawrence. "For months I have been in search of her; and was beginning to fear that she was dead."

"She is not very long for this world; but, if I read her face aright, she is growing purer for the next," said Doctor Wheatland. He then related what the reader already knows of his meeting with Madeline, adding:—

"I think this attack of pneumonia under control. Fortunately, I was called early. I shall see her again before night."

"Do you think, doctor," asked Mrs. Lawrence, "that it would be safe to remove her at once?"

"Remove her where?"

"To my house."

Doctor Wheatland bent his brows thoughtfully.

"Are you in earnest?" he asked. His surprise was not concealed.

"Altogether so, doctor. If it will be safe to remove her, I will order a carriage, and go for her without a moment's delay."

The doctor considered again.

"The day is cold," he said. "If she were to be chilled again! And then, I am not sure as to the condition of her lungs. The frosty air might be too stimulating."

"How far away is she?"

"A dozen blocks — not more."

"Don't you think it might be ventured, doctor? Say yes. I'm sure all ill effects will be more than compensated by the higher care and comfort of my house. I will nurse her as tenderly as if she were my own sister."

"She would be better here — a great deal better. Perhaps it might be ventured. To-morrow, I have no doubt it would be safe."

"Don't say to-morrow, doctor! To-day — now! Let me go for her at once."

"I shall have to see her first. In two hours I will visit her again," said Doctor Wheatland.

"Not for two hours! Oh, doctor!"

"What then, Mrs. Lawrence?"

"There are things that cannot wait, doctor. I will order a carriage at once, and half fill it with pillows, if needed. You shall go with me and if on seeing Madeline again, you decide that it will not be risking too much to remove her, we will bring her away.".

Mrs. Lawrence prevailed. Madeline was asleep when she entered softly, but with a disturbed heart and dim eyes, the small, close room where she lay, and bent down over her, only repressing the sobs that shook her inwardly, by a painful effort. There was now no fever-flush on Madeline's face, which was white and thin — almost ghostly — but very pure, and still preserving its finely cut outlines. Doctor Wheatland stood by her side.

The movements in Madeline's room were not wholly noiseless. She was sleeping but lightly, and opened her eyes upon the faces of the doctor and her old friend.

"Jessie!" There was no start, but a deep and tender surprise in her low voice.

"Madeline! Dear Madeline!" Mrs. Lawrence signed for silence and quiet with her finger upon her lips. Love could find no sweeter tones by which to reveal herself.

Doctor Wheatland took Madeline's hand and felt of her pulse.

"Scarcely any fever," he said. "How is the tightness in your chest?"

"I don't feel it now." She heard the doctor, but only saw Mrs. Lawrence, from whose face and eyes she was drinking the very wine of life.

"I have come to take you away from here," said Mrs. Lawrence. Madeline did not answer. Will and thought were quiescent. She had ceased her struggle for life. She was a frail leaf floating with the current. It might bear her whither it would.

Immediate preparations were made for her removal. She offered no resistance — asked no questions — made only one remark.

"She has been kind to me"—looking towards Mrs. Jackman, who, with a gratified, busy manner, was helping to get Madeline ready.

"And shall not be forgotten," said Mrs Lawrence.

When all was prepared, Madeline, well wrapped up left her room, leaning on the doctor and Mrs. Lawrence. She was weaker than had been supposed. At the head of the stairway, she became so faint that she had to sit down and some minutes passed before she was able to rise again.

Jackman—hard, coarse, and rough, had kept himself aloof from these proceedings, yet still within the line of observation. He was by no means an uninterested party. Two quite opposite feelings were at work in his mind. Always looking out for some advantage to himself, the question as to what gain might come to him through these new friends of Mrs. Spencer, gave to his dull blood a quicker motion. But, on the other hand, the human in him had been stirred from its almost death-sleep. Something about Mrs. Spencer, since he had come near enough to feel the sphere of her quality, had impressed him in a way never felt before. He was softened to a true manliness in her presence.

Madeline had risen, and was about attempting again to descend the stairs, supported by Doctor Wheatland and Mrs. Lawrence, when Jackman pressed forward, saying, with all the pity and gentleness he could throw into a voice unused to such intonations—

"There's no strength in her, poor thing! Let me carry her down."

And taking her up in his great arms as easily as most men would lift a child, he bore her down stairs and out to the carriage, placing her gently among the pillows with which it was lined.

"Oh, thank you, Mr. Jackman," Madeline said, feebly. "I wont forget this."

The man stood half shame-faced. He had been betrayed into an act of genuine kindness.

"Nor will *I* forget you, sir," said Doctor Wheatland, giving Jackman his hand as he stood by the carriage door.

"You will find her at No. —— Fourteenth street. Come to-morrow. We shall both want to see you." Mrs. Lawrence leaned from the carriage window, and spoke to Mrs. Jackman, who promised to call as desired.

"It is better so, John," said Mrs. Jackman, as the carriage drove away, and they went back across the pavement, "than if we had sent her to the alms-house."

Jackman did not reply. The remembrance of what he had meditated against Madeline hurt him interiorly. At the same time, there dawned into his mind a new conviction. He saw, dimly, it is true, that there might come loss, as well as gain, from a too eager seeking of our own. Mrs. Spencer in the alms-house! The thought gave him pain, and he pushed it aside, hastily.

"I'm so glad we were kind to her, poor thing!" continued Mrs. Jackman, when they were back again in the house. "It wasn't any loss to us. And I'm sure I feel a great deal better. It was just right in you, John, to take her up as you did and carry her down stairs. She might have fainted before getting to the carriage. She wont forget it. Poor dear soul! It is strange how I feel towards her."

Jackman kept silence while his wife talked, his thoughts echoing her words far oftener than she imagined.

CHAPTER XXXI.

THE Lawrences had neither seen Mr. Jansen nor heard of him for weeks. After the cold, damp, November weather set in, his calls at the store of Mr. Lawrence ceased. It was understood between the two men, that if Madeline were discovered, Mr. Jansen was to be at once informed of the fact.

The first day of the new year had arrived. It was nearly a week since Madeline had found peace and safety with her old friend, since the weary and fainting wanderer amid barren wastes, had rested on soft green banks by cooling waters. But, she had not rallied, physically, although but few symptoms of the serious attack of illness from which she was suffering when Doctor Wheatland found her, remained. The weak body had, for a long period, been sustained by the mind. The very necessity for effort, had kept her from fainting and falling by the way. Now that struggle had ceased, there was no return of vital power to the body's over-taxed forces. She lay very quiet, sometimes almost lethargic. She talked but little. Her mind, apparently not very active, seemed dwelling, half dreamily, half consciously, amid memories or hopes that were too dimly revealed to awaken in her heart a quicker pulsation.

Mrs. Lawrence did not seek to disturb this condition of mind; but ministered to her state with a care and tenderness born of purest affection. Doctor Wheatland saw her every day, lingering in her room, and watching over her with a far more than professional concern. After years of wandering amid desert vales and barren mountains, the days of suffering and loneliness were over. No more bruised and bleeding feet — torn flesh — terror of wild beasts — shiverings in the storm. Peace, safety, love!— these instead. Whether sleeping or waking — in the body, or out of the body, Madeline scarcely knew. Oh, the sweetness, the calmness, the serenity of that rest, after years of lonely struggle and pain, whose climax of despair had been almost reached!

"I will call at Mr. Jansen's." It was New Years day. Mr. Lawrence looked in at the room where his wife was sitting.

"You'll see Mr. Jansen?"

"Oh, yes. I am going for that purpose alone, not to call on the ladies." And he went out

At Mr. Jansen's he found the New Year's table spread with cold turkey, oysters, tongue, biscuit, brandy, wine, cake, fruit, etc., in liberal abundance, and Mrs. Jansen and her two oldest daughters, pranked out in jewels and finery to receive company. He thought it best to assume the attitude of a New Year's day caller, and so made his compliments to the ladies, sipped from a glass of wine, and took a mouthful or two of cake. Then he asked about the health of Mr. Jansen.

"He's miserable," was answered, with assumed concern, Mr. Lawrence saw that it was assumed.

"Does he ride out this weather?" he inquired.

"Oh, no indeed," replied the wife. "He hasn't been down stairs for a week."

The bell rung. Fresh callers were at the door. It was Mr. Lawrence's opportunity.

"Can I see him?" he said.

The countenance of Mrs. Jansen changed. She had not expected this. What did he want with her husband? She had an instinct of danger; or, not to use so strong a sentence, a suspicion that something was to be communicated not intended for her ears. She thought to a conclusion rapidly, and answered, with a bland smile —

"Oh yes, certainly," and she spoke to a servant who was in the room, who went up stairs, and immediately returned with word from Mr. Jansen, that Mr. Lawrence should come to his room. In the meantime, fresh callers had arrived, to the number of four or five, and they happened to be personages from whom Mrs. Jansen could not possibly excuse herself, and leave them to be entertained by her daughters. In the flutter of their reception, Mr. Lawrence, signed to by the servant, left the parlors and went to the room of Mr. Jansen.

It was a comfortless, neglected room, yet with every means of comfort in profusion. The hand of a loving, thoughtful wife, was nowhere visible. It was eleven o'clock, and yet the chamber had not been set in order. Mr. Jansen was sitting in a large easy chair, near a table on which books and papers were lying about in disorder.

Ashes and cinders covered the grate hearth; the window curtains were drawn awry; dust bedimmed everything; the floor was littered in many places; the air was close and impure for lack of ventilation.

Mr. Jansen had changed considerably. His face was whiter, his eyes sunk farther back in their orbits. It was plain that he had been wasting rapidly. A light broke over his face as Mr. Lawrence came in.

"Have you heard of her?" It was his first question, asked eagerly, as he took his visitor's hand.

"Yes."

A tremor thrilled the hand that still clasped that of Mr. Lawrence.

"What of her?" There was a look of painful suspense in the countenance of Mr. Jansen.

"She is at my house."

"Oh! Thank God!" He had been leaning eagerly forward; now he sunk back in his chair, shutting his eyes. The whole expression of his face had changed. Pain was gone, and in its stead relief blended with satisfaction.

"At your house?" he opened his eyes, and looked gratefully at Mr. Lawrence.

"Yes, where she will remain."

"How is she?"

"She was sick when we found her; but is recovering."

"Where did you find her?"

"She was taken suddenly ill, and the people with whom she lodged called in a physician, who happened to be Doctor Wheatland, by whom she was recognized. He told Mrs. Lawrence, who had her removed at once to our house."

"God's good providence," said Mr. Jansen. "Oh, how

12

thankful I am! And now, what of her? How does she come up out of her fiery trial?"

"Pure."

Jansen shut his eyes very tightly. The lashes quivered on his pale cheeks. When he opened them, the lashes were wet, but the eyes had a new light in them.

"Pure." He echoed the word, with a deep satisfaction in his voice.

"Meet for heaven; so my wife says, and she has looked down into her heart."

"Pure and meet for heaven." Jansen spoke to himself in an undertone, feebly, again shutting his eyes; but started in a moment afterwards, with shadows of disappointment on his brow, as the door swung open, and his wife, radiant in satin, gold and diamonds, burst in upon them as if they were conspirators. Suspicion was plainly marked on her face. She eyed the two men sharply, but discovered nothing. A new feeling quickly dominated. Mortification at the shameful condition of her husband's room, into which she had not before entered on this particular morning. That it would be described to Mrs. Lawrence, she did not doubt. The best she could do, was to break out in a coarse tirade against the neglectful servant, and to lay blame upon the head of her husband for permitting things to remain in that state.

Mr. Jansen made no reply; but his visitor saw disgust and repulsion on his face. It was plain to Mr. Lawrence, that Mrs. Jansen would not leave them alone, and so rising, he said —

"I hope to see you better when I call again," and bowing to both Mr. and Mrs. Jansen, withdrew. There passed between the two men a look of intelligence which the hawk-eyes of Mrs. Jansen did not fail to detect.

CHAPTER XXXII.

FOR a week or two Madeline continued in this half slumberous condition, tranquil and peaceful, as one who lingers in the morning hours between sleeping and waking. It was a question in the minds of her friends whether life would calmly recede, or the vital forces take up again their partly abandoned work.

Very slowly life appeared to gain on death. Thought was unveiled — her mental vision grew clearer. She looked into the face of her new condition, understood it, and became troubled. To this state of mind, which Mrs. Lawrence had seen must come in the natural evolution of things, it was a delicate and doubtful task to minister.

One day, after Madeline had so far regained strength as to be able to sit up, Mrs. Lawrence found her in tears. She had noted, for some time, the gradual stealing of a shadow over her face.

"I can't have this!" she said, cheerily, bending over Madeline and kissing her.

But, Madeline's tears only gushed afresh. Mrs. Lawrence sat down, and drawing her head against her bosom, held it there until a calmer state of mind was gained.

"What troubles you, dear?" she then asked.

Madeline sighed heavily, but remained silent.

"Let me give you a lesson"—Mrs. Lawrence looked tenderly at her friend. "It is two thousand years old but as clearly applicable to your case, as if just spoken. 'Take no thought for the morrow. Let the the morrow take thought for the things of itself. Sufficient unto the day is the evil thereof.' You were thinking of to-morrow."

"And why not?"

"To-day only is yours. Take the good of to-day; and do not spoil its sweetness with the imagined evils of tomorrow. Is not all right with you to-day? Is there any good thing wanting that I can supply?"

"Oh, my friend! You burden me with good things. You fill my cup until it runs over. You have already made me a debtor even to bankruptcy."

"Love keeps no account books. She stands creditor to none. I have already received more than I have given. My heart has been full to overflowing with delight ever since you have been here. Do not mar this pleasure — do not hinder the work of love."

"But your husband, Jessie?"

"It is of his good pleasure that you are here. For a long time we have sought for you — my husband and I. He has taken great pains to find you."

Madeline raised herself up, and turned to Mrs. Lawrence with a look of puzzled inquiry on her face.

"I do not just understand this," she said.

"Why should Mr. Lawrence take an interest in me? It was not so in the years gone by."

"Time works changes in us all," Mrs. Lawrence answered, with slight evasion, " and my husband has changed."

Madeline showed, by the way in which she looked at Mrs. Lawrence, that she was far from being satisfied. Not seeing the way clear for pursuing this subject, Mrs. Lawrence changed it by saying —

"Another time, when you are strong enough to help yourself, and go out, we will talk of this again. It would be fruitless now." Then, after a little pause, " I've wanted to know how it has been with you in the long years that have passed since you went out from your home and friends, with such a daring and desperate spirit, to walk through the world alone."

Madeline did not answer.

"If it would be very painful to uncover this past," added Mrs. Lawrence, " do not lift the veil. If the book is shut, do not open it again."

"I have shut the book, and would not open it again; for, to open it, would be to live over what I have not strength to bear," replied Madeline. "No doubt the discipline was needed. It was hard — very hard — this lonely, friendless life, out in the wilderness, with beasts of prey all around me, thirsting for innocent blood. But, out of it, in God's providence, I have come, a purer and better woman, I think, and fitter for heaven. It may be, that the end would not have been as well for me, if I had walked with beauty and brightness — cared for and housed amid luxuries. There may have been that in me which needed, for correction, all I have suffered. I know not. But this I know, that God has not permitted my wilfulness to work out destruction. In my distresses, I turned to Him, and he often gave light and even comfort. He was my defence on the right hand and on the left. In sorest trials and temptations, He did not suffer my feet to be moved.

"What has troubled me deepest at times," she continued, "is the evil consequences to another that have followed my ill-considered act."

Her voice trembled; she shut her eyes, and kept silence for a few moments. Then resumed with a singular calmness, considering the subject and her weakness —

"And yet, to both, it may be, that the painful discipline was needed. Life, in this world, is as nothing to the duration of life in the next; and all pain and suffering here, if they help us to put aside the things that would stand in the way of our happiness through eternity, are to be considered blessings in disguise. To this view, my mind has been, for some time, gradually rising. We cannot stand alone in this world; we cannot act for ourselves alone. No deed is fruitless of consequences; and the consequences rarely, if ever, limit themselves to the individual actor. So, in our passion and our pride, as well as in our love and humility, God makes of us instruments for good; and where our work is evil in the present, he controls the results and turns them into benefits. So, even in self-condemnation, I find a degree of comfort."

The pale cheeks of Madeline were beginning to flush, and her eyes to grow unnaturally bright. Mrs. Lawrence took her hand and found that it was trembling.

"Your thought is too strong for your body," she said; "and you must let it rest. I understand you clearly; and believe that you have solved the question aright. What we do, may seem to hurt another — nay, may hurt him in some degree of his life; but God's wise and unerring providence will cause the hurt of a lower degree, to become the minister of good to some higher degree of the mind. And so, where blindly, or of set purpose, we have wrought a present evil, He will work out a future good."

"It must be so," returned Madeline. "If God is infinitely good and wise, and His providence over all, even to the minutest things of life — 'the very hairs of your head are numbered' — will he not so control the results of our blindness and ignorance; of our self-will and passion; nay, even of our evil purpose, so that real harm shall not be done. There may be external, and apparent harm; harm such as the surgeon effects in order that a higher and nobler benefit may be secured; but it will be as nothing to the good results. 'For,' in the words of Paul, 'our light affliction, which is but for a moment, worketh for us a far more exceeding, and eternal weight of glory.' It is only through tribulation, that some of us can be purified; and they through whose agency we suffer tribulation, become really the ministers of blessing."

"I can give you no lessons, my dear friend, in this school," said Mrs. Lawrence. "There was a time, when I might have been your teacher; but you have learned from a better Instructor. Keep near to His side. Trust in Him, and recognize His providence in your presence here, as much as in any other event of your life. While we live, our lives affect other lives. You have not ceased to act upon others. Your work is not yet done. Not by any purpose of yours are you here to-day. The hand of Providence, that led you, is not disguised. Be passive, then, and wait."

"You are my teacher," replied Madeline, with moistening eyes. "Wise, true friend, I will be passive; I will wait."

CHAPTER XXXIII.

FTER a certain degree of convalescence, there came a pause in Madeline's condition. She was able to sit up for a portion of each day, and even to walk about her room; but, there improvement stopped.

"I am so weak, doctor," she said one day, early in the spring, to her physician, who found her in bed instead of sitting up. She spoke in a tone of discouragement.

"The warm season will soon be here," he replied. "Fresh air, and change, and exercise, will benefit wonderfully. At the first mild change in the weather, you must ride out."

A shadow came over her face. She sighed, and partly turned away.

"Are you so anxious to get well?" said the doctor.

"I shall never be well again," replied Madeline.

"Don't say that. You will find new life and health in

the warm summer breezes. As soon as the spring is well advanced, and you can ride out every day, your strength will come rapidly. I shall order you sent into the country as early as the middle of June.

"Doctor Wheatland," said Madeline, turning towards the physician, and taking his hand. She looked at him with a sober expression of countenance — "You talk to me as if I had a right to be here — as if I were mistress of the house, and not a helpless, penniless stranger, living day by day on charity. I have no carriage or servants."

"Not a penniless stranger! — not living on charity!" replied the doctor, with a warmth of manner that caused a gleam of surprise to pass over Madeline's face.

"You speak in an unknown language, Doctor Wheatland," she said.

"You understand my words?"

"I understand what your words mean, but not as applied to myself. As you utter them, they have no significance."

"On the contrary," replied the doctor, "they have the fullest significance. You are not a penniless stranger in this house, nor living day by day on charity. Lay that up in your heart, and so far as the question of independence is concerned, be at peace."

"I cannot understand you, doctor." The pale face of Madeline was beginning to grow warm from rising excitement. There was a look of startled inquiry in her eyes, and a shade of alarm as at the approach of something that would give pain.

"My dear madam," said the doctor, with impressive earnestness of manner, "put faith in what I say, and, for the present, while you are weak and helpless, give yourself no fruitless trouble. All is right. You owe nothing to Mr. and Mrs. Lawrence, but love and gratitude."

"Still the unknown tongue," she answered. "Will you not speak in a language that my thought can reach?"

Doctor Wheatland found himself in a delicate position. In the effort to give repose to the mind of his patient, he had only disturbed her deeply. She was not to be satisfied with these general assurances.

"You are neither poor nor friendless," he said, slowly and calmly. "There has been a long search for you, in order that you might be placed in possession of property justly your own. It is in the hands of Mr. Lawrence, in trust, and subject to your disposal. I can only say this to you now. Let your mind be at rest, then. Put aside the thought of dependence. When you are better and stronger, you can ask more questions. As your physician I must assert my authority here."

The flush went out of Madeline's face, and with it the ardor of inquiry. Her thought looked inward. A new fact, which was to effect all her future life, had been communicated. What was the broad significance of that fact? Property in her own right! A long search! Mr. Lawrence the trustee! Under the pressure of so strange a communication, there fell upon her spirit a deep calm. Not a pause in thought, but a cessation of all excitement.

As if she had said to herself — "I must be still — I must look at this communication on all sides, and see what it means."

What it really did mean, her quick instincts had already suggested. Was she pained, or pleased? — indignant or gratified? Doctor Wheatland endeavored to look down into her state of mind, but was not able.

"I am scarcely strong enough for this," she murmured.

"You are not strong enough," replied the doctor; "and so, I must insist upon it, that you ask no more questions. This is, for the present, your home — in right as well as in love. Mr. Lawrence is both friend and guardian.

When health returns, it will be time enough for you to question farther, and act as your judgment and sense of right may determine."

What passed in Madeline's thoughts was not communicated. The doctor saw that her mind was absorbed.

"I will see you again to-morrow," he said, rising to go.

"One thing, doctor."

"What is it?"

"Neither Mr. nor Mrs. Lawrence has given me the slightest intimation of this."

"I am aware of it," replied the doctor.

"I would rather not have them know that I have been informed."

"It shall be as you desire."

"Thank you."

The doctor lingered, but Madeline said nothing more.

After this it was noticed by Mrs. Lawrence that Madeline had passed into a new state of mind. She was more tranquil and indrawn; and less inclined to conversation.

Before, there had been a looking forward to the warm summer days, and to periods in the future, accompanied by a certain uneasiness born of uncertainty. All this vague unrest was gone now. Peace seemed to have folded her pinions.

"I'm afraid," said Mrs. Lawrence, on meeting Doctor Wheatland, a few days afterwards, "that Madeline is losing instead of gaining. I'm sure she is weaker to-day than she was a fortnight ago."

Doctor Wheatland looked serious, but did not respond.

"Don't you see a change?" asked Mrs. Lawrence.

"In what respect?"

"Don't you see that she is failing?"

"I can hardly say that she is gaining," replied the doctor.

"She seems all at once, to have lost her interest in life," said Mrs. Lawrence. "Last week she was troubling herself about the future, and showing a restless sense of obligation. But, this state has passed from her as completely as if her life were a dream."

The doctor stood silent.

"I don't like her present state."

"Why not, Mrs. Lawrence?"

"Evidently, life is receding."

"You think so?"

"Am I not right in my apprehension?" Mrs. Lawrence sought to read the doctor's face.

"There has come, seemingly, a pause in the tide of life," answered the physician. "It may flow on again; or it may recede. Better, perhaps, that it should recede."

"Doctor Wheatland!"

"Better, assuredly, if it be God's will. All the issues of life are in his hands."

"I cannot think of this, doctor. After the long night through which she has passed, does it not seem hard that she should die at daybreak?"

"And rise into the beauty, and brightness, and joy of an eternal morning," said the doctor.

"Then you think her case hopeless!" exclaimed Mrs. Lawrence.

"I cannot tell what may be the healing influences of

nature, when the air is filled with summer sweetness; but, in medicine, I find little to give encouragement. There is scarcely any response to the remedies I administer."

When the doctor went away, the heart of Mrs. Lawrence was heavier than when he came. She had looked to him to strengthen her failing hopes, and he had only removed another stay, and left them weaker.

CHAPTER XXXIV.

SPRING was advancing towards summer. It was early in June. There had been a few warm days in May, and under the doctor's advice, Madeline had taken advantage of them to ride out. But, the effort and excitement drew too heavily on her strength. She came back exhausted, and did not react from the fatigue, as well as the doctor had hoped.

"The promise of spring has failed," she said, smiling feebly. Mrs. Lawrence was sitting by her, as she lay on a sofa in the parlor, after one of these drives. She had not sufficient strength to walk up stairs, after coming in from the carriage, and rested in the parlor until she could gain a little for the effort.

"Oh, no," quickly answered her friend.

"The soft, warm air comes gratefully to my cheeks. I look upon the greenness and beauty of nature, and it refreshes my soul. But, new life does not flush my veins. The pulses are quickened; but only from fever."

Tears filled the eyes of Mrs. Lawrence. Her heart was so burdened that she could not reply. Madeline continued —

"I shall go from you in a little while, dear friend! The struggle is over. After a year of pain, I have ease — after wearying toil, I am at rest — after the bitterness of a long strife, there is peace. I lie awake, sometimes, for hours, in the night, thinking over the past, and looking at the present. The road along which I journeyed led me down into gloomy vales; through wildernesses, where dwelt all manner of evil beasts; over rocky and barren places. I have had sorrow, and repentance, and pain that seemed more than human strength could bear. But, God has brought my feet at last into a plain way. The ground is soft beneath them. The air is filled with light and fragrance. The journey is over, and looking down into my heart, I can say in truth, that it has been better for me that I have suffered. For the rest, God's love and wisdom are infinite. I shall no longer afflict my soul with the question — 'What might have been?' Out of what is, I will seek to draw the highest comfort."

From that time, a loss of strength was perceived, daily. Madeline never rode out again.

About the middle of June, Mr. Lawrence received a note from Mr. Jansen, asking him to call, and mentioning a certain hour when he would be alone. Mr. Lawrence could scarcely repress an exclamation of surprise when he entered the invalid's presence. Elsewhere, he would scarcely have recognized the wan and wasted face, that met him. The hand he took gave back only a feeble pressure.

"You see," he said, "that I am going rapidly."

While Mr. Lawrence was hesitating on the words of his answer, Mr. Jansen asked, with an interest not to be repressed —

"How is Madeline?"

"Failing," was answered.

"Does she go out?"

"No. She is too weak for that."

"Does she sit up?"

"Yes; for two or three hours at a time."

"You think her failing?"

"Yes. The doctor has no hope of her recovery. She may linger for a while — how long is uncertain."

"What is her state of mind?"

"She is very peaceful — waiting for the end."

Mr. Jansen clasped his hands together, and shut his eyes. There was a glow of thankfulness in his countenance.

"The long night of suffering is over. The pain all gone!" he murmured, with satisfaction.

"Yes, all gone," said Mr. Lawrence.

"I have sent for you to ask a favor — a great favor." The face of Mr. Jansen grew earnest.

"You will not deny me?"

"Say on." Mr. Jansen had paused.

"I want to see Madeline. Now don't say no! I must see her before I die. Oh, Mr. Lawrence!"— and the sick man trembled with excitement — "you cannot know how I am pining just to look once again into her face. Maybe it is wrong; but, I am to weak too discuss that question. I dream of her every night; I think of her all day — all night and all day in my loneliness! I say *loneliness*, Mr. Lawrence. Perhaps you understand me."

Mr. Lawrence dropped his eyes to the floor. Mr. Jansen, who was reading his face eagerly, saw disapproval there. The sick man leaned towards him —

"Just once! Only once." The pleading of his tone was touching in its eloquence.

"It might not be right," answered Mr. Lawrence. "It would not be right!" he added more firmly. "The peace of Madeline must not be so disturbed. It would be a violence to her state — a great wrong. She is in rest and tranquillity, waiting for the end. Oh, no, no, Mr. Jansen! It cannot be!"

"You are right as to Madeline. I do not ask an interview; I do not desire it. Even if both of us had strength to bear it, the act would be wrong. I recognize this."

"What then," said Mr. Lawrence.

"It might be arranged so that I could see her."

"How?"

"She is able to sit up?"

"Yes, for short periods at a time."

"She would not know me, I am so changed. I could ride past, and look upon her if she were at the window. This is all I meant."

After a little reflection, Mr. Lawrence said —

"Are you strong enough?"

"Oh, I'll risk all that!" answered the sick man.

"Do you ride out?"

"I haven't been out for two or three weeks. But, you know the weather has not been favorable."

"I will think it over," said Mr. Lawrence.

Mr. Jansen laid his white, almost transparent hand, on the arm of Mr. Lawrence, and spoke with considerable eagerness —

"My dear sir the sword is cutting into the scabbard!

"For a long time, I have resisted this desire to see Madeline; but, I have not the strength of will to put it from me any longer. It is so strong that it is exhausting me. Our days are numbered — hers and mine. She is declining peacefully — thank God, that I have been instrumental in affording that peace! — while my day is going out, dark and dreary. To look into her face, will be just so much of sunlight. You can bring it to pass if you will."

"I will put no hindrances in your way," answered Mr. Lawrence, who was considerably moved.

"If to-morrow is a fair day, I will ride out," said Mr. Jansen.

"But are you strong enough? Can you bear the fatigue?"

"I shall be strong enough — no fear of that!" he answered, quickly. "All I ask is, that you have Madeline so placed at the window that I can look into her face as I ride slowly by. She will not know me; and therefore no harm will be done. Her soul will remain peaceful; and mine will be satisfied. The thirsty lips of my spirit will bend to a spring of water."

CHAPTER XXXV.

HE day following was bright and balmy; the air soft and warm. Madeline felt its influence, and as the morning advanced towards noon, had her chair drawn to the open window, the sash of which came down to the floor.

At one o'clock, Mr. Jansen was to go by in an open carriage. Mr. Lawrence was to call for him; and it was arranged that he (Mr. Lawrence, should leave the carriage at the entrance of the block, and join it again as soon as it turned the corner of the next cross street.

On calling for Mr. Jansen at the time agreed upon Mr. Lawrence found him alone, his wife having gone out on her daily round of visits. He did not look so pale as on the day before. Ardor of feeling gave quicker and stronger pulsations to his heart, and actually touched his cheeks with color.

"Do you feel strong enough?" asked Mr. Lawrence, as

he took the hand of Mr. Jansen, and felt it thrill within his own.

"Oh, yes," he replied, quickly. "I have not felt so toned up for weeks. Is all arranged? Will she be at the window?"

"Yes."

He was very eager, and as they went down stairs, Mr. Lawrence had to bear him back gently and retard his hasty steps. On reaching the pavement, his strength was nearly gone, and it was with difficulty that he could support his own weight to the carriage. It was an open barouche, with extra cushions, among which he sunk back, on entering, while a sudden paleness overspread his face.

"I'm afraid this is too much for you," said Mr. Lawrence, half repenting his acquiescence in Mr. Jansen's wishes.

"Oh, no! no! It will pass over in an instant," was replied.

Mr. Lawrence got into the carriage, and the vehicle moved slowly away. No farther word passed between them. At the entrance of the block in which he lived Mr. Lawrence left the barouche.

"You know the house," he said.

"Yes."

"I will join you in the next street."

There was, now, no signs of agitation about Mr. Jansen. He was calm and indrawn, with a certain brightness of countenance which Mr. Lawrence had never before seen. He lay back among the cushions, with his face a little elevated.

In less than five minutes, Mr. Lawrence was again by his side.

"Did you see her?"

He had taken the sick man's hand on entering the carriage.

"Yes." There was a quick, strong pressure on the hand of Mr. Lawrence.

Mr. Jansen said no more, and Mr. Lawrence would not disturb him with questions. When they reached home, Mr. Jansen's strength was all gone. On getting down from the barouche, his limbs sunk under him, and he had to be carried to his room. A little wine revived him.

"This has been all wrong, I fear," said Mr. Lawrence. The only reply was a smile of satisfaction.

"I think," said Mr. Lawrence, to one of the servants, as he was about leaving the house, "that you had better send for the doctor. This ride has exhausted him considerably."

The servant promised to do so, and Mr. Lawrence went away. He was not at ease in his mind. In yielding to Mr. Jansen's wishes, he had felt that the ground they were about to tread was hardly safe; and so doubts had continually intruded themselves. From Mr. Jansen, his thought now turned to Madeline. Had the recognition been mutual? And if so, what had been the effect? With such thoughts and questionings in his mind, Mr. Lawrence walked homeward. His wife met him with a serious face.

"What of Madeline?" he asked.

"I can hardly answer the question," was replied.

"Did she recognize Mr. Jansen?"

"I think so."

"What was the effect? Tell me all about it."

They sat down, and Mrs. Lawrence said —

"As the time approached when Mr. Jansen was to go by, I began to feel very nervous. Madeline had been sitting up for a long time, and I was fearful that her strength would give way. But, she was unusually bright, and enjoyed the air and sunshine. It may be, that my state of mind affected hers, for as one o'clock drew near, she became quiet and thoughtful. She had been musing for some minutes, when she looked up at me, and remarked, in a grave, half wondering way, 'I have a singular kind of an impression, Jessie; as if I were going to see a stranger, and yet not a stranger.' We heard the bell ring at the moment. 'There,' she said, and leaned, listening, as Ellen went to the door. She almost held her breath. 'Who is it?' I asked of Ellen, who came up with a card in her hand. 'Mrs. Jordan.' I answered my own question, as I took the card. 'Say to her that I am particularly engaged this morning, and must ask to be excused.' As Ellen turned to leave the room, I looked at Madeline. The light had gone out of her face.

"'Why, Madeline!' I exclaimed, 'did you really put such a strong faith in this impression?'

"She smiled and tried to rally herself.

"'The impression is here, and I cannot remove it,' she answered.

"In a little while she grew very calm and sweet. There was a spiritual elevation in her eyes, and a tenderness about her mouth, that was inexpressible. I said to myself—'Angels are with her.' She looked up at the sky, which was of the softest blue, and singularly translucent, then back into my face, saying—'Heaven is not very far off. We just go to sleep, like tired children, and 'waken on the other side.'

"Tears came into my eyes. I could not keep them back. It was now only a few minutes to one o'clock. With difficulty I repressed the agitation that was steadily increasing. I had moved her chair so that she could look in the direction from which Mr. Jansen was to come Presently I heard the sound of wheels approaching slowly. My heart seemed to stand still. We had ceased talking. Madeline was looking out of the window—I put my hands upon her chair, and pushed her closer to the open casement. At that instant Mr. Jansen came in sight. He reclined a little back, with his head against a cushion which had been elevated in the carriage, and his eyes fixed on Madeline. I noticed a slight movement on her part, as if she had repressed a sudden emotion. I could not see her countenance. No sign of recognition was made by Mr. Jansen. His face was white and still, and his eyes resting steadily on Madeline. He turned his head just a little, as the carriage moved by, as if to prolong the vision that was before him.

"The moment he was past, I saw Madeline shrink in her chair, as though overstrained nerves had given way. I spoke to her, but she did not reply. I drew her back from the window, and saw that her long lashes had fallen upon her cheeks. There lingered on her countenance a look of half painful surprise, though the sweetness had not departed from her lips. 'You have been sitting up too long, I said, and wheeled her chair hastily across the room. She made no resistance, as I drew off the wrapper in which she had been dressed, and got her into bed. Not a word escaped from her lips. Her lashes lay trembling on her cheeks, and as her head touched the pillow, she shut her eyes closely and turned her face away. Since then, she has neither moved nor spoken."

"She recognized him," said Mr. Lawrence.

"Yes; I am sure of it."

"And, as I feared, the shock has been too much for her. I was wrong to have permitted this. I felt that it would be wrong from the beginning."

"You had no selfish end to gain replied Mrs. Lawrence. "You tried to serve another. What may seem an evil result to our limited vision, may be only the completion of some higher good. They are both in God's hands."

And they passed to God. That bright June day, on which they had looked once more into each other's faces, went down serene and cloudless; but their eyes did not see its evening beauty.

When day broke again, two white faces, and two shrouded forms, lay in separate dwellings, far apart, and there was no external bond between them. But, in the new morning that broke for their chastened souls, who will say that they stood not close together?

THE END.

www.ingramcontent.com/pod-product-compliance
Lightning Source LLC
Chambersburg PA
CBHW022053230426
43672CB00008B/1159